Instructor's Guide for

MICROCOMPUTER BASIC

Structures, Concepts, and Techniques

Edward J. Coburn

This comprehensive Instructor's Guide is also designed for use by instructors who have adopted:

- **AN INTRODUCTION TO BASIC: STRUCTURED PROGRAMMING FOR MICROCOMPUTERS, Coburn**
- **ADVANCED BASIC: STRUCTURED PROGRAMMING FOR MICROCOMPUTERS, Coburn**

 DELMAR PUBLISHERS INC.®

For information address Delmar Publishers Inc.,
2 Computer Drive West, Box 15-015
Albany, NY 12212-9985

Printed in the United States of America
Published simultaneously in Canada
by Nelson Canada,
a division of International Thomson Limited

10 9 8 7 6 5 4 3 2 1

Library of Congress Catalog Card Number: 85-16108
ISBN: 0-8273-2479-0

TABLE OF CONTENTS

NOTE: The numbers in parentheses correspond to the chapter
numbers as they are found in the INTRODUCTION TO BASIC (I)
and ADVANCED BASIC (A).

INTRODUCTION

This instructor's guide was prepared for use with MICROCOMPUTER BASIC: Structures, Concepts, and Techniques by Edward J. Coburn. This book is a combination of two other books; An Introduction to BASIC: Structured Programming for Microcomputers and Advanced BASIC: Structured Programming for Microcomputers by the same author.

This instructor's guide was prepared to assist the instructor in preparing classroom materials and exams. It should allow the instructor to spend less time preparing classroom lectures and more time preparing supplementary material so valuable to an in depth understanding of any subject. Each chapter is broken into several different sections:

1. Lecture outlines - I have found that an outline is much easier to use when lecturing than written out notes. I have also discovered it is beneficial to give the students a copy of the lecture notes so they can spend less time scribbling and more time listening. Figures and tables to be found in the text are referenced in the guide by page number rather than figure number. For example, a figure to be found on page 44 in the text would be shown as (F-44) in the guide.

2. Answers to the questions to aid understanding, including the ones already answered in the text. To keep the size of this guide to manageable one, flowcharts are not shown. Pseudocode is listed only when it is not redundant. All programs were coded and tested on an IBM PC and though the differences are not listed, the instructor should have no difficulty translating from the IBM version to either of the others needed.

After all the chapters are listed, there is a test bank consisting of 375 questions of five different varieties; true-false, multiple choice, short answer, program debugging, and program lines with possible errors. This test bank is also listed by chapter with the answers following immediately after each group of questions.

After the test bank, there is a collection of pages suitable for overhead reproduction. Many of the flowcharts and other figures are in the collection to enable the instructor to demonstrate points that the students found difficult to follow in the text.

It is suggested that the instructor teaching from this text have the students turn in either a flowchart or pseudocode list (or both) with every program. It is my feeling that design is one of the most important aspects of programming and too often neglected.

I would appreciate any suggestions for improving either the book or instructor's guide. You should send any such suggestions to:

Edward J. Coburn
% Delmar Publishers Inc.
2 Computer Drive, West
Albany, NY 12212

SUGGESTED COURSE OUTLINES

It has been my experience that the BASIC courses vary from school to school depending on the length of the course, how much programming experience the students already have, etc. The three books in this series allow the instructor the most flexibility in the design of the course. The following outlines suggest only a few of the possible organizations of the material. The instructor should note that many of the chapters should not be used out of sequence since the books were written to allow the maximum amount of continuity from chapter to chapter. Those chapters that may be used virtually anywhere interest dictates have been so indicated.

SUGGESTED OUTLINES FOR THOSE USING THE SEPARATE BOOKS

INTRODUCTORY BASIC (one quarter or semester)

CH. 1 . . MICROCOMPUTERS AND BASIC
CH. 2 . . FLOWCHARTS, PSEUDOCODE, AND STRUCTURES
CH. 3 . . BEGINNING BASIC
CH. 4 . . DOCUMENTATION AND INPUT
CH. 5 . . DECISIONS AND LOOPS
CH. 6 . . ARRAYS AND READ-DATA
CH. 7 . . STRING HANDLING AND FUNCTIONS
CH. 8 . . SEQUENTIAL FILE HANDLING
CH. 9 . . MENUS AND REPORTS

Chapters 7, 8, and 9 are optional and may be covered in this course if time permits, otherwise they may be saved and covered in the Advanced course.

ADVANCED BASIC (one quarter or one semester)

CH. 1 . . MICROCOMPUTERS AND STRUCTURES
CH. 2 . . A REVIEW OF BASIC
CH. 3 . . SEQUENTIAL FILE HANDLING
CH. 4 . . MENUS AND REPORTS
CH. 5 . . PROMPTS AND ERRORS
CH. 6 . . RANDOM ACCESS FILE PROCESSING
CH. 7 . . INDEXED FILE PROCESSING
CH. 8 . . TREE STRUCTURES
CH. 9 . . SORTING
CH. 10 . . GRAPHICS AND COLOR

Chapters 1 through 4 may be covered as new material or may be assigned as review material if the topics were covered in the Introductory course.
Chapters 9 and 10 may be considered optional or may be moved and used when the instructor feels it is appropriate. Care needs to be taken when doing this, however, as some of the exercises at the end of the chapters require some file handling techniques.

SUGGESTED OUTLINES FOR THOSE USING THE COMBINED BOOK

EXTENDED BASIC COURSE (one quarter or semester - following some
BASIC coverage in another course such as Intro to Computers)

CH. 1 . . MICROCOMPUTERS AND BASIC
CH. 2 . . FLOWCHARTS, PSEUDOCODE, AND STRUCTURES
CH. 3 . . BEGINNING BASIC
CH. 4 . . DOCUMENTATION AND INPUT
CH. 5 . . DECISIONS AND LOOPS
CH. 6 . . ARRAYS AND READ-DATA
CH. 7 . . STRING HANDLING AND FUNCTIONS
CH. 8 . . SEQUENTIAL FILE HANDLING
CH. 9 . . MENUS AND REPORTS
CH. 10 . . PROMPTS AND ERRORS
CH. 11 . . RANDOM ACCESS FILE PROCESSING
CH. 12 . . INDEXED FILE PROCESSING
CH. 13 . . TREE STRUCTURES
CH. 14 . . SORTING
CH. 15 . . GRAPHICS AND COLOR

Some or all of chapters 1 through 6 may be assigned as review
material, depending upon depth of students knowledge.
Chapters 14 and 15 may be considered optional or may be moved and
used when the instructor feels it is appropriate. Care needs to
be taken when doing this, however, as some of the exercises at
the end of the chapters require some file handling techniques.

TWO COURSE SEQUENCE (two quarters or semesters)

CH. 1 . . MICROCOMPUTERS AND BASIC
CH. 2 . . FLOWCHARTS, PSEUDOCODE, AND STRUCTURES
CH. 3 . . BEGINNING BASIC
CH. 4 . . DOCUMENTATION AND INPUT
CH. 5 . . DECISIONS AND LOOPS
CH. 6 . . ARRAYS AND READ-DATA
CH. 7 . . STRING HANDLING AND FUNCTIONS
CH. 8 . . SEQUENTIAL FILE HANDLING
CH. 9 . . MENUS AND REPORTS
CH. 10 . . PROMPTS AND ERRORS
CH. 11 . . RANDOM ACCESS FILE PROCESSING
CH. 12 . . INDEXED FILE PROCESSING
CH. 13 . . TREE STRUCTURES
CH. 14 . . SORTING
CH. 15 . . GRAPHICS AND COLOR

Chapters 1 through 6 should be used for the introductory course.
If time permits, chapters 7, 8, and 9 may be added, otherwise,
they may be used for the advanced course.
Chapters 14 and 15 may be considered optional or may be moved and
used when the instructor feels it is appropriate. Care needs to
be taken when doing this, however, as some of the exercises at
the end of the chapters require some file handling techniques.

CHAPTER 1 . . . . . MICROCOMPUTERS AND BASIC

1-1 Introduction

1. Discuss what is to be covered in the chapter

   A. **Hardware** - the equipment

   B. The machines to be used:

      1) IBM PC (F-2)

      2) Radio Shack Model III and 4 (F-3)

      3) Apple II line (II, II+, IIe, IIc) (F-4, F-5)

1-2 In the Beginning

1. **Software** (also **programs**) - the instructions that direct the hardware

2. **BASIC** - Beginners All-purpose Symbolic Instruction Code

   A. developed by John Kemeny and Thomas Kurtz of Dartmouth in 1964

   B. Easy to learn, yet powerful

   C. Used for **interactive programming**

1-3 Storage Concepts

1. **Memory** is used to store information

   A. Switches called **bits** or **BI**nary digi**Ts**

   B. Eight bits make a **byte** which is enough storage for a **character**

   C. Microcomputer use the **ASCII** code or American Standard Code for Information Interchange

1-4 Input and Output Functions

1. All computers have three functions

   A. **Input** - getting information into the computer

   B. **Process** - manipulating the information

   C. **Output** - getting information out of the computer

1-5 The Display Screen

　　1. The **cursor** is the display indicator

　　　　A. IBM uses blinking underline

　　　　B. Radio Shack uses blinking half box

　　　　C. The Apple cursor is a blinking square

　　　　D. IBM and Radio Shack can be changed (see Appendix A)

　　2. Prompt is on the screen to indicate the machine is ready

　　　　A. IBM uses **Ok** (this is used throughout the book)

　　　　B. Radio Shack displays READY and uses the > symbol

　　　　C. Apple uses the] symbol

　　3. Upper left-hand corner is **home position** (F-7)

　　4. Screen size is:

　　　　A. IBM screen is 40 or 80 columns by 24 rows

　　　　　　1) 25th row is not normally used

　　　　　　2) Can change widths with **WIDTH** command

　　　　B. Radio Shack

　　　　　　1) Model III is 64 columns by 16 rows

　　　　　　2) Model 4 is 80 columns by 24 rows

　　　　C. Apple is 40 columns by 24 rows (hardware can be
　　　　　　adapted for 80 columns)

1-6 **The Keyboards**

　　1. The communication key is the **RETURN** key

　　　　A. IBM has a key with an arrow <----

　　　　B. Radio Shack key is ENTER

　　　　C. Apple uses RETURN key

　　2. **BREAK** key will stop the execution of a program

　　　　A. IBM uses Ctrl (control) and Scroll Lock keys together

B. Radio Shack has BREAK key

C. Apple uses RESET key

3. Only the Apple II and II+ do not use lower case letters. All the others have shift keys and a lock key

4. All but the Apple II and II+ have an automatic **repeat function** on the keys. The II and II+ have a **repeat key.**

5. The **CLEAR** key will clear the screen

A. The IBM uses the Ctrl and Home keys together

B. The Radio Shack has a CLEAR key

C. The Apple has no key to clear the screen

1-7 Getting Started on the Machines

It is best to show the students how to get started on the machines with a demonstration. You will need a DOS disk for each student and it is best if they are allowed to copy the disk themselves.

1-8 External Storage

1. Though cassettes are used, they are too slow and unreliable for practical use and will not be dealt with.

2. We will use **diskettes** (F-10)

A. Also called **floppy disk** or simply **disk**

B. Housed in protective cover called **jacket**

C. Magnetic coating is broken up into **tracks** (F-11)

D. Tracks are broken into **sectors** (F-11)

E. Storage on our machines is:

MACHINE	BYTES/SECTOR	SECTORS	TRACKS	TOTAL BYTES
IBM	512	9	40	184,320
Radio Shack	256	18	40	184,320
Apple	256	16	35	143,360

Note: What is listed for the IBM is only one side. The IBM PC uses double sided disk drives so the actual disk storage is twice what is listed.

        F. Information about **files** and programs is in **directory** that can be examined with the following commands:

           1) IBM uses the command **FILES A:** or **FILES B:**

           2) Radio Shack uses **CMD"D:0"** or **CMD"D:1"**

           3) Apple uses **CATALOG,D1** or **CATALOG,D2**

1-9 An Important Note

Remember that each student should have a copy of the DOS disk on which to store their programs.

1-10 Storing Programs on Disk

    1. To store programs on the disk requires **SAVE**

        A. IBM and Radio Shack use quotes SAVE "PROGTEST"

        B. The Apples require no quotes SAVE PROGTEST

1-11 Retrieving Programs From Disk

    1. To retrieve the programs requires the **LOAD**

        A. IBM and Radio Shack again use quotes LOAD "PROGTEST"

        B. The Apple does not LOAD PROGTEST

ANSWERS TO QUESTIONS TO AID UNDERSTANDING

     1. Hardware is the computer equipment itself while the
software is the instructions that guide the hardware.

     2. Memory is the place in the computer where information is
stored while it is being processed. A bit is a single on-off
location in memory. A byte is eight bits which is enough storage
space for a character.

     3. Input is getting information into the computer.
Processing is manipulating that data in some manner. Output is
getting the results of the processing out of the computer.

     4. The cursor is the positional marker on the video display
screen. It is important to the user as an indicator of where the
next information will be put on the screen.

     5. The RETURN key is the key to press when you are done
keying your information. It is the signal to the machine that
you have finished. The BREAK key is used to stop the functioning
of a program that is executing.

     * 6. A diskette is a small plastic disk that is coated with a
magnetic material. The disk has concentric circles of storage
known as tracks. Each track is broken logically into groups
known as sectors. Each sector contains 256 bytes of storage.
The size of the storage for each machine can be seen on page 1-12
in the text.

     * 7. A directory is a single track on the diskette reserved
for the storage of the names and locations of all the files and
programs stored on the disk. It is important because this is
what allows the computer to keep track of where everything is
stored.

     8. The command to store a program on disk is SAVE and to
retrieve it is LOAD.

     9. This exercise is a program to key in. See the book for
the programs.

     10. An exercise to give the student practice in saving and
loading a program.

CHAPTER 2 . . . . . FLOWCHARTS, PSEUDOCODE, AND STRUCTURES

2-1 Introduction

1. Communication is always difficult

2. Symbol diagram called **flowchart** is used to help communication

3. **Program flowchart** is used to design a program

4. Also use informal language called **pseudocode**

5. **System** is group of programs that perform function

6. **System flowchart** diagrams the system

7. **Systems analysts** use systems flowcharts

8. Flowcharts have become mainly a tool for systems analysts

9. Flowchart symbols used are **ANSI** or **American National Standards Committee**

2-2 A Word About Structured Concepts

1. Programming used to be a haphazard task

2. **Structured programming** is helping overcome this

3. Three different structures (as proposed by Edsger Dijkstra)

   A. The simple sequence

   B. The selection

   C. The repetitive block

4. Structured programming is a disciplined way of putting programs together

5. Structured programming in book will follow guidelines

   A. All programming will be done using the recommended structures.

   B. All programs will be well documented as an aid to understanding.

   C. All programs will be modular (when appropriate).

2-3 Beginning Symbols and Pseudocode

   1. Terminal symbol - the START and END of the chart (F-23)

   2. Process symbol - denotes data manipulation (F-23)

   3. I/O symbol - for input and output (F-24)

2-4 Our First Structure

   1. Show the students an example of a SIMPLE SEQUENCE. You
      may wish to reproduce the example in the book on page 24 (F-25).

   2. Flow lines are used to connect symbols (F-25)

   3. A loop or iteration can allow reuse of commands

2-5 The IF-THEN-ELSE Structure

   1. Pseudocode form of IF-THEN-ELSE is (F-26)

        IF a THEN
            b
        ELSE
            c
        END-IF

   2. You should give students several examples (pages 27, 28)

   3. The book uses the connector symbol as a collector

   4. Null ELSE has form of (F-29)

        IF a THEN
            b
        (ELSE)
        END-IF

2-6 The DO-WHILE Structure

   1. Pseudocode form of DO-WHILE is (F-30)

        DO-WHILE a
            b
        END-DO

   2. Loop continues as long as condition "a" is true

   3. The first thing in the loop is the test

   4. Should show example like that on page 30

5. **Preparation symbol** is used to **initialize** a counter

6. DO-WHILE structures can be **nested** either in themselves or in an IF-THEN-ELSE

2-7 Another DO-WHILE

1. This one uses an **end-of-data marker** (F-33, 34)

2. The program is on page 33 with only one input

3. And on page 34 with two inputs (the proper way)

2-8 Other Symbols

1. **Connector** can connect one area of chart to another (F-35)

2. **Annotation** is used for comments (F-36)

3. **Predefined process** indicates routine defined elsewhere. It allows modular programs. (F-36, 37 in program)

4. Program example on page 38

****

ANSWERS TO QUESTIONS TO AID UNDERSTANDING

1. A flowchart is a symbolic diagram of the flow of data through a program or system. They are important because it is many times helpful to be able to visualize the solution to a problem.

* 2. There are system charts and program charts. The system charts are constructed by the systems analyst and use many more symbols than do the program flowcharts. The program flowcharts are created by programmers to get a visual image of the logic of the program.

3. Pseudocode is an informal language that is used to lay out a program before it is coded. It is important as an aid to the design and debugging of a program before it is coded.

4. The flowchart symbols are shown in the chapter, they are: Terminal, Process, I/O, Flow lines, Decision test, Connector, Preparation, Annotation, and Predefined process. See the chapter for the Flowcharts.

5. The structures are:

   A. Simple sequence - shows the procedures in a linear fashion

   B. IF-THEN-ELSE or selection - allows the program to make decisions

   C. DO-WHILE - allows the program to reuse program lines by creating a loop

* 6. A counter is used to determine how many times a loop has been executed. A counter is used in the DO-WHILE structure.

7. An end-of-data marker is used to signal the end of a loop. It is used in the DO-WHILE structure.

8. The pseudocode would be:

```
Start
Get notes
Get one page
DO-WHILE there are pages left
    Study page
    Get one page
END-DO
Study last page
End
```

9. This instructor's guide contains no flowcharts.

10. The pseudocode is:

```
Start
Initialize counter to 1.
DO-WHILE counter is less than 6.
    Input miles traveled.
    Computer the mileage rate.
    Print out the results.
    Increment counter by 1
END-DO
End
```

* 11. The flowchart can be seen in Figure F-1 (in the book) and the pseudocode is:

```
Start
Input the miles traveled
DO-WHILE miles not negative
    Computer the mileage rate
    Print out the results
    Input the miles traveled
END-DO
End
```

12. The pseudocode should be:

```
Start
Initialize counter to 1
DO-WHILE counter is less than 51
    Input name, hours, and pay rate
    Calculate gross pay
    Make deductions
    Print the payroll check
    Increment the counter by 1
END-DO
End
```

CHAPTER 3 . . . . . BEGINNING BASIC

3-1 Introduction

1. Introduce BASIC as easy-to-learn language.

2. Assure them that mistakes are forgiven by the computer.

3. Remind them about the RETURN key.

3-2 The Immediate Mode and Print Command

1. The **immediate mode** causes commands to execute immediately and does not store commands in memory.

2. **Syntax errors** mean the computer doesn't understand.

3. **PRINT** is one of the most common commands used.

   A. Used to print things on the screen.

      1) Print calculations.

      2) Printed numbers leave a blank in front and behind numbers (except on Apple).

      3) Front blank in front is for sign (negative numbers have no leading blank).

   B. Blanks generally don't matter to BASIC.

      1) Imbedded in **keywords** will cause error.

      2) Will print as-is in **literals**.

   C. Data enclosed in quotes is called a **literal**.

      1) Will print without the quotes.

      2) Any printable character can be printed.

   D. PRINT command uses **delimiters** to print multiple items.

      1) **Semicolon** will cause items to print together.

      2) **Comma** will print in **print zones**.

         a) IBM, Radio Shack Model 4, and Apple use print zones of 14 columns (5 zones of 14 and the last has 10)

         b) Radio Shack Model III uses zones 16 columns wide.

3) A blank (or no delimiter) is not recommended.

    E. TAB statement much more flexible.

        1) Will position cursor to indicated column.

        2) A space between TAB and the () will cause an error (**subscript out of range error**).

    F. IBM and Radio Shack also use **SPC** statement.

        1) Will move cursor over specified number of columns.

3-3 Mathematical Operators

1. The **mathematical operators** are:

    A. + for addition

    B. - for subtraction

    C. * for multiplication

    D. / for division

    E. ^ for exponentiation (up arrow on Radio Shack)

    F. () for parentheses

2. The order of operations is:

    A. For operations with the same weight, proceed left to right.

    B. parentheses

    C. Exponentiation

    D. Multiplication and division

    E. Addition and subtraction

3-4 The Program Mode

1. **Program mode** causes statements to be stored in memory.

2. Statement consists of:

    A. **line number** from 0 to:

        1) 65529 on IBM and Radio Shack

        2) 63999 on Apple

B. Command to be executed

3. To execute stored program requires **RUN** command.

3-5 Line Numbering

1. We number by 10's so there is room to insert new lines.

2. A few examples might be helpful.

3-6 Additional Commands

1. The **LIST** will display the program lines on the screen.

   A. LIST <u>line</u> <u>number</u> will list only that line.

   B. LIST -<u>line</u> <u>number</u> will list from the beginning to that line (including the listed line).

   C. LIST <u>line</u> <u>number</u>- will list from that line to the end of the program (including the listed line).

   D. LIST <u>line</u> <u>number</u>-<u>line</u> <u>number</u> will list the two listed line numbers and all the lines in between.

2. To delete one line simply enter the line number and press RETURN

3. **DELETE command** will remove listed section of program.

   A. Such as DELETE 30-50

   B. Apple uses **DEL** 30,50

4. **NEW** will erase entire program from memory.

3-7 Printing on the printer

1. On the IBM and Radio Shack you merely use LPRINT.

2. The Apple requires **PR#1** to turn on the printer and **PR#0** to turn it back off.

3-8 Clearing the screen

1. On the IBM and Radio Shack the command is **CLS**.

2. On the Apple the command is **HOME**.

3-9 Variables

1. Can use either **constants** or **variables** in a program.

2. Two type of constants, numeric and literal.

3. Two type of variables, numeric and string.

4. Variable names

A. All variables must begin with a letter.

B. Next is letter or number.

C. In Radio Shack and Apple, only these first two characters are recognized as the variable name.

D. IBM allows variable names unique up to 40 characters.

E. IBM also allows names to contain periods.

F. String variables end with a dollar sign ($).

5. Examples are helpful here.

6. Radio Shack has only a limited amount of string space (50 characters).

A. When used, you get **Out of string space error**.

B. To reserve additional space **CLEAR** is used.

3-10 Assignment

1. The **assignment statement** uses the optional word **LET**.

2. Form is   10 LET variable = expression

3. Equal sign is assignment operator.

4. The variable is **assigned** not **equal to**.

5. Expression can be:

A. Numerical calculation

B. Literal

C. Numeric variable

D. String variable

6. Both sides of the operator must be the same type, either both numeric types or string types.

7. No type of expression is allowed on the left side of assignment.

8. Variables are automatically assigned a value.

   A. Numeric variables automatically begin as zero.

   B. String variables begin as **null** (empty).

3-11 One Final Program Statement

1. Though BASIC does not require it, an **END statement** should be put at the end of the program..

3-12 Putting It All Together

1. An example or two will be necessary to get the students started.

2. You may wish to use the one in the book on page 64 (F-64, F-65, F-66).

****

ANSWERS TO QUESTIONS TO AID UNDERSTANDING

1. The immediate mode allows commands to be executed immediately upon the pressing of the RETURN key.

2. The program mode stores the statements (by line number) until the execution command (RUN) is given.

* 3. In the immediate mode the commands are executed immediately upon pressing RETURN. The commands are not stored in memory, so when the screen is cleared, all the information generated is lost. In the program mode, each command has a line number on it which causes the command to be stored in memory. Then, in order for the commands to execute, a RUN command must be issued.

4. We number our programs by 10's so that there is room between the lines to insert additional lines.

5. The answers are:

   a. LIST

   b. LIST 10-50

   c. LIST 30-

   d. LIST -60

6. 10 followed by the RETURN key.

* 7. a. correct

   b. incorrect- no special symbols

   c. correct

   d. incorrect - cannot lead off with number

   e. incorrect - number, not variable

   f. correct

   g. correct

   h. correct

   i. incorrect - variable will not allow special characters

* 8. a. correct

   b. incorrect - only a single variable should be on the left-hand side of the equal sign

   c. incorrect - numeric cannot be assigned to string

   d. incorrect - should be an operator between the 6 and the (

   e. correct

   f. correct

   g. incorrect - string cannot be assigned to numeric

   h. incorrect - "5" not compatible with the rest

   i. incorrect - cannot have two symbols together

   j. incorrect - incompatible since TEST is not a string

9.
```
10 A=10
20 B=25
30 C=A * B
40 PRINT  "THE PRODUCT OF THE NUMBERS IS";C
```

10.
```
10 A=41
20 B=68
30 C=A + B
40 PRINT "THE SUM OF THE NUMBERS IS";C
```

* 11. The flowchart can be seen in Figure F-2 (in the book)
  and the pseudocode follows:

```
Start
Assign variables (5)
Add the variables
Divide total by 5
Print the result
End
```

The program should look like the following:

```
10 A=80
20 B=90
30 C=95
40 D=63
50 E=75
60 T=A+B+C+D+E
70 A=T/5
80 PRINT "THE AVERAGE IS";A
90 END
RUN
THE AVERAGE IS 80.6
Ok
```

12.
```
10 N$="EDWARD J. COBURN"
20 A$="1400 SOUTH STREET"
30 C$="EL PASO, TEXAS  76708"
40 PRINT N$
50 PRINT A$
60 PRINT C$
70 END
RUN
EDWARD J. COBURN
1400 SOUTH STREET
EL PASO, TEXAS  76708
Ok
```

```
13.  10 PRINT "MULTIPLICATION TABLE"
     20 PRINT "    !  1    2    3    4"
     30 PRINT "--------------------"
     40 PRINT "1   !  1    2    3    4"
     50 PRINT "2   !  2    4    6    8"
     60 PRINT "3   !  3    6    9   12"
     70 PRINT "4   !  4    8   12   16"
     80 END
     RUN
     MULTIPLICATION TABLE
          !  1    2    3    4
     --------------------
     1    !  1    2    3    4
     2    !  2    4    6    8
     3    !  3    6    9   12
     4    !  4    8   12   16
     Ok


14.  10 PRINT "   X"
     20 PRINT "  XXX"
     30 PRINT " XXXXX"
     40 PRINT "XXXXXXX"
     50 PRINT "  XXX"
     60 PRINT "  XXX"
     70 END
     RUN
        X
       XXX
      XXXXX
     XXXXXXX
       XXX
       XXX
     Ok


15.  The pseudocode should be:

     Start
     Assign name, hourly wage, and number of hours
     Calculate gross pay
     Make deductions
     Print check
     End
```

The program should look like the following:

```
10 N$="JOHN SMITH"
20 W=4.56
30 H=40
40 G=W*H
50 S=G*.09
60 F=G*.2
70 ST=G*.05
80 N=G-S-F-ST
90 PRINT "XYZ Corporation"
100 PRINT "854 South Street"
110 PRINT "El Paso, Texas  78678"
120 PRINT
130 PRINT "PAY TO THE ORDER OF ";N$
140 PRINT
150 PRINT TAB(30);"$";N
160 END
RUN
XYZ Corporation
854 South Street
El Paso, Texas  78678

PAY TO THE ORDER OF JOHN SMITH

                              $ 120.384
Ok
```

CHAPTER 4 . . . . . DOCUMENTATION AND INPUT

4-1 Introduction

1. This chapter will explore several more commands.

2. We will also pseudocode, flowchart, and code more programs.

4-2 Program Documentation

1. There are three types of **documentation:**

   A. **Program documentation** is comments put into a program.

   B. **Programmer documentation** is documents that help the programmer understand the workings of the program.

      1) Flowcharts

      2) Pseudocode

      3) Disk storage layouts (file layouts)

      4) Written comments about the program

   C. **User documentation** is a manual prepared for the user.

   D. Program documentation in BASIC is **REM** or remark **statement.**

      1) Form is   10 REM with anything else on line

      2) Can be used to modularize the program.

      3) Can be used to identify the program.

         a) Program name.

         b) Who programmed it.

         c) When it was programmed.

         d) Explanation of program purpose.

         e) Variable list.

      4) Can mark important statements.

         a) Can be used on end with colon (:).

         b) Example   10 P=P+1 : REM P is page counter

c) The apostrophe (') can substitute for : REM
(Not on the Apple).

    5) Only problem with REM is too many can cause the
program to run out of memory.

4-3 Input

1. The **INPUT** is a variable way of making assignments.

2. Form is   10 INPUT variable

3. When executed, question mark (called **prompt**) will appear
on the screen indicating the user should make an entry.

4. If variable is numeric, entry will have to be numeric
If not, a **Redo from start** message will appear and another
prompt.

5. String variable will accept any entry.

6. Literal prompt can be used to give message to user.

    A. Form is   10 INPUT "prompt";variable

    B. Prompt is any normal literal but should be appropriate
message.

    C. Prompt will appear with question mark and blank following
(On Apple neither the question mark nor blank show up).

7. More than one variable can be used on INPUT statement.

    A. Separate them with commas.

    B. Responses to prompt should be separated by commas if
they are to be entered on one line.

    C. One line is the only way the IBM will accept the entry.

    D. Radio Shack and Apple will accept on multiple entry
lines. Each prompt line after the first will be
indicated by two question marks.

    E. Quotation marks are not needed around literal entries
unless a comma is needed as part of the data.

8. Examples should be shown throughout discussion.
Gas mileage program shown on page 84 (F-85).

4-4 Unconditional Branch

 1. The **GOTO** is the unconditional branch.

 2. Form is   100 GOTO line number

 3. Simply branches to listed line number.

 4. If line number is not in program an **Unidentified line number error** will occur.

 5. We will create a **non-ending** or **infinite loop**.

 6. To get out of loop use the **BREAK** key.

 7. Program example shows **accumulator** or running total.

 8. Special care should be exercised when using the GOTO to structure program.

 9. Example in book on page 87 (F-88).

4-5 STOP Versus END

 1. The **STOP** can be used to pause your program when testing.

 2. It can be started up again with **CONT** statement.

 3. CONT also works after BREAK key is pressed.

 4. CONT can cause problems on Apple.

 5. Example in book on page 90.

ANSWERS TO QUESTIONS TO AID UNDERSTANDING

 * 1. Program documentation is remarks put in the program to help the programmer follow the logic of the coding. Programmer documentation is pseudocode, flowcharts, and other devices that help the programmer to understand the logic of the program without looking at the actual code. User documentation is a manual that is prepared to help the user understand how the program functions and what is expected when the program is executed.

 2. The REM or remark statement allows comments to be put into a BASIC program.

 * 3. The INPUT statement can be used with a PRINT statement used prior to the INPUT statement to print the prompt on the screen. Or the INPUT statement can have the prompt within the statement itself with no prior print statement necessary.

4. When the program encounters an END statement, it merely halts execution. When a STOP statement is executed, the program not only halts but prints the line number of the STOP statement on the screen.

5. The STOP statement can be quite helpful in debugging programs since it can be placed anywhere in the program and will tell you which line number stopped the program.

* 6. 10 incorrect - RME is misspelled.

   20 correct

   30 correct

   40 incorrect - PRINT is misspelled, YOUR is misspelled
                  (not really an error)

   50 correct

   60 incorrect - INPUT is misspelled

   70 incorrect - the quote is missing in front of MY

   80 incorrect - line 25 doesn't exist in the program

   90 correct

* 7. a. correct

   b. incorrect - the semicolon should be a comma

   c. incorrect - first quote is an apostrophe

   d. incorrect - the statement needs delimiters

   e. incorrect - the word LINE is extra (also an infinite
                  loop would be created by the line
                  branching to itself.)

   f. incorrect - there is no command, INPUT is in quotes

8.
```
10 REM ***** PROGRAM NAME: MAINT
20 REM
30 REM ***** WRITTEN BY EDWARD J. COBURN
40 REM
50 REM THIS PROGRAM WILL DO MAINTENANCE TO THE RECORDS
60 REM IN THE PAYROLL SYSTEM.  THE FUNCTIONS ARE:
70 REM    A. ADD RECORDS
80 REM    B. CHANGE RECORDS
90 REM    C. DELETE RECORDS
100 REM   D. PRINT THE FILE
110 REM
120 REM ********* VARIABLE LIST *************
130 REM
140 REM CANNOT LIST VARIABLES SINCE THERE IS NO PROGRM
```

9. The pseudocode would look like:

```
Start
Input information
Print label
End
```

The program should look like:

```
10 REM ***** PROGRAM NAME: LABEL
20 REM
30 REM ***** WRITTEN BY EDWARD J. COBURN
40 REM
50 REM THIS PROGRAM WILL PRODUCE A MAILING LABEL
60 REM
70 INPUT "NAME";N$
80 INPUT "ADDRESS";A$
90 INPUT "CITY";C$
100 INPUT "STATE";S$
110 INPUT "ZIP CODE";Z$
120 PRINT
130 PRINT
140 PRINT N$
150 PRINT A$
160 PRINT C$;", ";S$;"  ";Z$
170 END
RUN
NAME? ED COBURN
ADDRESS? 1400 SOUTH STREET
CITY? EL PASO
STATE? TEXAS
ZIP CODE? 76708


ED COBURN
1400 SOUTH STREET
EL PASO, TEXAS  76708
Ok
```

*   10.   The flowchart can be seen in Figure F-3 (in the book)
and the pseudocode follows:

    Start
    Input the grades (3)
    Total the grades
    Divide the total by 3
    Print the result
    End

The program should look like the following:

```
10 REM ***** PROGRAM NAME: F-4-10
20 REM
30 REM ***** GRADE PROGRAM - EXERCISE 4-10
40 REM
50 INPUT "KEY IN THREE GRADES";A,B,C
60 T=A+B+C
70 A=T/3
80 PRINT "THE AVERAGE IS";A
90 END
RUN
KEY IN THREE GRADES? 100, 90, 80
THE AVERAGE IS 90
Ok
```

    11. Since this is an unstructured loop, there is no
pseudocode possible for this program.

```
10 REM ***** PROGRAM NAME: BANKBAL
20 REM
30 REM ***** WRITTEN BY EDWARD J. COBURN
40 REM
50 REM THIS PROGRAM WILL FIGURE A BANK BALANCE
60 REM
70 INPUT "WHAT IS THE BEGINNING BALANCE";B
80 INPUT "WHAT IS THE AMOUNT OF THE CHECK";C
90 B=B-C          ' REDUCE THE BALANCE BY THE CHECK
100 PRINT "THE CURRENT BALANCE IS";B
110 PRINT          ' A BLANK LINE
120 GOTO 80        ' NONENDING LOOP
130 END
```

```
RUN
WHAT IS THE BEGINNING BALANCE? 100
WHAT IS THE AMOUNT OF THE CHECK? 10
THE CURRENT BALANCE IS 90

WHAT IS THE AMOUNT OF THE CHECK? 25
THE CURRENT BALANCE IS 65

WHAT IS THE AMOUNT OF THE CHECK? 32
THE CURRENT BALANCE IS 33

WHAT IS THE AMOUNT OF THE CHECK? 15
THE CURRENT BALANCE IS 18

WHAT IS THE AMOUNT OF THE CHECK?
Break in 90
```

12. The pseudocode is:

```
Start
Input numbers
Print numbers
End
```

The program is:

```
10 REM ***** PROGRAM NAME: NUMBERS
20 REM
30 REM ***** WRITTEN BY EDWARD J. COBURN
40 REM
50 REM THIS PROGRAM WILL PRINT NUMBERS AS A TOTAL
60 REM
70 INPUT "FIRST NUMBER";N1
80 INPUT "SECOND NUMBER";N2
90 INPUT "THIRD NUMBER";N3
100 INPUT "FOURTH NUMBER";N4
110 INPUT "FIFTH NUMBER";N5
120 T=N1+N2+N3+N4+N5               ' TOTAL THE NUMBERS
130 PRINT T;"=";N1;"+";N2;"+";N3;"+";N4;"+";N5
END
RUN
FIRST NUMBER? 1
SECOND NUMBER? 2
THIRD NUMBER? 4
FOURTH NUMBE? 7
FIFTH NUMBER? 10
24 = 1 + 2 + 4 + 7 + 10
Ok
```

13. The pseudocode would be:

```
Start
Input name, rate of pay, hours worked for first employee
Calculate gross pay
Calculate deductions
Calculate net pay
Print gross pay, deductions, and net pay
Total gross pay and deductions
Repeat above steps for all four other employees
Print total gross pay and deductions
Calculate total net pay
Print total net pay
End
```

The program should look like the following:

```
10 REM ***** PROGRAM NAME: PAYROLL
20 REM
30 REM ***** WRITTEN BY EDWARD J. COBURN
40 REM
50 REM THIS PROGRAM WILL PREPARE A PAYROLL LIST
60 REM
70 INPUT "EMPLOYEE NAME";N$
80 INPUT "RATE OF PAY";R
90 INPUT "HOURS WORKED";H
100 G=R*H                 ' GROSS PAY
110 S=G*.09               ' SOCIAL SECURITY
120 F=G*.2                ' FEDERAL INCOME TAX
130 ST=G*.05              ' STATE INCOME TAX
140 N=G-S-F-ST            ' NET PAY
150 D=S+F+ST              ' TOTAL DEDUCTIONS
160 PRINT "GROSS PAY =";G;"      DEDUCTIONS =";D
170 PRINT "NET PAY    =";N
180 TG=TG+G               ' TOTAL GROSS PAY
190 TD=TD+D               ' TOTAL DEDUCTIONS
200 PRINT                 ' BLANK LINE
210 INPUT "EMPLOYEE NAME";N$
220 INPUT "RATE OF PAY";R
230 INPUT "HOURS WORKED";H
240 G=R*H                 ' GROSS PAY
250 S=G*.09               ' SOCIAL SECURITY
260 F=G*.2                ' FEDERAL INCOME TAX
270 ST=G*.05              ' STATE INCOME TAX
280 N=G-S-F-ST            ' NET PAY
290 D=S+F+ST              ' TOTAL DEDUCTIONS
300 PRINT "GROSS PAY =";G;"      DEDUCTIONS =";D
310 PRINT "NET PAY    =";N
320 TG=TG+G               ' TOTAL GROSS PAY
330 TD=TD+D               ' TOTAL DEDUCTIONS
340 PRINT                 ' BLANK LINE
350 INPUT "EMPLOYEE NAME";N$
```

(Program continued on next page)

```
360 INPUT "RATE OF PAY";R
370 INPUT "HOURS WORKED";H
380 G=R*H                ' GROSS PAY
390 S=G*.09              ' SOCIAL SECURITY
400 F=G*.2               ' FEDERAL INCOME TAX
410 ST=G*.05             ' STATE INCOME TAX
420 N=G-S-F-ST           ' NET PAY
430 D=S+F+ST             ' TOTAL DEDUCTIONS
440 PRINT "GROSS PAY =";G;"      DEDUCTIONS =";D
450 PRINT "NET PAY   =";N
460 TG=TG+G              ' TOTAL GROSS PAY
470 TD=TD+D              ' TOTAL DEDUCTIONS
480 PRINT                ' BLANK LINE
490 INPUT "EMPLOYEE NAME";N$
500 INPUT "RATE OF PAY";R
510 INPUT "HOURS WORKED";H
515 G=R*H                ' GROSS PAY
520 S=G*.09              ' SOCIAL SECURITY
530 F=G*.2               ' FEDERAL INCOME TAX
540 ST=G*.05             ' STATE INCOME TAX
550 N=G-S-F-ST           ' NET PAY
560 D=S+F+ST             ' TOTAL DEDUCTIONS
570 PRINT "GROSS PAY =";G;"      DEDUCTIONS =";D
580 PRINT "NET PAY   =";N
590 TG=TG+G              ' TOTAL GROSS PAY
600 TD=TD+D              ' TOTAL DEDUCTIONS
610 PRINT                ' BLANK LINE
620 INPUT "EMPLOYEE NAME";N$
630 INPUT "RATE OF PAY";R
640 INPUT "HOURS WORKED";H
650 G=R*H                ' GROSS PAY
660 S=G*.09              ' SOCIAL SECURITY
670 F=G*.2               ' FEDERAL INCOME TAX
680 ST=G*.05             ' STATE INCOME TAX
690 N=G-S-F-ST           ' NET PAY
700 D=S+F+ST             ' TOTAL DEDUCTIONS
710 PRINT "GROSS PAY =";G;"      DEDUCTIONS =";D
720 PRINT "NET PAY   =";N
730 TG=TG+G              ' TOTAL GROSS PAY
740 TD=TD+D              ' TOTAL DEDUCTIONS
750 PRINT                ' BLANK LINE
760 PRINT                ' BLANK LINE
770 PRINT "TOTAL GROSS PAY  =";TG
780 PRINT "TOTAL DEDUCTIONS =";TD
790 PRINT "TOTAL NET PAY    =";TN
800 END
```

```
RUN
EMPLOYEE NAME? JOHN SMITH
RATE OF PAY? 3.56
HOURS WORKED? 40
GROSS PAY = 142.4      DEDUCTIONS = 48.416
NET PAY   = 93.984

EMPLOYEE NAME? LESLIE THOMPSON
RATE OF PAY? 4.56
HOURS WORKED? 35
GROSS PAY = 159.6      DEDUCTIONS = 54.264
NET PAY   = 105.336

EMPLOYEE NAME? SARA HARRISON
RATE OF PAY? 7.89
HOURS WORKED? 40
GROSS PAY = 315.6      DEDUCTIONS = 107.304
NET PAY   = 208.296

EMPLOYEE NAME? JILL GEORGE
RATE OF PAY? 3.90
HOURS WORKED? 38
GROSS PAY = 148.2      DEDUCTIONS = 50.388
NET PAY   = 97.812

EMPLOYEE NAME? HENRY STEVENS
RATE OF PAY? 10.75
HOURS WORKED? 40
GROSS PAY = 430       DEDUCTIONS = 146.2
NET PAY   = 283.8

TOTAL GROSS PAY  = 1195.8
TOTAL DEDUCTIONS = 406.572
TOTAL NET PAY    = 789.228
Ok
```

CHAPTER 5 . . . . . Decisions and Loops

5-1 Introduction

1. In this chapter we learn the decision test.

2. Also an easier way of creating a DO-WHILE.

5-2 Decision Test

1. The BASIC decision test is the IF-THEN.

2. Form is   10 IF condition THEN action

3. If condition is true, action is done otherwise program drops to next line.

4. The conditionals are (T-98):

    =   <   >   <>   <=   >=

5. Action can be any valid BASIC command such as:

    A. Assignment - page 99 (F-100)

    B. STOP - page 101 (F-101)

    C. PRINT - page 102 (F-103)

    D. GOTO (conditional branch) - page 102 (F-103)

6. Introduce the **REPEAT-UNTIL** or **DO-UNTIL** - page 105.

    A. First thing in loop is the process (test is last).

    B. Not used as often as DO-WHILE - page 105 (F-106).

5-3 The Actual IF-THEN-ELSE

1. Form is 10 IF condition THEN action ELSE action

2. If condition is true, THEN action is done otherwise ELSE action is done.

3. Examples on pages 107, 108 (F-107).

5-4 **Using the Colon to Continue the Action**

    1. Multiple statements on action is done with colon.

    2. Example   10 IF A=5 THEN P=6 : R=5 - page 109 (F-109)

5-5 **Boolean Operators**

    1. **Boolean operators** or **logical operators**.

    2. Normally use **AND, OR,** and **NOT**.

        A. AND condition is true only when both conditions are true.

        B. OR condition is true when either or both are true.

        C. NOT gives the opposite of test.

5-6 **A Couple of Program Segments**

    1. Male/Female test (error trap) shown on page 111 (F-112).

    2. Password test on page 114 (F-115).

5-7 **A Complete Program**

    1. Pseudocode on page 116 (F-117).

    2. Program on page 118.

5-8 **Another Method of Looping**

    1. The **FOR-NEXT** loop is basically a DO-WHILE.

    2. Form is:

        10 FOR counter variable = start point TO end point

            body of loop (what the loop accomplishes)

        100 NEXT counter variable

    3. Counter variable begins with the value in start point.

    4. Counter increases by one each time through the loop.

    5. After each loop, the counter is compared to end point
       until it exceeds the end point and the loop ends by
       branching to line after the NEXT statement.

    6. Loop can be anything that is appropriate.

7. Printing the counter variable is not necessary, just convenient.

8. Spacing is necessary on IBM   FOR I = 1 TO 10

9. Loop will <u>always</u> function once (not true DO-WHILE).

10. Start and end points can be constants or variables.

11. Changing the values of the start and end points makes no difference.

12. Changing the counter variable in the loop should only be done with caution.

13. **STEP** command can be used to change increment.

    A. Negative numbers can be used.

    B. STEP can be constant or variable.

    C. Changing STEP value in loop has no effect.

5-9 One Final Note About the FOR-NEXT

1. Make note that the student should only use the FOR-NEXT when it is appropriate.

2. Other times a simple GOTO, IF-THEN loop is better.

5-10 Putting It All Together

1. The pseudocode is on page 127 (F-128, 129).

2. Program is coded on page 130.

****

Answers to Questions to Aid Understanding

1. Any valid BASIC statement may be used as an action of an IF-THEN statement. Some of the possibilities are:

    A. PRINT

    B. GOTO (understood)

    C. Assignment

    D. STOP

    E. Another IF-THEN (nested IF-THEN)

2. The six relational operators are:

A. = for equal

B. < for less than

C. > for greater than

D. <> for not equal to

E. <= for less than or equal to

F. >= for greater than or equal to

The three Boolean operators are:

A. AND which is true only when both tests are true

B. OR which is true if either of the tests are true

C. NOT which is true if the test itself is false

* 3. a. branch to 110

branch to 110

cannot branch to 110 since branch is to 50

branch to 110

b. branch to 110

branch to 110

error - incompatible variables

branch to 110

no branch since A=5 and B=9

* 4. a. A=10

b. A=0 (not assigned)

c. A=1

d. A=10

5. A. An automatic counter

B. An end-point test

C. An automatic branch

* 6. We should use the counter on the NEXT statement because it helps us match the FOR with the appropriate NEXT. This will become more important when we begin nesting the loops.

7. As soon as the FOR statement is executed, the start and end point values are stored in special memory locations and the variables (or constants) in the FOR statement are not used anymore.

8. Changing the counter variable within the loop can cause the loop to end prematurely or loop endlessly. We can change it, but we need to be careful that we know exactly what we are intending to do.

* 9. a. incorrect - A and "5" are not compatible

b. correct

c. incorrect - THEN B is not a proper action

d. correct (to will be changed to TO by the machine)

e. incorrect - FRO should be FOR

f. incorrect - variable missing

g. incorrect - incorrect symbol

h. incorrect - action should be assignment not inequality

i. correct

10. A. IF-THEN-ELSE structure is for tests.

B. DO-WHILE is used for loops where the first thing done in the loop is the test.

C. REPEAT-UNTIL is used for loops where the test is the last thing done in the loop.

11.

I	A	J
1	0	0
1	1	1
3	2	2
3	3	9

```
12. Start
    Initialize I to 1
    DO-WHILE I < 5
           DO-WHILE J <= I
                  PRINT I,J,A
                  Increment J by 1
                  A = I * J
           END-DO
           Increment I by 1
    END-DO
    End


13. 10 REM ***** EXERCISE 5-13
    20 REM
    30 FOR I = 10 TO 5 STEP -.25
    40      PRINT I
    50 NEXT I
    RUN
     10
     9.75
     9.5
     9.25
     9
     8.75
     8.5
     8.25
     8
     7.75
     7.5
     7.25
     7
     6.75
     6.5
     6.25
     6
     5.75
     5.5
     5.25
     5
    Ok
```

14. The pseudocode would be:

```
Start
Initialize counters and accumulators
DO-UNTIL user indicates no more
     Input a grade
     DO-WHILE grade is not negative
          Add grade to accumulator
          Increment counter by 1
          Input a grade
     END-DO
     Calculate the average by accumulator divided by counter
     Print the average
     Accumulate grand totals
     Zero out accumulator fields for group
     Ask user if there are more
END-DO
Calculate and print final average
End
```

The program should be:

```
10 REM ***** PROGRAM NAME: EXERCISE 5-14
20 REM
30 REM CALCULATE GRADE AVERAGES FOR MANY STUDENTS
40 REM END-OF-DATA MARKER IS NEGATIVE NUMBER
50 REM
60 REM ***** WRITTEN BY EDWARD J. COBURN
70 REM
80 T=0                 ' INITIALIZE ACCUMULATOR
90 N=0                 ' INITIALIZE COUNTER
100 GT=0               ' INITIALIZE GRAND TOTAL
110 TN=0               ' INITIALIZE TOTAL NUMBER OF GRADES
120 INPUT "WHAT IS THE GRADE";G
130 IF G<0 THEN 200 ' END INPUT - GO CALCULATE
140 T=T+G              ' TOTAL THE GRADES
150 N=N+1              ' GET THE NUMBER OF GRADES
160 GOTO 120           ' RETURN FOR ANOTHER GRADE
170 REM
180 REM ***** GRADE CALCULATION AND PRINT
190 REM
200 A=T/N              ' CALCULATE AVERAGE
210 PRINT "YOUR AVERAGE FOR";N;"GRADES IS";A
220 GT=GT+T            ' ACCUMULATE GRAND TOTAL
230 T=0                ' ZERO OUT GRADE TOTAL
240 TN=TN+N            ' ACCUMULATE TOTAL NUMBER OF GRADES
250 N=0                ' ZERO OUT NUMBER OF GRADES
260 REM
270 REM ***** GET NEW GROUP
280 REM
290 PRINT
300 INPUT "ANOTHER GROUP (Y OR N)";A$
```

(Program continues)

```
310 IF A$="Y" THEN 120
320 REM
330 REM ***** END PROGRAM
340 REM
350 PRINT
360 PRINT "THE AVERAGE OF ALL STUDENTS IS";GT/TN
370 END
RUN
WHAT IS THE GRADE? 100
WHAT IS THE GRADE? 95
WHAT IS THE GRADE? 97
WHAT IS THE GRADE? 90
WHAT IS THE GRADE? -1
YOUR AVERAGE FOR 4 GRADES IS 95.5

ANOTHER GROUP (Y OR N)? Y

WHAT IS THE GRADE? 100
WHAT IS THE GRADE? 90
WHAT IS THE GRADE? 80
WHAT IS THE GRADE? -1
YOUR AVERAGE FOR 3 GRADES IS 90

ANOTHER GROUP (Y OR N)? N

THE AVERAGE OF ALL STUDENTS IS 93.1429
```

* 15. The pseudocode follows:

```
Start
Input table size
Print table heading
Initialize counter to 1
DO-WHILE counter is not greater than table size
     Print the counter variable and the counter variable
          multiplied by itself
     Increment the counter by 1
END-DO
End
```

The program should look like the following:

```
10 REM ***** PROGRAM NAME: F-5-15
20 REM
30 REM ***** SQUARE TABLE - EXERCISE 5 - 15
40 REM
50 INPUT "WHAT IS THE TABLE SIZE";A
60 PRINT "NUMBER","SQUARE"
70 FOR I = 1 TO A
80     PRINT "  ";I,"  ";I*I
90 NEXT I
100 END
```

(Output on next page)

```
RUN
WHAT IS THE TABLE SIZE? 5
NUMBER          SQUARE
    1               1
    2               4
    3               9
    4              16
    5              25
Ok
```

16. The pseudocode is:

```
    Start
    Print the first line
    Initialize counter to 1
    DO-WHILE counter less than 4
        Print the line
        Increment counter by 1
    END-DO
    End
```

The program should look like:

```
10 REM ***** PROGRAM NAME: EX-5-16
20 REM
30 REM ***** WRITTEN BY EDWARD J. COBURN
40 REM
50 REM EXERCISE 5-16 - MULTIPLICATION TABLE
60 REM
80 PRINT ,1,2,3
100 FOR I=1 TO 3
110     PRINT I,I*1,I*2,I*3
120 NEXT I
130 END
RUN
            1           2           3
1           1           2           3
2           2           4           6
3           3           6           9
Ok
```

17. The pseudocode should look like:

```
    Start
    Input the password
    IF password input is correct THEN
        Initialize counter to 1
        DO-WHILE counter < 11
            Print message
            Increment counter by 1
        END-DO
    (ELSE)
    END-IF
    End
```

The program should look like the following:

```
10 REM ***** PROGRAM NAME: EX-5-17
20 REM
30 REM ***** WRITTEN BY EDWARD J. COBURN
40 REM
50 REM EXERCISE 5-17 - PASSWORD PROTECTION
60 REM
70 INPUT "WHAT IS THE PASSWORD";P$
80 IF P$<>"ED COBURN" THEN 120
90 FOR I=1 TO 10
100    PRINT "PASSWORD ACCEPTED"
110 NEXT I
120 END
RUN
WHAT IS THE PASSWORD? JOHN
Ok
RUN
WHAT IS THE PASSWORD? ED COBURN
PASSWORD ACCEPTED
PASSWORD ACCEPTED
PASSWORD ACCEPTED
PASSWORD ACCEPTED
PASSWORD ACCEPTED
PASSWORD ACCEPTED
PASSWORD ACCEPTED
PASSWORD ACCEPTED
PASSWORD ACCEPTED
PASSWORD ACCEPTED
Ok
```

18. The pseudocode should look like the following:

```
Start
Input the number of words
Initialize price to $1.60
IF number of words > 5 THEN
    Calculate how many additional words there are
    Add the cost of the additional ones to the price
(ELSE)
END-IF
Print the price
End
```

The program should look like the following:

```
10 REM ***** PROGRAM NAME: EX-5-18
20 REM
30 REM ***** WRITTEN BY EDWARD J. COBURN
40 REM
50 REM EXERCISE 5-18 - TELEGRAM COST
60 REM
70 INPUT "HOW MANY WORDS";W
80 P=1.6                                ' START WITH 1.60
90 IF W<6 THEN 120                      ' NO ADDITIONAL WORDS
100    AW=W-5                           ' ADDITIONAL WORDS
110    P=P+AW*.12                       ' .12 EACH
120 PRINT "THE TELEGRAM HAS";W;"WORDS AND THE COST IS";P
130 END
RUN
HOW MANY WORDS? 5
THE TELEGRAM HAS 5 WORDS AND THE COST IS 1.6
RUN
HOW MANY WORDS? 2
THE TELEGRAM HAS 2 WORDS AND THE COST IS 1.6
RUN
HOW MANY WORDS? 8
THE TELEGRAM HAS 8 WORDS AND THE COST IS 1.96
Ok
```

19. The pseudocode should look like the following:

```
Start
Input month
DO-WHILE month not valid
     Print error message
     Input month
END-DO
Input day
DO-WHILE day not valid
     Print error message
     Input day
END-DO
Input year
DO-WHILE year not valid
     Print error message
     Input year
END-DO
Print date
End
```

And the program should look like the following:


```
10 REM ***** PROGRAM NAME: EX-5-19
20 REM
30 REM ***** WRITTEN BY EDWARD J. COBURN
40 REM
50 REM EXERCISE 5-19 - DATE COMPARISON
60 REM
70 INPUT "ENTER THE MONTH";MM
80 IF MM<1 OR MM>12 THEN PRINT "THE MONTH IS IN ERROR" : GOTO 70
90 INPUT "ENTER THE DAY";DD
100 IF DD<1 OR DD>31 THEN PRINT "THE DAY IS IN ERROR" : GOTO 90
110 INPUT "ENTER THE YEAR";YY
120 IF YY<1 OR YY>86 THEN PRINT "THE YEAR IS IN ERROR" : GOTO 110
130 PRINT
140 PRINT MM;"/";DD;"/";YY
150 END
RUN
ENTER THE MONTH? 13
THE MONTH IS IN ERROR
ENTER THE MONTH? 11
ENTER THE DAY? 30
ENTER THE YEAR? 86

 11 / 30 / 86
Ok
```

20. The pseudocode should look like the following:

```
Start
Initialize counter to 1
DO-WHILE counter < 6
     Print counter without carriage return
     Increment counter by 1
END-DO
Print the percentages (on the same line)
Initialize counter to 100
DO-WHILE counter < 1001
     Print table line
     Increment counter by 100
END-DO
End
```

The program might look like:

```
10 REM ***** PROGRAM NAME: EX-5-20
20 REM
30 REM ***** WRITTEN BY EDWARD J. COBURN
40 REM
50 REM EXERCISE 5-20 - TAX TABLE
60 REM
70 FOR I=1 TO 5
80      PRINT TAB(I*10);I;
90 NEXT I
100 PRINT
110 PRINT TAB(10);"15%";TAB(20);"13%";TAB(30);
                  "11%";TAB(40);"9%";TAB(50);"7%"
140 FOR I=100 TO 1000 STEP 100
150      PRINT "$";I;TAB(10);I*.15;TAB(20);I*.13;
160      PRINT TAB(30);I*.11;TAB(40);I*.09;TAB(50);I*.07
170 NEXT I
RUN
```

	1	2	3	4	5
	15%	13%	11%	9%	7%
$ 100	15	13	11	9	7
$ 200	30	26	22	18	14
$ 300	45	39	33	27	21
$ 400	60	52	44	36	28
$ 500	75	65	55	45	35
$ 600	90	78	66	54	42
$ 700	105	91	77	63	49
$ 800	120	104	88	72	56
$ 900	135	117	99	81	63
$ 1000	150	130	110	90	70

Ok

21. The pseudocode should look like the following:

```
Start
Initialize counter to 5
DO-WHILE counter < 6
     Input the name
     Input the rate
     Input the hours
     Calculate the gross pay
     Accumulate total gross
     IF hours > 40 THEN
          Calculate overtime hours
          Calculate 1/2 pay using overtime hours
          Accumulate overtime pay
          Add overtime pay to gross pay
     (ELSE)
     END-IF
     Calculate FICA
     Calculate federal tax
     Calculate state tax
```

```
          Calculate net pay
          Accumulate total deductions
          Print regular pay, overtime pay, deductions, and net pay
          Zero out overtime pay
          Increment counter by 1
END-DO
Print totals
End
```

The program should look like:

```
10 REM ***** PROGRAM NAME: EX-5-21
20 REM
30 REM ***** WRITTEN BY EDWARD J. COBURN
40 REM
50 REM EXERCISE 5-21 - XYZ PAYROLL
60 REM
70 FOR I=1 TO 5
80     INPUT "ENTER EMPLOYEE NAME";N$
90     INPUT "ENTER RATE OF PAY";P
100    INPUT "ENTER HOURS WORKED";H
110    GP=P*H                           ' GROSS PAY (NORMAL)
115    TGP=TGP+GP                        ' TOTAL GROSS PAY
120    IF H<40 THEN 160                  ' NO OVERTIME
130        OH=H-40                       ' OVERTIME HOURS
140        OP=OH*P/2                     ' 1/2 PAY
145        TOP=TOP+OP                    ' TOTAL OVERTIME PAY
150        GP=GP+OP                      ' ADD OVERTIME PAY
160    SS=GP*.09                         ' SOCIAL SECURITY
170    FT=GP*.2                          ' FEDERAL TAX
180    ST=GP*.05                         ' STATE TAX
190    NP=GP-SS-FT-ST                    ' NET PAY
200    D=SS+FT+ST                        ' SUM OF DEDUCTIONS
210    TD-TD+D                           ' TOTAL DEDUCTIONS
220    PRINT "REGULAR PAY =";GP-OP;"   OVERTIME =";OP
230    PRINT "DEDUCTIONS =";D;"   NET PAY =";NP
240    PRINT
245    OP=0                              ' ZERO OUT OVERTIME PAY
250 NEXT I
260 PRINT "TOTAL REGULAR PAY =";TGP
270 PRINT "TOTAL OVERTIME =";TOP
280 PRINT "TOTAL DEDUCTIONS =";TD
290 PRINT "TOTAL NET PAY =";TGP+TOP-TD
300 END
```

```
RUN
ENTER EMPLOYEE NAME? SAM SMITH
ENTER RATE OF PAY? 5.65
ENTER HOURS WORKED? 45
REGULAR PAY = 254.25    OVERTIME = 14.125
DEDUCTIONS = 91.2475    NET PAY = 177.1275

ENTER EMPLOYEE NAME? TOM JEFFERIES
ENTER RATE OF PAY? 4.25
ENTER HOURS WORKED? 50
REGULAR PAY = 212.5    OVERTIME = 21.25
DEDUCTIONS = 79.47501    NET PAY = 154.275

ENTER EMPLOYEE NAME? SAM SPADE
ENTER RATE OF PAY? 10.35
ENTER HOURS WORKED? 35
REGULAR PAY = 362.25    OVERTIME = 0
DEDUCTIONS = 123.165    NET PAY = 239.085

ENTER EMPLOYEE NAME? LISA HARRIS
ENTER RATE OF PAY? 6.75
ENTER HOURS WORKED? 40
REGULAR PAY = 270    OVERTIME = 0
DEDUCTIONS = 91.8    NET PAY = 178.2

ENTER EMPLOYEE NAME? TATA SIMPSON
ENTER RATE OF PAY? 5.85
ENTER HOURS WORKED? 36
REGULAR PAY = 210.6    OVERTIME = 0
DEDUCTIONS = 71.60401    NET PAY = 138.996

TOTAL REGULAR PAY = 1309.6
TOTAL OVERTIME = 35.375
TOTAL DEDUCTIONS = 457.2915
TOTAL NET PAY = 887.6835
Ok
```

CHAPTER 6 . . . . . ARRAYS AND READ-DATA

6-1 Introduction

    1. This chapter will cover three more areas

        A. Arrays

        B. READ-DATA

        C. Subroutines

6-2 Arrays

    1. **Arrays** can take the place of many assignments.

    2. Array pointer is called **index** or **subscript**.

    3. Array must be **DIM**ensioned.

        A. Number of elements defaults to 11 (0 thru 10).

        B. Access outside of DIM size will cause error.

            1) **Subscript out of range error** on IBM and Radio Shack.

            2) **Bad subscript error** on Apple.

        C. Dimension can be done with variable.

    4. Arrays and loops are natural companions.

    5. It is best to DIM only what you will need, but there is no harm in reserving more elements than you will use (except memory limits).

    6. String arrays are useful also.

6-3 **Program Example Using Arrays**

    1. Pseudocode is on page 145 (F-146).

    2. Inventory program is on page 147.

6-4 **The READ and DATA Statements**

    1. Arrays and **READ-DATA** work well together.

    2. **READ statement:**

A. Form is   10 READ variable, variable, ...

B. Variables may be either string or numeric.

3. **DATA** statement:

A. Form is   10 DATA constant, constant, ...

B. Only a storage place for constant data.

C. Non-executable statement.

D. All DATA statement should be kept together in the program, usually at the end.

E. Any type of data can be used.

4. Important points:

A. If READ variable is numeric, only numeric data may be used.

B. There must be enough data for all the variables on the READ statements, if not, **Out of data error** occurs.

C. Quotes are necessary for literals if a comma is to be imbedded since delimiter is comma.

5. **RESTORE** is used to reset DATA pointer.

A. IBM can RESTORE to particular line number.

B. Radio Shack and Apple cannot.

6-5 **An Example Using Arrays and the READ-DATA**

1. Pseudocode is on page 153 (F-154).

2. Program is on page 153, 155.

6-6 **Using Multi-dimensional Arrays**

1. Two or more dimensions let array appear as table.

2. Generally use variable(row,column) though how you input the data will determine the row and column.

3. Example program on page 157, 160 - pseudocode on page 158 (F-159).

6-7 **GOSUB (Subroutine)**

1. Subroutine is done with **GOSUB** statement.

2. Form is   10 GOSUB line number

3. At the end of subroutine use **RETURN** statement.

4. Subroutine will execute and send program back to line following GOSUB statement.

5. If program encounters RETURN without using GOSUB, a **Return without GOSUB error** will occur.

6. Advantages of subroutine are:

   A. Reuse of code.

   B. Since code is there only once, changes are easy.

   C. Modularity of programming.

6-8   The Case Structure

1. **Case** is series of IF-THEN tests (F-165 and F-166).

2. BASIC case is the **ON...GOSUB** or **ON...GOTO**

3. Form is   10 ON numeric expression GOSUB line number, ...

4. If the numeric expression is zero or larger than number of line numbers listed, control falls through to next line.

6-9   Sorting for Practice

1. **Sorting** is arranging a list in sequence.

2. **Bubble sort** is the most common.

3. **Selection sort** is used.

   A. Begin at beginning and scan for smallest element.

   B. That element is then switched with first element.

   C. Search begins at next element.

   D. Searches continue until only the last element is left.

   E. Search requires a save variable - it begins with value larger than largest value in list.

4. Exchange requires temporary storage variable.

5. Pseudocode on page 170 (F-171, 172).

6. Program on page 173.

7. More sorts in Chapter 14.

Answers to Questions to Aid Understanding

1. 11 elements (0 thru 10)

2. The DIM (dimension) statement.

* 3. When you want to change a value that is stored in a DATA
statement, if you always put them in either the top or bottom of
the program, they will be easy to locate. Otherwise, you will
have to look through the entire program to find the DATA
statements in order to change them.

4. There is no limit beyond the line length of the version
of BASIC.

5. Out of data error

* 6. The RESTORE statement specifies that the DATA statement
pointer should be placed at the beginning of the first DATA
statement.

7. It allows you to test for many different items with only
one statement instead of a multitude of nested IF-THEN
statements.

8. a. B(1) = 5

   B(3) = 0 (not assigned)

   B(4) = 7

   B(8) = 0 (not assigned)

   B(10) = 1

   B(13) = 0 (not assigned - error)

   b. Subscript out of range error (not dimensioned)

   c. DIM B(50)

   d. 17

* 9. a. incorrect - there is no line number on the RETURN
            statement.

   b. incorrect - no amount to be dimensioned

   c. incorrect - the GOSUB is misspelled

d. incorrect - semicolon between A and B

e. incorrect - incomplete statement

f. incorrect - type mismatch (C$)

g. correct   - though there are two H's in a row

h. incorrect - wrong specification for READ

i. correct

j. incorrect - variable on ON...GOSUB must be numeric

* 10. a. correct

b. incorrect - A cannot contain HI and B cannot contain BYE

c. correct

d. incorrect - there is no DATA statement

e. correct

f. incorrect - A cannot contain MARY

11. The pseudocode for this program should look like:

```
Start
Initialize counter to 1
DO-WHILE counter < 4
    Read numbers to print
    Print numbers
END-DO
End
```

The program should look like:

```
10 REM ***** PROGRAM NAME: EX-6-11
20 REM
30 REM ***** WRITTEN BY EDWARD J. COBURN
40 REM
50 REM EXERCISE 6-11 - TABLE FROM READ-DATA
60 REM
70 FOR I=1 TO 3
80     READ A,B,C,D
90     PRINT A,B,C,D
100 NEXT I
110 DATA 1,3,7,15
120 DATA 6,5,9,89
130 DATA 5,8,14,22
140 END
```

```
RUN
 1          3          7          15
 6          5          9          89
 5          8          14         22
Ok
```

12. The pseudocode for this program should look like:

```
Start
Print heading
Initialize counter to 1
DO-WHILE counter < 4
     Read data to print
     Print data
     Increment counter
END-DO
End
```

The program should look like:

```
10 REM ***** PROGRAM NAME: EX-6-12
20 REM
30 REM ***** WRITTEN BY EDWARD J. COBURN
40 REM
50 REM EXERCISE 6-12 - WAGES REPORT
60 REM
65 PRINT "LAST NAME","FIRST NAME","WAGES EARNED"
70 FOR I=1 TO 5
80     READ N$,LN$,W
90       PRINT LN$,N$,W
100 NEXT I
110 END
500 DATA ED,COBURN,1000,JOHN,SMITH,3000
510 DATA TAMMY,SIMPSON,4000,STEVE,WOODS,1500
520 DATA AMY,THOMPSON,3500
RUN
LAST NAME          FIRST NAME          WAGES EARNED
COBURN             ED                  1000
SMITH              JOHN                3000
SIMPSON            TAMMY               4000
WOODS              STEVE               1500
THOMPSON           AMY                 3500
Ok
```

13. The pseudocode for this program should look like:

```
Start
Assign values
Initialize counter to 1
DO-WHILE counter < 21
     Set array variable to zero
     Increment counter
END-DO
Initialize counter to 1
DO-WHILE counter < 21
     Print array variable
     Increment counter
END-DO
End
```

The program should look like:

```
10 REM ***** PROGRAM NAME: EX-6-13
20 REM
30 REM ***** WRITTEN BY EDWARD J. COBURN
40 REM
50 REM EXERCISE 6-13 - ZERO ARRAY
60 REM
70 DIM B(20)
80 B(1)=15
90 B(4)=25
100 B(19)=0
110 FOR I=1 TO 20
120     B(I)=0
130 NEXT I
140 FOR I=1 TO 20
150     PRINT I;"=";B(I)
160 NEXT I
170 END
RUN
 1 = 0
 2 = 0
 3 = 0
 4 = 0
 5 = 0
 6 = 0
 7 = 0
 8 = 0
 9 = 0
 10 = 0
 11 = 0
 12 = 0
 13 = 0
 14 = 0
 15 = 0
 16 = 0
 17 = 0
```

(Output continues)

```
 18 = 0
 19 = 0
 20 = 0
Ok
```

  *   14. The flowchart can be seen in Figure F-5 (in the book)
and the pseudocode follows:

```
Start
Initialize counter to 1
DO-WHILE counter not greater than 5
     Read DATA into three arrays (LR, HR, D)
     Increment counter by 1
END-DO
Initialize counter to 1 (I)
Input employee name into array
DO-WHILE name not "END"
     Input rest of data
     IF deductions > 3 THEN
         Set deductions to 3 (has to fit calculations)
     (ELSE)
     END-IF
     Calculate gross pay
     Initialize tax to zero
     Initialize counter to 1 (J)
     REPEAT-UNTIL tax is not zero
         IF gross pay is within range THEN
                 Set Tax to table amount
         (ELSE)
         END-IF
         Increment counter by 1 (J)
     END-REPEAT
     Calculate Net pay
     Increment counter by 1 (I)
     Input employee name into array
END-DO
Print report using arrays
End
```

The program should look like the following:

```
10 REM ***** PROGRAM NAME: F-6-14
20 REM
30 REM ***** PAYROLL PROGRAM - EXERCISE 6 - 14
40 REM
50 DIM N$(25),GP(25),TAX(25)
55 FOR I = 1 TO 5
60 ' LR IS LOW RANGE, HR IS HIGH RANGE AND D IS DEDUCTIONS
70     READ LR(I),HR(I),D(I*3-2),D(I*3-1),D(I*3)
80 NEXT I
90 I=1                                ' LOOP COUNTER
100 INPUT "EMPLOYEE NAME";N$(I)
```

(Program continues)

```
110        IF N$(I)="END" THEN 235    ' END-OF-DATA MARKER
120        INPUT "HOURLY RATE";R
130        INPUT "HOURS WORKED";H
140        INPUT "DEDUCTIONS";DED
150        IF DED>3 THEN DED=3        ' NECESSARY TO FIT TABLE
160        GP(I)=R*H                  ' NO WORRY ABOUT OVERTIME
170        J=1                        ' COUNTER FOR NEW LOOP
180            IF GP(I)>=LR(J) AND GP(I)<HR(J) THEN
                   TAX(I) = D((J-1) * 3 + DED)
190            J=J+1                  ' INCREMENT COUNTER
200            IF TAX(I) = 0 THEN 180 ' LOOP
210        I=I+1
220 GOTO 100
225 REM
227 REM ***** READY FOR REPORT
230 REM
235 PRINT                            ' BLANK LINE
240 PRINT "NAME         GROSS PAY           TAX    NET PAY"
250 PRINT                            ' BLANK LINE
260 FOR I = 1 TO I-1                 ' NUMBER OF ENTRIES
270     NP=GP(I)-TAX(I)
280       PRINT N$(I);TAB(13);GP(I);TAB(32);TAX(I);TAB(39);NP
290 NEXT I
300 DATA 0,100,0,0,0
310 DATA 100,200,12,9,6
320 DATA 200,400,42,30,24
330 DATA 400,800,168,120,96
340 DATA 800,99999,580,394,300
350 END
RUN
EMPLOYEE NAME? ED COBURN
HOURLY RATE? 10
HOURS WORKED? 25
DEDUCTIONS? 5
EMPLOYEE NAME? TOM SMITH
HOURLY RATE? 5.25
HOURS WORKED? 40
DEDUCTIONS? 1
EMPLOYEE NAME? SAM GRID
HOURLY RATE? 3.56
HOURS WORKED? 35
DEDUCTIONS? 2
EMPLOYEE NAME? TAMMY JONES
HOURLY RATE? 13.62
HOURS WORKED? 40
DEDUCTIONS? 2
EMPLOYEE NAME? END

NAME             GROSS PAY      TAX    NET PAY

ED COBURN        250            24     226
TOM SMITH        210            42     164
SAM GRID         124.6          9      115.6
TAMMY JONES      544.8          120    424.8
Ok
```

15. The pseudocode for this program should look like:

```
Start
Initialize counter to 1
DO-WHILE counter < 10
     Read data item
     Increment counter
END-DO
Initialize counter to 9
DO-WHILE counter > 0
     Print data item
     Decrement counter by 1
END-DO
End
```

The program should look like:

```
10 REM ***** PROGRAM NAME: EX-6-15
20 REM
30 REM ***** WRITTEN BY EDWARD J. COBURN
40 REM
50 REM EXERCISE 6-15 - REVERSAL
60 REM
70 FOR I=1 TO 9
80     READ A(I)
90 NEXT I
100 FOR I=9 TO 1 STEP -1
110     PRINT A(I);
120 NEXT I
130 END
140 DATA 10,11,6,12,54,76,43,65,9
RUN
 9  65  43  76  54  12  6  11  10
Ok
```

16. The pseudocode for this program should look like:

```
Start
Print heading
Initialize counter to 1
DO-WHILE counter < 6
     Read number into array
     Increment counter
END-DO
Input number to check
DO-WHILE number not 0
     Initialize counter to 1
     DO-WHILE counter < 6
          IF input number = array item (counter) THEN
               Print number matched message
               Increase counter to 6
          (ELSE)
```

(Pseudocode continues)

```
            END-IF
        END-DO
        IF counter = 6 THEN
              Print numbers didn't match message
        (ELSE)
        END-IF
END-DO
End
```

The program should look like:

```
10 REM ***** PROGRAM NAME: EX-6-16
20 REM
30 REM ***** WRITTEN BY EDWARD J. COBURN
40 REM
50 REM EXERCISE 6-16 - INPUT CHECK
60 REM
70 FOR I=1 TO 5
80      READ A(I)                       ' GET THE DATA
90 NEXT I
100 INPUT "ENTER NUMBER TO CHECK";N
110 IF N=0 THEN 180                     ' END OF DATA MARKER
120 FOR I=1 TO 5
130      IF N<>A(I) THEN 160            ' TO END OF LOOP
140              PRINT "THE NUMBER MATCHED"
150              I=6                     ' INCREASE COUNTER TO MAX
160 NEXT I
170 IF I=6 THEN PRINT "THE NUMBER DIDN'T MATCH"
180 END
190 DATA 100,15,68,95,45
RUN
ENTER NUMBER TO CHECK? 2
THE NUMBER DIDN'T MATCH
Ok
RUN
ENTER NUMBER TO CHECK? 100
THE NUMBER MATCHED
Ok
RUN
ENTER NUMBER TO CHECK? 96
THE NUMBER DIDN'T MATCH
Ok
RUN
ENTER NUMBER TO CHECK? 95
THE NUMBER MATCHED
Ok
```

17. The pseudocode for this program should look like:

```
Start
Initialize outside counter to 1
DO-WHILE counter < 6
    Initialize inside counter to 1
    DO-WHILE counter < 7
        Read number into array
        Increment inside counter by 1
    END-DO
    Increment outside counter by 1
END-DO
Input product number to check
DO-WHILE product number not 0
    Input quantity
    IF input product number <> array item (counter) THEN
        Print error message
    (ELSE)
    END-IF
    Calculate raw materials and parts
    Print raw materials and parts
    Accumulate totals
END-DO
Print total raw materials and parts
End
```

The program should look like:

```
10 REM ***** PROGRAM NAME: EX-6-17
20 REM
30 REM ***** WRITTEN BY EDWARD J. COBURN
40 REM
50 REM EXERCISE 6-17 - XYZ RAW MATERIALS
60 REM
70 DIM T(5,6)                         ' DIMENSION TABLE
80 FOR I=1 TO 5
90     FOR J=1 TO 6
100        READ T(I,J)                 ' READ TABLE
110    NEXT J
120 NEXT I
130 INPUT "WHAT IS THE PRODUCT NUMBER";P
140 IF P=0 THEN 390                    ' END-OF-DATA MARKER
150    INPUT "WHAT IS THE QUANTITY";Q
160    I=1                             ' INITIALIZE COUNTER
170    IF T(I,1)=P THEN 220            ' TO END OF LOOP
180        I=I+1                       ' INCREMENT COUNTER
190        IF I<6 THEN 170             ' END OF LOOP
200        PRINT "NO SUCH PRODUCT NUMBER"
210        GOTO 130                    ' RETURN FROM ERROR
220    RA=T(I,2)*Q                     ' RAW A
230    RB=T(I,3)*Q                     ' RAW B
240    PA=T(I,4)*Q                     ' PART A
```

(Program continues)

```
250       PB=T(I,5)*Q                        ' PART B
260       PC=T(I,6)*Q                        ' PART C
270       PRINT "RAW A =";RA;"     RAW B =";RB
280       PRINT "PART A =";PA;"     PART B =";PB;"PART C =";PC
290       PRINT "TOTAL RAW =";RA+RB;"     TOTAL PARTS =";PA+PB+PC
300       TRA=TRA+RA                         ' TOTAL RAW A
310       TRB=TRB+RB                         ' TOTAL RAW B
320       TPA=TPA+PA                         ' TOTAL PART A
330       TPB=TPB+PB                         ' TOTAL PART B
340       TPC=TPC+PC                         ' TOTAL PART C
350       TQ=TQ+Q                            ' TOTAL QUANTITY
360       PRINT                              ' BLANK LINE
370       GOTO 130
380 REM
390 PRINT
400 PRINT
410 PRINT "TOTAL RAW A =";TRA;"     TOTAL RAW B =";TRB
420 PRINT "TOTAL PART A =";TPA;"     TOTAL PART B =";TPB
430 PRINT "TOTAL PART C =";TPC
440 PRINT "TOTAL QUANTITY PRODUCED =";TQ
450 END
460 DATA 1597,100,200,3,4,5
470 DATA 1497,3,1500,2,0,17
480 DATA 12478,15,25,10,0,0
490 DATA 1342,2,0,0,0,9
500 DATA 1458,2,2,5,6,0
RUN
WHAT IS THE PRODUCT NUMBER 1400
WHAT IS THE QUANTITY 100
NO SUCH PRODUCT NUMBER
WHAT IS THE PRODUCT NUMBER 1597
WHAT IS THE QUANTITY 10
RAW A = 1000      RAW B = 2000
PART A = 30      PART B = 40 PART C = 50
TOTAL RAW = 3000      TOTAL PARTS = 120

WHAT IS THE PRODUCT NUMBER 12478
WHAT IS THE QUANTITY 25
RAW A = 375      RAW B = 625
PART A = 250      PART B = 0 PART C = 0
TOTAL RAW = 1000      TOTAL PARTS = 250

WHAT IS THE PRODUCT NUMBER 1597
WHAT IS THE QUANTITY 100
RAW A = 10000      RAW B = 20000
PART A = 300      PART B = 400 PART C = 500
TOTAL RAW = 30000      TOTAL PARTS = 1200

WHAT IS THE PRODUCT NUMBER 1342
WHAT IS THE QUANTITY 35
RAW A = 70      RAW B = 0
PART A = 0      PART B = 0 PART C = 315
TOTAL RAW = 70      TOTAL PARTS = 315

(Output continues)
```

```
WHAT IS THE PRODUCT NUMBER 1458
WHAT IS THE QUANTITY 20
RAW A = 40        RAW B = 40
PART A = 100       PART B = 120 PART C = 0
TOTAL RAW = 80        TOTAL PARTS = 220

WHAT IS THE PRODUCT NUMBER 0


TOTAL RAW A = 11485        TOTAL RAW B = 22665
TOTAL PART A = 680        TOTAL PART B = 560
TOTAL PART C = 865
TOTAL QUANTITY PRODUCED = 190
```

CHAPTER 7 . . . . . STRING HANDLING AND FUNCTIONS

7-1 Introduction

1. A computer differs from a calculator because it can handle characters.

2. This chapter covers many different ways to handle strings.

7-2 Concatenation

1. **Concatenation** is combining of strings into a larger string.

2. The symbol is plus sign (+).

3. Example would be   10 A$ = B$ + C$

7-3 String Manipulation

1. We can capture a **substring** with one of three functions.

2. **LEFT$** gets the characters from the left.

   A. Form is:
      string variable = LEFT$(string, number of characters)

   B. Same string can be used on both sides of an assignment.

   C. Function can be part of another statement (such as IF).

3. **RIGHT$** gets the characters from the right.

   A. Form is:
      string variable = RIGHT$(string, number of characters)

4. **MID$** gets the characters from the middle.

   A. Form is:
      string variable = MID$(string, beg. position, no. of chara.)

   B. If beginning position is 1, MID$ is same as LEFT$ function.

   C. Power is getting from the middle of string.

   D. IBM BASIC will also allow assignment of MID$.

      1) Such as MID$(B$,3,4)=A$

2) In Radio Shack and Apple such an assignment requires:
B$=MID$(B$,1,2)+A$+MID$(B$,5,2) (B$ is 6 long)

E. Name reversal program on page 187.

7-4 INSTR (String Search Function)

1. The INSTR function will search for a particular string in another string (not for Apple).

2. Form is   10 INSTR(beg. position, search string, string)

3. Example is   10 A$=INSTR(1,B$,",")

4. Beginning position is optional - if 1 unnecessary.

5. Search function for Apple on page 188.

7-5 LEN (String Length Function)

1. The LEN function gives the length of a string.

2. Form is   numeric variable = LEN(string)

3. Name reversal program page 189.

4. Pseudocode on page 191 (F-192, 193).

5. Program on page 191.

7-6 String Conversion

1. Can convert string to numeric or numeric to string.

2. VAL will convert string to numeric.

   A. Form is numeric variable = VAL(string)

   B. Can be used in other statements (ON...GOSUB program 195).

3. STR$ will convert numeric to string.

   A. Form is   string variable = STR$(numeric)

   B. Demonstration program on page 196.

4. ASC will convert character to ASCII code.

   A. Form is   numeric variable = ASC(string)

   B. Demonstration program on page 196.

C. Useful on statements like ON...GOSUB.

5. **CRH$** will convert ASCII code to character.

    A. Form is   string = CHR$(numeric < 255)

    B. Demonstration program on page 198.

7-7 Filling a String

1. IBM and Radio Shack use **STRING$** function.

2. It will fill a string with a specified character.

3. Form is
string variable = STRING$(number, "character" or number)

4. Example would be   A$=STRING$(5,"A") or STRING$(5,65)

5. Apple does not have function. To create one use:

```
50 A$="-"
60 FOR I = 1 TO 6
70    A$=A$+A$
80 NEXT I
```

Sample programs on page 199.

7-8 Inputting a Character

1. The character input function inputs one character at a time.

    A. **INKEY$** is used on the IBM and Radio Shack.

    B. **GET** is used on the Apple.

2. Doesn't stop to wait for input (except Apple IIe and IIc).
Need to use loop such as:

```
10 A$=INKEY$
20 IF A$="" THEN 10
```

3. Doesn't echo character input. Need to PRINT character.

4. Password entry program on page 202.

7-9 Integer Function

1. The **INT** function will give integer of numeric.

2. Form is   10 numeric variable = INT(numeric variable)

3. Can use for **MOD** function program on page 203.

4. Can also use as **rounding** function such as:

   A. Two decimals   10 A=INT((A+.005)*100)/100

   B. One decimal   10 A=INT((A+.05)*10)/10

7-10 Random Numbers

1. A **random number** is an unpredictable number produced by chance.

2. We actually get **pseudorandom numbers**.

3. Useful for games and **sampling**.

4. Form is   10 numeric variable = RND(1)
                                    (RND(0) on Radio Shack)

5. This will give us a decimal from 0 to 1 which we need to convert: A=INT(RND(1)*6)+1

6. Random names pseudocode and program on page 205 (F-206).

7. To produce a different set of random numbers, IBM requires **RANDOMIZE** statement.

8. An example of its use would be:

   10 RANDOMIZE VAL(RIGHT$(TIME$,2))

****

Answers to Questions to Aid Understanding

1. A. RIGHT$ makes a substring of the specified number of characters counting from the middle to right end of the string.

    B. LEFT$ makes a substring of the specified number of characters beginning at the beginning of the string.

    C. MID$ makes a substring of the specified number of characters beginning at the specified location in the string.

2. It is the string search command allowing one string to be searched for a specified group of characters. The Apple has no such command.

3.   The LEN function will allow the programmer to determine the length of a string variable. This is useful as many times loops need to be executed through the number of characters in a string. This, of course, is only one example of the many uses for the length of a string.

4. VAL

5. STR$

* 6.   The ASCII decimal code is the mathematical equivalent of the binary code assigned the that particular character. It is significant in that there are many character codes that are not printable keys (such as the RETURN key) and in order to use those keys in comparisons, etc. we need to be able to indicate to the machine which character we are referencing.

7. ASC

8. CHR$

9. It is the command that allows a string to be filled with a specified character. The Apple has no such command.

* 10.   The INPUT command stops execution and waits for the user to key some data, the INKEY$ doesn't. The INPUT command automatically prints a prompt on the screen, the INKEY$ doesn't. The length of the input on the INPUT command is virtually unlimited, the INKEY$ inputs only one character.

11. It yields pseudorandom numbers.

12. The pseudocode should look like the following:

```
Start
Initialize counter to 65
DO-WHILE counter < 91
    Print character using CHR$ function
    Increment counter
END-DO
End
```

The program should look like the following:

```
10 REM ***** PROGRAM NAME: EX-7-12
20 REM
30 REM ***** WRITTEN BY EDWARD J. COBURN
40 REM
50 REM EXERCISE 7-12 - PRINT THE ALPHABET
60 REM
70 FOR I=65 TO 90
80     PRINT CHR$(I);" ";
90 NEXT I
100 END
```

```
RUN
A B C D E F G H I J K L M N O P Q R S T U V W X Y Z
Ok
```

13. The pseudocode should look like the following:

```
Start
Assign alphabet
Initialize counter to length of alphabet
DO-WHILE counter > 0
    Print character using MID$ function
    Decrement counter
END-DO
End
```

The program should look like the following:

```
10 REM ***** PROGRAM NAME: EX-7-13
20 REM
30 REM ***** WRITTEN BY EDWARD J. COBURN
40 REM
50 REM EXERCISE 7-13 - PRINT THE ALPHABET BACKWARDS
60 REM
70 A$="ABCDEFGHIJKLMNOPQRSTUVWXYZ"
80 FOR I=LEN(A$) TO 1 STEP -1
90      PRINT MID$(A$,I,1);" ";
100 NEXT I
110 END
RUN
Z Y X W V U T S R Q P O N M L K J I H G F E D C B A
Ok
```

  * 14. The flowchart can be seen in Figure F-6 (in the book) and the pseudocode follows:

```
Start
Initialize the counter to 90
DO-WHILE counter is not less than 65
    Print the character code
END-DO
End
```

The program should look like the following:

```
10 REM ***** PROGRAM NAME: F-7-14
20 REM
30 REM ***** BACKWARDS ALPHABET - EXERCISE 7 - 14
40 REM
50 FOR I = 90 TO 65 STEP -1
60      PRINT CHR$(I);" ";
70 NEXT I
80 END
```

```
RUN
Z Y X W V U T S R Q P O N M L K J I H G F E D C B A
Ok
```

15. The flowchart can be seen in Figure F-6 (in the book) and the pseudocode follows:

```
Start
RANDOMIZE
DO-UNTIL input = yes for end
   Generate a year randomly
   IF mod 4 of year THEN
     Print leap year message
   ELSE
     Print not leap year message
   END-IF
   Input yes or no to continue
END-DO
End
```

The program should look like the following:

```
10 REM ***** PROGRAM NAME: EX-7-15
20 REM
30 REM ***** WRITTEN BY EDWARD J. COBURN
40 REM
50 REM EXERCISE 7-15 - RANDOMLY GENERATE YEARS
60 REM
70 RANDOMIZE VAL(RIGHT$(TIME$,2))
80 YY=INT(RND(1)*101)+1900
90 IF YY/4=INT(YY/4) THEN PRINT YY;"IS A LEAP YEAR"
100 PRINT
110 INPUT "DO YOU WANT ANOTHER (Y OR N)";A$
120 PRINT
130 IF A$="Y" THEN 80
140 END
RUN
  48 IS A LEAP YEAR

DO YOU WANT ANOTHER (Y OR N)? Y

  31 IS NOT A LEAP YEAR

DO YOU WANT ANOTHER (Y OR N)? N

Ok
```

* 16. The pseudocode follows:

```
Start
Input word
DO-WHILE word not "END"
    Restore data pointer
    Initialize code to 0
    Initialize counter to 1
    DO-WHILE counter is less than 11
        Read data word
        IF input data word = read data word THEN
            Set code to 1
        (ELSE)
        END-IF
    END-DO
    IF code = 0 THEN
        Print misspelled message
    (ELSE)
    END-IF
    Input word
END-DO
End
```

The program should look like the following:

```
10 REM ***** PROGRAM NAME: F-7-16
20 REM
30 REM ***** SPELLING CHECKER - EXERCISE 7 - 16
40 REM
50 INPUT "WHAT WORD";W$
60   IF W$="END" THEN 170      ' END-OF-DATA MARKER
70 C=0                         ' CODE
80 RESTORE
90 FOR I = 1 TO 10
100    READ D$
110    IF W$=D$ THEN C=1 : GOTO 120
120 NEXT I
130 IF C=0 THEN PRINT "WORD ";W$;" WAS MISSPELLED"
140 GOTO 50
150 REM
160 DATA HI,BYE,TOM,HELLO,PASSWORD,UP,DOWN,AROUND,IN,OUT
170 END
RUN
WHAT WORD? GEORGE
WORD GEORGE WAS MISSPELLED
WHAT WORD? HELLO
WHAT WORD? HI
WHAT WORD? HY
WORD HY WAS MISSPELLED
WHAT WORD? END
Ok
```

17. The pseudocode follows:

```
Start
Input a character
IF character < 32 (using ASC function) THEN
   Print message
(ELSE)
END-IF
End
```

The program should look like the following:

```
10 REM ***** PROGRAM NAME: EX-7-17
20 REM
30 REM ***** WRITTEN BY EDWARD J. COBURN
40 REM
50 REM EXERCISE 7-17 - FIND NON-PRINTABLE KEYS
60 REM
70 A$=INKEY$
80 IF A$="" THEN 70                        ' LOOP
90 IF ASC(A$)<32 THEN PRINT "NOT PRINTABLE CHARACTER - CODE IS";ASC
100 END
RUN
NOT PRINTABLE CHARACTER - CODE IS 13
Ok
RUN
NOT PRINTABLE CHARACTER - CODE IS 8
Ok
```

18. The pseudocode follows:

```
Start
DO-UNTIL total value of characters >= 300
   Input a character
   DO-WHILE character < A or > Z
     Print message
     Input a character
   END-DO
   Accumulate value of character
   Print value of character
END-DO
Print end of loop message
End
```

The program should look like the following:

```
10 REM ***** PROGRAM NAME: EX-7-18
20 REM
30 REM ***** WRITTEN BY EDWARD J. COBURN
40 REM
50 REM EXERCISE 7-18 - ACCUMULATE VALUE OF ALPHABETIC CHARACTERS
60 REM
70 INPUT "WHAT CHARACTER";A$
80 IF A$<"A" OR A$>"Z" THEN PRINT "NOT A-Z" : GOTO 70
90 T=T+ASC(A$)
100 PRINT "CHARACTER = ";A$;"  DECIMAL VALUE =";ASC(A$)
                           ;"  ACCUMULATED TOTAL =";T
105 PRINT
110 IF T<300 THEN 70
120 PRINT "300 WAS REACHED.  THE LOOP IS OVER."
130 END
RUN
WHAT CHARACTER? A
CHARACTER = A  DECIMAL VALUE = 65  ACCUMULATED TOTAL = 65

WHAT CHARACTER? D
CHARACTER = D  DECIMAL VALUE = 68  ACCUMULATED TOTAL = 133

WHAT CHARACTER? Z
CHARACTER = Z  DECIMAL VALUE = 90  ACCUMULATED TOTAL = 223

WHAT CHARACTER? 1
NOT A-Z

WHAT CHARACTER? G
CHARACTER = G  DECIMAL VALUE = 71  ACCUMULATED TOTAL = 294

WHAT CHARACTER? A
CHARACTER = A  DECIMAL VALUE = 65  ACCUMULATED TOTAL = 359

300 WAS REACHED.  THE LOOP IS OVER.
Ok
```

19. The pseudocode follows:

```
Start
RANDOMIZE
Initialize counter to 1
DO-WHILE counter is < 101
   Null word accumulator
   Initialize inner counter to 1
   DO-WHILE inner counter < 4
      Generate a character
      Concatenate to create the word
   END-DO
   Print the word
END-DO
End
```

The program should look like the following:

```
10 REM ***** PROGRAM NAME: EX-7-19
20 REM
30 REM ***** WRITTEN BY EDWARD J. COBURN
40 REM
50 REM EXERCISE 7-19 - PRINT RANDOMLY GENERATED 3 LETTER WORDS
60 REM
70 RANDOMIZE VAL(RIGHT$(TIME$,2))
80 FOR I=1 TO 100
90     W$=""                            ' EMPTY THE WORD
100     FOR J=1 TO 3
110         R=INT(RND(1)*26)+65
120         W$=W$+CHR$(R)                ' CONCATENATE THE WORD
130     NEXT J
140     PRINT W$;"    ";
150 NEXT I
160 END
RUN
ARD   HGU   JWE   JJF   KGJ   QIU   NVK   JSU   JSO   JSH
JSH   JFI   KKS   JFU   KWO   MOS   PWQ   KWI   QOK   XPO
JDO   SKH   QKO   JDI   JDK   MSO   MWN   ZMI   ZMA   MNS
HFJ   IWJ   LSP   LOT   MKJ   JIU   YTG   GDD   KWK   JHU
KIT   HGE   WQH   GLO   MKJ   GUY   TGR   DEC   BHG   KJI
LOI   JNH   WLY   BOR   TLM   OIG   BVR   XCD   XKJ   HLO
LOI   YHT   GBI   EVI   LOK   SDE   HGT   NJH   LKI   VGT
NHI   KIU   HGY   WSE   FRT   HGY   KIN   BGT   FDE   BHP
IJU   YTM   NSX   ZSU   QZF   DMH   PLD   THN   DEL   OPM
GTF   GBV   VCX   MKI   JKN   BGO   PLI   AWS   FRD   UHJ
Ok
```

20. The pseudocode follows:

```
Start
Print heading
Initialize counter to 1
DO-WHILE counter is < 7
   Read inventory number
   Find dash
   Get color (MID$)
   Find slash
   Get Quantity (MID$)
   Print part number and color code
   Check code and print appropriate color
   Print quantity
END-DO
End
```

The program should look like the following:

```
10 REM ***** PROGRAM NAME: EX-7-20
20 REM
30 REM ***** WRITTEN BY EDWARD J. COBURN
40 REM
50 REM EXERCISE 7-20 - XYZ INVENTORY PART NUMBERS
60 REM
70 PRINT "NUMBER",,"COLOR DES.","COLOR","QUANTITY"
80 FOR I=1 TO 6
90     READ I$
100    J=1                                    ' INITIALIZE COUNTER
110    IF MID$(I$,J,1)="-" THEN 140           ' EXIT LOOP
120        J=J+1                               ' INCREMENT COUNTER
130        GOTO 110                            ' LOOP
140    C$=MID$(I$,J+1,2)                       ' GET COLOR
150    J=J+4                                   ' ADJUST COUNTER
160    IF MID$(I$,J,1)="/" THEN 190            ' EXIT LOOP
170        J=J+1                               ' INCREMENT COUNTER
180        GOTO 160                            ' LOOP
190    Q=VAL(MID$(I$,J+1,LEN(I$)-J+1))         ' GET QUANTITY
200    PRINT I$;TAB(29);C$,                    ' PRINT NUMBER AND COLOR DES.
210    IF C$="RE" THEN PRINT "RED",            ' PRINT COLOR
220    IF C$="GR" THEN PRINT "GREEN",          ' PRINT COLOR
230    IF C$="YE" THEN PRINT "YELLOW",         ' PRINT COLOR
240    IF C$="BL" THEN PRINT "BLACK",          ' PRINT COLOR
250    PRINT Q                                 ' PRINT QUANTITY
255    PRINT                                   ' BLANK LINE
260 NEXT I
270 END
280 DATA 123-RE-BG45/15,133-BL-GD67/95,147-YE-HQ668/46
290 DATA 1-BL-4/67,33574-GR-TG/456,4569-RE-HH/78
RUN
```

NUMBER	COLOR DES.	COLOR	QUANTITY
123-RE-BG45/15	RE	RED	15
133-BL-GD67/95	BL	BLACK	95
147-YE-HQ668/46	YE	YELLOW	46
1-BL-4/67	BL	BLACK	67
33574-GR-TG/456	GR	GREEN	456
4569-RE-HH/78	RE	RED	78

Ok

CHAPTER 8 . . . . . SEQUENTIAL FILE HANDLING

8-1 Introduction

1. Use of DATA statements has practical limits.

2. We need file processing.

3. We will not discuss Cassette processing - Only diskette.

4. Thus far BASIC versions have been quite similar.
   Disk processing is very different.
   In practice only, not in concept - concepts are the same.

8-2 Storage Methodology

1. Bit is on-off switch.

2. Byte is eight bits -- room for one character.

3. We have used two different variable types:

   A) **Numeric**

   B) **String**

   C) In data storage, variables are called **fields**
      Two types of fields; numeric and character.

4. **Related** fields make up **record**.

5. Groups of related records make up a **file**.

6. Inventory example might have the following fields:
   a) Inventory item number
   b) Item name
   c) Item description
   d) Quantity-on-hand
   e) Cost at last purchase
   f) Sales price per item
   g) Date of last purchase of item

8-3 File Names

1. File names must begin with a letter.

2. Can be up to 8 characters long on IBM and Radio Shack.
   On Apple they can be up to 30 and can have embedded blanks.

3. **File extensions** can be used on IBM and Radio Shack.

   A. On IBM:
      1) Up to three characters following a period.
      2) .BAS for BASIC programs - .DAT for data files are samples.

   B. On Radio Shack:
      1. Up to three characters following a slash (/).
      2. /CMD for system files - /BAS for BASIC programs.

4. Applesoft uses no extensions (file names are long enough).

8-4   How to Use a File

1. First the file must be opened. If you open the file for
   output and it is not there, the machine will create it
   for you automatically.

2. Second records are put into the file.
   Two methods for this:

   A. Sequential access

   B. Random access -- also knows as direct access

3. Third the file must be closed.

The OPEN command

IBM

1. Form of OPEN statement is:

   10 OPEN "file name" FOR mode AS #file number.

2. OPEN, FOR, and AS must be used as shown.

3. "file name" is programmers choice (must be in quotes).

4. Mode is for type of file processing:

   A. INPUT - for input files

   B. OUTPUT - for output files

                C. APPEND - for appending to the end of files
                           (OUTPUT will write from the beginning)

        5. File number is 1 thru 3 (special commands allow > 3).

        6. Sample statement would be:

           10 OPEN "SAMPLE" FOR OUTPUT AS #1

Radio Shack

        1. Form of OPEN statement is:

           10 OPEN "code",file number,"file name"

        2. The only statement word is OPEN.

        3. "Code" specified the type of processing:

           A. I is used for inputs

           B. O is used for outputs

           C. E is for extending the file (appending)

           D. R is for random file processing (Chapter 11)

        4. File number is 1 thru 3 (special commands for > 3).

        5. "file name" is programmers choice (must be in quotes).

        6. Sample command is:

           10 OPEN "O",1,"SAMPLE"

Apple

        1. Control of peripheral devices is through PRINT statement.

        2. Device signal:

           A. Must be used before each PRINT statement to a device.

           B. Use Control-D which is also CHR$(4).

           C. The usual use is   10 D$=CHR$(4)   (used in book)

        3. OPEN statement is of the form:

           10 PRINT D$;"OPEN file name"

        4. The file name is the programmers choice.

5. Sample OPEN statement would be:

   10 PRINT D$;"OPEN SAMPLE"

6. When reusing a data file, it must be **deleted** first with:

   10 PRINT D$;"DELETE file name"

7. The sequence to reuse a file would be:

   10 PRINT D$;"OPEN SAMPLE"
   20 PRINT D$;"DELETE SAMPLE"
   30 PRINT D$;"OPEN SAMPLE"

8. Can use **APPEND** to replace OPEN and write to end of file:

   10 PRINT D$;"APPEND file name"

The PRINT# command

1. The form of the command for IBM and Radio Shack is:

   10 PRINT#file number,field

2. A sample would be:

   10 PRINT#1,A,B,C

3. On the Apple we must issue a **WRITE** command:

   10 PRINT D$;"WRITE file name"

4. Then PRINT variables as normal:

   20 PRINT A,B,C

5. The above type of PRINT would give only one field when
   read back in. We need to PRINT with either of the following:

   A. Three separate statements:

      10 PRINT#1,A   Or (Apple)   20 PRINT A
      20 PRINT#1,B   30 PRINT B
      30 PRINT#1,C   40 PRINT C

   B. Or with embedded commas:

      10 PRINT#1,A,",",B,",",C

      Or (Apple)

      20 PRINT A,",",B,",",C

6. On the Apple, when finished, issue another PRINT D$.

The INPUT # command

    1. Form of the statement on IBM and Radio Shack is:

       10 INPUT#file number,field,field,field,...

    2. A sample would be:

       10 INPUT#1,A,B$,C

    3. Apple needs additional **READ** statement:

       10 PRINT D$;"READ file name"

    4. Then simply INPUT:

       20 INPUT A,B$,C

    5. Apple then needs additional PRINT D$.

End-of-file check

    1. Needed to keep program from reading beyond the end-of-file.

IBM and Radio Shack

    1. Command is **EOF** as:

       EOF(file number)

    2. A statement using EOF would be (to keep loop going):

       100 IF NOT EOF(1) THEN 30

Apple

    1. No special command, we need to interpret an error:

       100 ONERR GOTO line number

    2. Cause branch to line number on error.

    3. Then in the error routine we use:

       1000 E=PEEK(222)

       Which returns the number of the error that occurred.

    4. If the error number (E in sample) is 5, it was end-of-file.

The CLOSE command

1. Form of the statement on IBM and Radio Shack is:

   10 CLOSE#file number OR   10 CLOSE

2. On the Apple use:

   10 PRINT D$;"CLOSE file name"   OR   10 PRINT D$;"CLOSE"

3. The singular CLOSE will close all open files.

4. On the IBM and Radio Shack open files are automatically closed by the machine upon exiting the program for another function. You should not allow this. All files should be explicitly closed.

5. On the Apple, files are not closed automatically and if you do not close them you may loose some information.

A simple example

1. You should demonstrate the use of the commands introduced in this chapter with a simple program.

2. Book example shown on pages 225-226.

A More Comprehensive Example

1. A more complicated example is generally a useful teaching technique.

2. The one to create the file is on pages 227-230 (F-228).

3. The one to read the records is on pages 231-232 (F-229).

Program Rewrite

1. It is a good idea to show better technique than that previously demonstrated wherever possible.

2. The book rewrite is on page 235.

****

Answers to Questions to Aid Understanding

   1. If programs are to be written with more than a few simply data items, there must be some method of storing this data. The disk is the best solution.

   2. A bit is a single on-off switch. A byte is eight bits

and enough room to store a single character. A field is a group
of related characters such as a name or amount. A record is a
group of related fields. A file is a group of related records
stored on some type of storage device (in this book a disk).

3. A file extension is a marker on the file name to specify
what type of file it is.

4. A sequential file stores records one after another and
they must be read back the same way. A random file allows access
to any record in the file without concern to sequence.

5. A disk file can be accessed either sequentially or
randomly. Sequential access means every record must be read in
the order they are stored on the disk. With random access, a
particular record may be accessed without having to access the
intervening records.

* 6A. a. incorrect - uses only output code "O"

     b. correct

     c. correct

     d. incorrect - should be CLOSE not DCLOSE

     e. incorrect - code comes first

     f. incorrect - conditional is type mismatched

     g. correct

     h. incorrect - an INPUT cannot be used as shown

     i. correct

     j. incorrect - the INPUT# statement cannot use a prompt

* 6B. a. incorrect - FOR option comes second

     b. correct

     c. correct

     d. incorrect - should be CLOSE not DCLOSE

     e. incorrect - EXTEND should be APPEND

     f. incorrect - conditional is type mismatched

     g. correct

     h. incorrect - an INPUT cannot be used as shown

     i. correct

j. incorrect - the INPUT# statement cannot use a prompt

* 6C. a. incorrect - cannot include special characters (')

b. correct

c. correct

d. incorrect - should be CLOSE not DCLOSE

e. incorrect - must have file name, not number

f. incorrect - conditional is type mismatched

g. incorrect - ONERR is command, not variable name

h. incorrect - an INPUT cannot be used as shown

i. incorrect - must be used on PRINT statement

j. correct

7. The pseudocode for the first program should be:

```
Start
Open the file
Input the social security number
DO-WHILE social security number <> "END"
   Print social security number into file
   Input name
   Print name into file
   Input class
   Print class into file
   Input 5 grades
   Print the 5 grades into file
   Input social security number
END-DO
Close the file
End
```

The program should look like the following:

```
10 REM ***** PROGRAM NAME: EX-8-71
20 REM
30 REM ***** WRITTEN BY EDWARD J. COBURN
40 REM
50 REM EXERCISE 8-7 - STUDENT RECORDS FILE CREATION
60 REM
70 OPEN "STUDENTS" FOR OUTPUT AS #1      ' OPEN THE FILE
80 INPUT "WHAT IS THE SS NUMBER";SS$
90 IF SS$="END" THEN 200                 ' END THE LOOP
100     PRINT #1,SS$
110     INPUT "WHAT IS THE NAME";N$
120     PRINT #1,N$
130     INPUT "WHAT IS THE CLASS";C$
140     PRINT #1,C$
150     FOR I=1 TO 5
160             INPUT "ENTER A GRADE";G
170             PRINT #1,G
180     NEXT I
190     GOTO 80                          ' LOOP
200 CLOSE #1
210 END
```

The pseudocode for the second program follows:

```
Start
Open the file
Initialize counter to 1
DO-WHILE counter < 5
   Input record from file
   Print student ID and name
   Print department using department code
   Print grades
   Calculate average
   Print average
   Print letter grade using average
END-DO
Close the file
End
```

The program should look like the following:

```
10 REM ***** PROGRAM NAME: EX-8-72
20 REM
30 REM ***** WRITTEN BY EDWARD J. COBURN
40 REM
50 REM EXERCISE 8-7 - STUDENT RECORDS FILE PRINT
60 REM
70 OPEN "STUDENTS" FOR INPUT AS #1
80 FOR I=1 TO 4
90     INPUT #1,SS$,NL$,NF$,C$,G1,G2,G3,G4,G5
100        PRINT "STUDENT ID = ";LEFT$(SS$,3);"-";MID$(SS$,4,2);"-";
                            RIGHT$(SS$,4);
110        PRINT "          STUDENT NAME =";NF$;" ";NL$
120        IF LEFT$(C$,2)="DP" THEN PRINT
           "DEPARTMENT = DATA PROCESSING      ";"CLASS = ";RIGHT$(C$,3)
130        IF LEFT$(C$,2)="EG" THEN PRINT
           "DEPARTMENT = ENGLISH              ";"CLASS = ";RIGHT$(C$,3)
140        IF LEFT$(C$,2)="MA" THEN PRINT
           "DEPARTMENT = MATH                 ";"CLASS = ";RIGHT$(C$,3)
150        PRINT "GRADES =";STR$(G1);",";STR$(G2);",";STR$(G3);",";
160        PRINT STR$(G4);",";STR$(G5)
170        AV=(G1+G2+G3+G4+G5)/5
180        PRINT "AVERAGE =";AV;"   FOR A GRADE OF ";
190        IF AV>=90 THEN PRINT "A"
200        IF AV>=80 AND AV<90 THEN PRINT "B"
210        IF AV>=70 AND AV<80 THEN PRINT "C"
220        IF AV>=60 AND AV<70 THEN PRINT "D"
230        IF AV<60 THEN PRINT "F"
240        PRINT
250 NEXT I
260 CLOSE #1
270 END
RUN
STUDENT ID = 555-66-7777          STUDENT NAME =ED COBURN
DEPARTMENT = DATA PROCESSING      CLASS = 100
GRADES = 100, 56, 75, 88, 95
AVERAGE = 82.8    FOR A GRADE OF B

STUDENT ID = 664-56-9899          STUDENT NAME =SAM HILL
DEPARTMENT = ENGLISH              CLASS = 205
GRADES = 88, 86, 85, 92, 76
AVERAGE = 85.4    FOR A GRADE OF B

STUDENT ID = 759-89-8878          STUDENT NAME =TERRY THOMAS
DEPARTMENT = MATH                 CLASS = 106
GRADES = 45, 88, 96, 92, 99
AVERAGE = 84    FOR A GRADE OF B

STUDENT ID = 878-20-0280          STUDENT NAME =TOM HARRISON
DEPARTMENT = ENGLISH              CLASS = 445
GRADES = 40, 60, 70, 55, 63
AVERAGE = 57.6    FOR A GRADE OF F
Ok
```

8. The pseudocode for the first program should be:

```
Start
Open the file
Read the data
DO-WHILE item number <> "END"
   Print the data into file
END-DO
Close the file
End
```

The program should look like the following:

```
10 REM ***** PROGRAM NAME: EX-8-81
20 REM
30 REM ***** WRITTEN BY EDWARD J. COBURN
40 REM
50 REM EXERCISE 8-8 - INVENTORY RECORDS FILE CREATION
60 REM
70 OPEN "INVENT" FOR OUTPUT AS #1 ' OPEN THE FILE
80 READ I$,D$,Q,P                ' READ ITEM, DESC., QTY, PRICE
90 IF I$="END" THEN 150          ' END-OF-DATA MARKER
100 PRINT #1,I$
110 PRINT #1,D$
120 PRINT #1,Q
130 PRINT #1,P
140 GOTO 80
150 CLOSE #1
160 END
170 DATA 123-RE-BG45/15,HORSE COLLAR,100,15.56
180 DATA 133-BL-GD67/95,BRIDLE,25,30.15
190 DATA 147-YE-HQ668/46,BLANKET,30,12.56
200 DATA 1-BL-4/67,ROPE,20,5.67
210 DATA 33574-GR-TG/456,RIFLE,10,257.85
220 DATA 4569-RE-HH/78,BOX SHELLS,100,3.56
230 DATA END,0,0,0
```

The pseudocode for the second program follows:

```
Start
Open the file
Print heading
DO-UNTIL EOF
   Input record from file
   Print detail line
   Accumulate total cost
END-DO
Print the total cost
Close the file
End
```

The program should look like the following:

```
10 REM ***** PROGRAM NAME: EX-8-82
20 REM
30 REM ***** WRITTEN BY EDWARD J. COBURN
40 REM
50 REM EXERCISE 8-8 - INVENTORY RECORDS FILE PRINT
60 REM
70 OPEN "INVENT" FOR INPUT AS #1  ' OPEN THE FILE
80 PRINT "ITEM NUMBER        ITEM NAME      QUANTITY";
          "COST      TOTAL COST"
90 IF EOF(1) THEN 140              ' EXIT LOOP
100 INPUT#1,I$,D$,Q,P              ' READ ITEM, DESC., QTY, PRICE
110     PRINT I$;TAB(20);D$;TAB(35);Q;TAB(46);P;TAB(58);Q*P
120     TC=TC+Q*P
130     GOTO 90
140 PRINT TAB(47);"TOTAL        ";TC
150 CLOSE #1
160 END
RUN
ITEM NUMBER          ITEM NAME      QUANTITY      COST      TOTAL COST
123-RE-BG45/15       HORSE COLLAR     100         15.56       1556
133-BL-GD67/95       BRIDLE           25          30.15       753.75
147-YE-HQ668/46      BLANKET          30          12.56       376.8
1-BL-4/67            ROPE             20          5.67        113.4
33574-GR-TG/456      RIFLE            10          257.85      2578.5
4569-RE-HH/78        BOX SHELLS       100         3.56        356
                                                  TOTAL       5734.45
Ok
```

9. The pseudocode should be:

```
Start
Open the files
DO-UNTIL EOF
   Input the data from the old file
   Print the name
   Input the new address
   Print the data into the new file
END-DO
Close the file
End
```

The program should look like the following:

```
10 REM ***** PROGRAM NAME: EX-8-9
20 REM
30 REM ***** WRITTEN BY EDWARD J. COBURN
40 REM
50 REM EXERCISE 8-9 - UPDATING THE FILE
60 REM
70 OPEN "MAILFILE" FOR INPUT AS #1          ' INPUT FILE
80 OPEN "NEWFILE"  FOR OUTPUT AS #2         ' OUTPUT FILE
90 IF EOF(1) THEN 150                       ' END-OF-FILE
100      INPUT #1,N$,A$,C$,S$,Z$
110      PRINT "NAME IS ";N$                ' SHOW NAME
120      INPUT "WHAT IS THE NEW ADDRESS";NA$    ' GET NEW ADDRESS
130      PRINT #2,N$,",",NA$,",",C$,",",S$,",",Z$
140      GOTO 90
150 END
```

* 10. The pseudocode for the first program follows:

```
Start
Open the file
Initialize counter to 1
DO-WHILE counter is less than 31
     Generate random number between 1 and 10
     Dump number into file
END-DO
Close the file
End
```

The program should look like the following:

```
10 REM ***** PROGRAM NAME: F-8-10-1
20 REM
30 REM ***** RANDOM NUMBERS - EXERCISE 8 - 10
40 REM
50 REM ***** THIS IS THE DATA INPUT PROGRAM
60 REM ***** PROGRAM 1
70 REM
80 REM ***** THIS IS THE IBM VERSION
90 REM
100 OPEN "RANDOM1" FOR OUTPUT AS #1
105 FOR I = 1 TO 30
110      R=INT(RND(0)*10)+1              ' NUMBER FROM 1 TO 10
120      PRINT #1,R
130 NEXT I
140 CLOSE
150 END
```

To create the second file, only the file name needs to be changed in the program and then the program should be rerun. The second pseudocode list follows:

```
Start
Open the files
Initialize counter to 1
DO-WHILE counter is less than 31
      Input one number from each file
      IF numbers match THEN
            Print number and match message
      ELSE
            Print both numbers, difference and mismatch message
      END-IF
END-DO
Close the files
End
```

The program should look like the following:

```
10 REM ***** PROGRAM NAME: F-8-10-2
20 REM
30 REM ***** RANDOM NUMBERS - EXERCISE 8 - 10
40 REM
50 REM ***** THIS IS THE FILE INPUT PROGRAM
60 REM ***** PROGRAM 2
70 REM
80 REM ***** THIS IS THE IBM VERSION
90 REM
100 OPEN "RANDOM1" FOR INPUT AS #1
110 OPEN "RANDOM2" FOR INPUT AS #2
115 FOR I = 1 TO 30
117     INPUT #1,N1
120     INPUT #2,N2
130     IF N1 = N2 THEN PRINT "THE NUMBER WAS";N1;
                      "AND THEY MATCHED"
        ELSE PRINT "MISMATCH, #1=";N1;" #2=";N2;
                  " DIFFERENCE=";N1-N2
140 NEXT I
150 CLOSE
160 END
```

A sample of the output of this program would be (only a few of the 30 are listed):

```
RUN
THE NUMBER WAS 10 AND THEY MATCHED
MISMATCH, #1= 9  #2= 4   DIFFERENCE= 5
MISMATCH, #1= 1  #2= 3   DIFFERENCE= -2
MISMATCH, #1= 4  #2= 8   DIFFERENCE= -4
MISMATCH, #1= 3  #2= 7   DIFFERENCE= -4
MISMATCH, #1= 6  #2= 1   DIFFERENCE= 5
THE NUMBER WAS 4 AND THEY MATCHED
```

* 11. The pseudocode for the first program follows:

```
Start
Open the file
Input the name
DO-WHILE name <> "END"
   Print name into file
   Input the rest of the data
   Print data into file
END-DO
Close the file
End
```

The program should look like the following:

```
10 REM ***** PROGRAM NAME: EX-8-111
20 REM
30 REM ***** SALARY FILE STORAGE PROGRAM
40 REM
50 REM ***** WRITTEN BY EDWARD J. COBURN
60 REM
70 REM THIS IS EXERCISE 8-11-1
80 REM
90 OPEN "SALARY" FOR OUTPUT AS #1    ' OPEN THE FILE
100 INPUT "WHAT IS THE NAME";N$
110 IF N$="END" THEN 250             ' END-OF-DATA MARKER
120     PRINT#1,N$                   ' PUT THE NAME IN FILE
130     INPUT "WHAT IS THE SS NUMBER";SS$
140     INPUT "WHAT IS THE SALARY CODE";C$
150     IF C$="S" THEN INPUT "WHAT IS THE SALARY";S
155     IF C$="H" THEN INPUT "WHAT IS THE HOURLY RATE";S
160     INPUT "WHAT IS THE NUMBER OF HOURS";H
170     PRINT#1,SS$
180     PRTNT#1,C$
190     PRINT#1,S
200     PRINT#1,H
210     GOTO 100                     ' RETURN FOR MORE INPUT
220 REM
230 REM ***** END OF THE PROGRAM
240 REM
250 CLOSE #1                         ' CLOSE THE FILE
260 END
RUN
WHAT IS THE NAME? ED COBURN
WHAT IS THE SS NUMBER? 497881906
WHAT IS THE SALARY CODE? S
WHAT IS THE SALARY? 450
WHAT IS THE NUMBER OF HOURS? 40.5
END
Ok
(Only one entry was demonstrated)
```

The pseudocode for the second program follows:

```
Start
Open the file
Print the heading
DO-WHILE not EOF
   Input data from file
   Print social security number, name, and salary code
   IF salary code = S THEN
      Print salary message
   ELSE
      Print amount
      Calculate hourly wages
   END-IF
   Print hours and salary amount (or wages)
   Accumulate total pay
END-DO
Print the total pay
Close the file
End
```

The program should look like the following:

```
10 REM ***** PROGRAM NAME: EX-8-112
20 REM
30 REM ***** SALARY FILE PRINT PROGRAM
40 REM
50 REM ***** WRITTEN BY EDWARD J. COBURN
60 REM
70 REM THIS IS EXERCISE 8-11-2
80 REM
90 OPEN "SALARY" FOR INPUT AS #1          ' OPEN THE FILE
100 PRINT "SOCIAL SEC. #    NAME            CODE    RATE";
           "     HOURS   WEEKLY PAY"
110 IF EOF(1) THEN 210                     ' END THE LOOP
120     INPUT #1,N$,SS$,C$,S,H
130     PRINT LEFT$(SS$,3);"-";MID$(SS$,4,2);"-";
           RIGHT$(SS$,4);"       ";N$;
140     PRINT TAB(35);C$;
150     IF C$="S" THEN PRINT "     SALARY"; ELSE PRINT "     ";S;
160     IF C$="H" THEN S=S*H               ' CALCULATE HOURLY
170     PRINT TAB(50);H;TAB(60);S
180     TP=TP+S                            ' TOTAL PAY
190     GOTO 110
200 REM
210 PRINT TAB(61);"--------"
220 PRINT TAB(50);"TOTAL      ";TP
230 CLOSE #1
240 END
```

```
RUN
SOCIAL SEC. #     NAME             CODE    RATE      HOURS    WEEKLY PAY
497-88-1906       ED COBURN        S       SALARY    40.5     450
687-95-8392       SARA SMITH       H       2.65      40       106
487-85-9374       TOM HARRIS       H       3.85      35.6     137.06
837-69-4872       SALLY THOMAS     S       SALARY    40       325
847-82-2929       FRED FILSTER     H       6.75      38.5     259.875
                                                              --------
                                                     TOTAL    1277.935
```

CHAPTER 9 . . . . . MENUS AND REPORTS

9-1 Introduction

   1. Explain **user-oriented programming.**

9-2 **Menu-oriented Programs**

   1. One method of user-oriented is **menu-driven programs.**

   2. Lets user pick among items displayed on menu.

   3. Example is shown on page 243.

   4. Use an error trap for those items outside of input range.

   5. Reuse of the input line requires **direct cursor addressing.**

IBM direct cursor addressing

   1. Form is

        10 LOCATE row, column

   2. Book uses subroutine in line 5000 (page 245).

Radio Shack direct cursor addressing

Model III

   1. Form is

        10 PRINT @(cursor position),item;item;...

   2. Row and column format is

        10 PRINT @((R-1)*64+C-1),"";

   3. Book uses subroutine in line 5000 (page 247).

Model 4

   1. Form is

        10 PRINT @(row,column),item;item;...

   2. Book uses subroutine in line 5000 (page 247).

Apple direct cursor addressing

    1. Apple uses VTAB and HTAB as

        10 VTAB row
        20 HTAB column

    2. Book uses subroutine in line 5000 (page 248).

9-3 **Back to the Menu Program**

    1. This section will add the cursor addressing to the routine being built (pages 248-249).

9-4 **A Few Guidelines About Screen displays**

    1. Every screen should have a heading.

    2. Screen should be balanced.

    3. Don't clutter the screen - use two if necessary.

    4. Use blank lines between, when appropriate.

    5. Prompts should appear in the same place on the screen. (Book uses the bottom of the screen.)

    6. Keep the prompts short but informative.

    7. Error messages should not be cryptic and never use codes.

    8. Error messages should be displayed in the same place. (Book uses bottom of screen for this also.)

    9. Error messages should attract the user's attention.
       A. Flashing (the method used in the book)
       B. In color
       C. Highlighting

9-5 **Displaying an Error Message**

    1. Error message routine is in line 6000 and shown on page 251.

    2. The entire screen display program is on page 252.

9-6 **Report Generation - General Information**

    1. There are three things to be concerned about:

       A. What the report should contain.

B. Whether the report should be printed or simply displayed on the screen.

C. What format the report should have.

1) Detail lines

2) Headings - page and column

3) Totals - subtotals and final totals

9-7 The Line Spacing Chart

1. A line spacing chart should be shown and demonstrated.

2. Figures 9-1 (page 254) and 9-2 (page 255) are examples.

9-8 Report Generation - Data Editing

1. BASIC automatically defaults to **single precision**

2. Up to seven significant digits -9,999,999 --- 9,999,999.

Different Precisions

1. Number larger or smaller than precision are represented with **scientific notation** --- 9.0097E15

2. Double precision

A. Apple does not have double precision

B. Variable is marked with # such as A#

C. Allows up to 17 significant digits

3. Integers

A. Sometimes improves program execution speed.

B. Variable is marked with % such as A%

C. Value range is from -32768 to 32768.

4. Other points

A. Main difference between precision is storage required.

1) Integer requires two bytes

2) Single precision requires four bytes

3) Double precision requires eight bytes

    B. All variables are different - A and A% or A# are not related.

The PRINT USING for IBM and Radio Shack

1. Data sample program is on page 256.

2. Form of **PRINT USING** is:

    10 PRINT USING "edit string";item;item;...

3. Edit string uses format characters of:

    A. # - for indicating position of numbers.

    B. . - for indicating decimal points.

    C. , - for indicating position of commas in long numbers.

    D. $ - for indicating positional dollar sign.

    E. $$ - for **floating dollar sign.**

    F. /blanks/ - for indicating position of literals will leave two additional blanks for slashes.

    G. There are other codes but these are the commonly used ones.

4. Sample table shown on page 258.

5. Program showing use is on page 258.

Programming Your Own Data Editing For Apple

1. The Apple has no PRINT USING so one must be created.

2. Program showing data editing routine is on page 260.

3. You may wish to add modifications to the routine or possibly make the modifications an assignment for the students.

9-9 Report Generation - Subtotals

1. A **subtotal** is sometimes called a **control total.**

2. Subtotals are written after **control break.**

3. Control breaks are keyed to a change in a **control field.**

4. Field saved for comparison against control field is called **test field**.

5. Sample inventory program is on page 262 (F-263).

9-10 Report Generation - A Final Consideration

1. Without the detail lines you have a **totals report** or **summary report**.

2. Sample summary report shown on page 265.

****

Answers to Questions to Aid Understanding

1. User-oriented programming simply means writing the programs so they are as easy to use as possible. It is important because too many programs are written without regard for the user and some are virtually worthless because they are too difficult to use.

2. A menu-driven program is one in which the program options are displayed in a menu on the screen.

3. A. Every screen should have a heading.

   B. Screen should be balanced.

   C. Don't clutter the screen - use two if necessary.

   D. Use blank lines between, when appropriate.

   E. Prompts should appear in the same place on the screen. (Book uses the bottom of the screen.)

   F. Keep the prompts short but informative.

   G. Error messages should not be cryptic and never use codes.

   H. Error messages should be displayed in same place. (Book uses bottom of screen for this also.)

   I. Error messages should attract the users attention.
      1) Flashing (the method used in the book)
      2) In color
      3) Highlighting

* 4. Error messages are important because they tell the user exactly what was entered incorrectly leaving no doubt in the user's mind about how to correct the error. Without error messages, program usage is a very frustrating experience.

5.   A. What the report should contain.

     B. Whether the report should be printed or simply
        displayed on the screen.

     C. What format the report should have.

        1) Detail lines

        2) Headings - page and column

        3) Totals - subtotals and final totals

6.   Control breaks are breaks in the normal flow of the
program caused by the changing on a particular key record. They
are used to generate subtotals.

7.   The pseudocode for the first program follows:

```
Start
Open the file
Read the inventory number and quantity
DO-WHILE inventory number <> "END"
   Print data into file
   Read the inventory number and quantity
END-DO
Close the file
End
```

The program should look like the following:


```
10 REM ***** PROGRAM NAME: EX-9-7
20 REM
30 REM ***** WRITTEN BY EDWARD J. COBURN
40 REM
50 REM EXERCISE 9-7 - INVENTORY SUBTOTALS
60 REM
70 OPEN "INVENT" FOR OUTPUT AS #1        ' INPUT FILE
80 READ I$,Q
90 IF I$="END" THEN 120                  ' END-OF-DATA MARKER
100     PRINT #1,I$,",",Q                 ' DUMP INTO FILE
110     GOTO 80
120 CLOSE #1
130 END
2000 DATA 123-BL-BG45/97,15,123-BL-HT32/132,25,123-RE-F4.6/2,32
2010 DATA 135-BL-RD46/2,765,135-RE-RE3/45,952
2020 DATA 400-GR-4/2,45,400-GR-15/3,46
2030 DATA 452-BL-RF15/2,386
2040 DATA 542-BL-TF45/24,34,542-RE-TF14/35,45
2050 DATA END,0
```

The pseudocode for the second program follows:

```
Start
Open the file
Print headings
DO-UNTIL EOF
   Read the data
   IF control field has changed THEN
      Execute control subroutine
   (ELSE)
   END-IF
   Accumulate quantity subtotal
   Print inventory number and department code
   Print the color based upon code
   Search for the slash
   Print the class (after the slash) and the quantity
   Assign the test field (for control break testing)
END-DO
Execute control subroutine
Print the plant total
Close the file
End

Start control subroutine
Print the subtotal line
Accumulate the total quantity
Zero out subtotal quantity
Assign the test field
End subroutine
```

The program should look like the following:

```
10 REM ***** PROGRAM NAME: EX-9-72
20 REM
30 REM ***** WRITTEN BY EDWARD J. COBURN
40 REM
50 REM EXERCISE 9-7 - INVENTORY SUBTOTALS REPORT
60 REM
70 OPEN "INVENT" FOR INPUT AS #1         ' OPEN THE FILE
80 CLS
90 PRINT TAB(20);"INVENTORY REPORT"
100 PRINT
110 PRINT "ITEM NUMBER        DEPT CODE     COLOR     ";
          "CLASS     QUANTITY"
120 IF EOF(1) THEN 290                    ' END-OF-FILE MARKER
130 INPUT #1,I$,Q                         ' READ INV. # AND QTY
140 IF T$<>"" AND T$<>LEFT$(I$,3) THEN GOSUB 360' CONTROL BREAK
150    S=S+Q                              ' ACCUMULATE SUBTOTAL
160    PRINT I$;TAB(24);LEFT$(I$,3);TAB(33);
170    IF MID$(I$,5,2)="RE" THEN PRINT "RED";
180    IF MID$(I$,5,2)="GR" THEN PRINT "GREEN";
190    IF MID$(I$,5,2)="BL" THEN PRINT "BLACK";
```

(Program continues)

```
200      IF MID$(I$,5,2)="YE" THEN PRINT "YELLOW;
210      A=INSTR(I$,"/")                   ' SEARCH FOR /
220      PRINT TAB(44);USING "###";VAL(MID$(I$,A+1,LEN(I$)-A+1));
230      PRINT TAB(54);USING "#####";Q
240      T$=LEFT$(I$,3)                     ' ASSIGN TEST FIELD
250      GOTO 120                           ' GET MORE DATA
260 REM
270 REM ***** END OF DATA ROUTINE
280 REM
290 GOSUB 360                               ' PRINT SUBTOTAL
300 PRINT "PLANT TOTAL";TAB(63);
310 PRINT USING "###### */*";T              ' PRINT TOTAL
315 CLOSE #1                                ' CLOSE THE FILE
320 END
330 REM
340 REM ***** CONTROL SUBROUTINE
350 REM
360 PRINT "DEPT TOTAL";TAB(24);LEFT$(T$,3);
        TAB(58);USING "###### *";S
370 T=T+S                                   ' ACCUMULATE TOTAL
380 S=0                                     ' ZERO OUT SUBTOTAL
390 T$=LEFT$(I$,3)                          ' SET UP TEST FIELD
400 RETURN
```

The execution of the program follows:

RUN
                    INVENTORY REPORT

ITEM NUMBER	DEPT CODE	COLOR	CLASS	QUANTITY		
123-BL-BG45/97	123	BLACK	97	15		
123-BL-HT32/132	123	BLACK	132	25		
123-RE-F4.6/2	123	RED	2	32		
DEPT TOTAL	123				72	*
135-BL-RD46/2	135	BLACK	2	765		
135-RE-RE3/45	135	RED	45	952		
DEPT TOTAL	135				1717	*
400-GR-4/2	400	GREEN	2	45		
400-GR-15/3	400	GREEN	3	46		
DEPT TOTAL	400				91	*
452-BL-RF15/2	452	BLACK	2	386		
DEPT TOTAL	452				386	*
542-BL-TF45/24	542	BLACK	24	34		
542-RE-TF14/35	542	RED	35	45		
DEPT TOTAL	542				79	*
PLANT TOTAL					2345	*/*

Ok

8. The pseudocode and program will look the same except for removing the lines that print the detail. In the program they are lines 160-240. The output should look like the following:

```
RUN
                     INVENTORY REPORT

ITEM NUMBER          DEPT CODE    COLOR    CLASS    QUANTITY
DEPT TOTAL              123                                      72 *
DEPT TOTAL              135                                    1717 *
DEPT TOTAL              400                                      91 *
DEPT TOTAL              452                                     386 *
DEPT TOTAL              542                                      79 *
PLANT TOTAL                                                    2345 */*
Ok
```

9. The pseudocode for the program follows:

```
Start
Open the file
Print headings
DO-UNTIL EOF
   Input the data
   Print the detail line
END-DO
Close the file
End
```

The program should look like the following:

```
10 REM ***** PROGRAM NAME: EX-9-9
20 REM
30 REM ***** WRITTEN BY EDWARD J. COBURN
40 REM
50 REM EXERCISE 9-9 - MAIL LIST
60 REM
70 OPEN "MAILFILE" FOR INPUT AS #1
80 PRINT TAB(30);"MAIL FILE LIST"
90 PRINT
100 PRINT "NAME                ADDRESS              ";
          "CITY          STATE     ZIP"
110 IF EOF(1) THEN 180                   ' CHECK FOR END OF FILE
120      INPUT #1,N$,A$,C$,S$,Z$
130      PRINT N$;TAB(18);A$;TAB(39);C$;TAB(53);S$;TAB(62);Z$
140      GOTO 110
150 REM
160 REM ***** END OF THE PROGRAM
170 REM
180 CLOSE #1                             ' CLOSE THE FILE
190 END
```

```
RUN
                         MAIL FILE LIST

NAME                ADDRESS             CITY        STATE    ZIP
ED COBURN           1400 SOUTH STREET   EL PASO      TX     76708
TOM SMITH           415 SOUTH STREET    CINCINNATI   OH     98705
AMY JOHNSON         458 WEST WESTWOOD   NASHVILLE    TN     64578
HARROLD ROBBINS     896 TERRANCE SQUARE NEW YORK     NY     10056
Ok
```

10. The pseudocode follows:

```
Start
Open the file
Print headings
DO-UNTIL EOF
   Read the data
   IF control field has changed THEN
      Execute control subroutine
   (ELSE)
   END-IF
   Print the social security number, name, and salary code
   IF salary code is S THEN
      Print salary message
   ELSE
      Print hourly rate
      Calculate the hourly pay
   END-IF
   Print the hours and gross pay
   Accumulate totals and subtotals
   Assign test field for control break
END-DO
Execute control subroutine
Print the grand total
Close the file
End

Start control subroutine
Print the subtotal line
Accumulate the total quantity
Zero out subtotal quantity
Assign the test field
End subroutine
```

The program should look like the following:

```
10 REM ***** PROGRAM NAME: EX-9-10
20 REM
30 REM ***** SALARY FILE CONTROL BREAK PROGRAM
40 REM
50 REM ***** WRITTEN BY EDWARD J. COBURN
60 REM
70 REM THIS IS EXERCISE 9-10
```

(Program continues)

```
80 REM
90 OPEN "SALARY" FOR INPUT AS #1           ' OPEN THE FILE
100 PRINT TAB(30);"PAYROLL REPORT"
110 PRINT
120 PRINT "SOC. SEC. #    NAME           CODE    ";
          "RATE    HOURS    GROSS PAY"
130 PRINT
140 IF EOF(1) THEN 350                     ' END THE LOOP
150     INPUT #1,N$,SS$,C$,S,H
160     IF T$<>"" AND T$<>C$ THEN GOSUB 430 ' CONTROL BREAK
170     PRINT LEFT$(SS$,3);"-";MID$(SS$,4,2);"-";
          RIGHT$(SS$,4);"   ";N$;
180     PRINT TAB(29);C$;
190     IF C$="S" THEN PRINT "     SALARY";
                ELSE PRINT USING"    #.##";S;
200     IF C$="H" THEN S=S*H               ' CALCULATE HOURLY
210     PRINT TAB(43);USING "##.#";H;
220     PRINT TAB(52);USING "###.##";S
290     TD=TD+D                            ' FINAL TOTAL OF DEDUCTIONS
300     TP=TP+S                            ' TOTAL PAY
310     TS=TS+S                            ' SUBTOTAL OF PAY
320     T$=C$                              ' SETUP TEST FIELD
330     GOTO 140
340 REM
350 GOSUB 430                              ' CONTROL SUBROUTINE
360 PRINT TAB(51);"-------"
370 PRINT TAB(51);"-------"
380 PRINT TAB(36);USING "GRAND TOTAL    #,###.##";TP
385 CLOSE #1
390 END
400 REM
410 REM ***** CONTROL SUBROUTINE
420 REM
430 PRINT TAB(51);"-------"
440 IF NOT EOF(1) THEN PRINT TAB(29);USING
                        "TOTAL FOR SALARIES    #,###.##";TS
                ELSE PRINT TAB(31);USING
                        "TOTAL FOR HOURLY    #,###.##";TS
450 PRINT
460 TS=0                                   ' ZERO OUT TOTAL
470 T$=C$
480 RETURN
```

```
RUN                       PAYROLL REPORT

SOC. SEC. #    NAME          CODE    RATE    HOURS   GROSS PAY

497-88-1906    ED COBURN      S     SALARY   40.5     450.00
837-69-4872    SALLY THOMAS   S     SALARY   40.0     325.00
                                                    -------
                            TOTALS FOR SALARIES      775.00

687-95-8392    SARA SMITH     H      2.65    40.0     106.00
487-85-9374    TOM HARRIS     H      3.85    35.6     137.06
847-82-2929    FRED FILSTER   H      6.75    38.5     259.88
                                                    -------
                            TOTALS FOR HOURLY        502.94

                                                    -------
                                                    -------
                            GRAND TOTAL            1,277.94
```

11. The pseudocode follows:

```
Start
Open the file
Print headings
DO-UNTIL EOF
    Read the data
    IF control field has changed THEN
        Execute control subroutine
    (ELSE)
    END-IF
    Print the social security number, name, and salary code
    IF salary code is S THEN
        Print salary message
    ELSE
        Print hourly rate
        Calculate the hourly pay
    END-IF
    Print the hours and gross pay
    Calculate the deductions
    Print the deductions and net pay
    Accumulate totals and subtotals
    Assign test field for control break
END-DO
Execute control subroutine
Print the grand totals
Close the file
End

Start control subroutine
Print the subtotal line
Accumulate the total quantity
Zero out subtotal quantity
Assign the test field
End subroutine
```

The program should look like the following:

```
10 REM ***** PROGRAM NAME: EX-9-11
20 REM
30 REM ***** SALARY FILE CONTROL BREAK PROGRAM WITH FICA AND NET
40 REM
50 REM ***** WRITTEN BY EDWARD J. COBURN
60 REM
70 REM THIS IS EXERCISE 9-11
80 REM
90 OPEN "SALARY" FOR INPUT AS #1          ' OPEN THE FILE
100 PRINT TAB(30);"PAYROLL REPORT"
110 PRINT
120 PRINT "SOC. SEC. #    NAME          CODE    ";
          "RATE   HOURS   GROSS PAY   DEDUCT.    NET PAY"
130 PRINT
140 IF EOF(1) THEN 350                    ' END THE LOOP
150     INPUT #1,N$,SS$,C$,S,H
160     IF T$<>"" AND T$<>C$ THEN GOSUB 430 ' CONTROL BREAK
170     PRINT LEFT$(SS$,3);"-";MID$(SS$,4,2);"-";
              RIGHT$(SS$,4);"   ";N$;
180     PRINT TAB(29);C$;
190     IF C$="S" THEN PRINT "      SALARY";
                  ELSE PRINT USING"   #.##";S;
200     IF C$="H" THEN S=S*H              ' CALCULATE HOURLY
210     PRINT TAB(43);USING "##.#";H;
220     PRINT TAB(52);USING "###.##";S;
230     F=S*.0965                         ' FICA TAX
240     TX=S*.22                          ' FEDERAL TAX
250     D=F+TX                            ' TOTAL DEDUCTIONS
260     SD=SD+D                           ' SUBTOTAL OF DEDUCTIONS
270     NP=S-D                            ' NET PAY
280     PRINT USING "  ###.##    ###.##";D;NP
290     TD=TD+D                           ' FINAL TOTAL OF DEDUCTIONS
300     TP=TP+S                           ' TOTAL PAY
310     TS=TS+S                           ' SUBTOTAL OF PAY
320     T$=C$                             ' SETUP TEST FILES
330     GOTO 140
340 REM
350 GOSUB 430                             ' CONTROL SUBROUTINE
360 PRINT TAB(51);"-------   ------   ------"
370 PRINT TAB(51);"-------   ------   ------"
380 PRINT TAB(36);USING
          "GRAND TOTAL   #,###.##   ###.##    ###.##";TP;TD;TP-TD
385 CLOSE #1
390 END
400 REM
410 REM ***** CONTROL SUBROUTINE
420 REM
430 PRINT TAB(51);"-------   ------   ------"
```

(Program continues)

```
     440 IF NOT EOF(1) THEN PRINT TAB(28);USING
         "TOTALS FOR SALARIES   #,###.##   ###.##    ###.##";TS;SD;TS-SD
                  ELSE PRINT TAB(30);USING
         "TOTALS FOR HOURLY   #,###.##   ###.##    ###.##";TS;SD;TS-SD
     450 PRINT
     460 TS=0                               ' ZERO OUT TOTAL
     465 SD=0                               ' ZERO OUT DEDUCTIONS
     470 T$=C$                                SUBTOTAL
     480 RETURN
RUN
                         PAYROLL REPORT

SOC. SEC. #    NAME          CODE    RATE    HOURS   GROSS PAY   DEDUCT.    NET PAY

497-88-1906    ED COBURN      S     SALARY   40.5      450.00    142.43     307.58
837-69-4872    SALLY THOMAS   S     SALARY   40.0      325.00    102.86     222.14
                                                      --------   ------     ------
               TOTALS  FOR SALARIES                    775.00    245.29     529.71

687-95-8392    SARA SMITH     H     2.65     40.0      106.00     33.55      72.45
487-85-9374    TOM HARRIS     H     3.85     35.6      137.06     43.38      93.68
847-82-2929    FRED FILSTER   H     6.75     38.5      259.88     82.25     177.62
                                                      --------   ------     ------
               TOTALS  FOR HOURLY                      502.94    159.18     343.76

                                                      --------   ------     ------
                                                      --------   ------     ------
                              GRAND TOTAL            1,277.94    404.47     873.47
Ok
```

* 12. This program is written using DATA statements although it could be used with the data files created previously. The purpose of this program is to practice using the screen formatting, not using data files. The flowchart can be seen in Figure F-10 (in the book), the line spacing chart in Figure F-11 (in the book), and the pseudocode follows:

```
     Start
     Read data items into array from DATA statements
     Read cursor positions into array from DATA statements
     Display item screen
     Input record number
     DO-WHILE record number not "END"
          Display record on screen using cursor positions
          Input item number to change
          DO-WHILE item number not zero
               Input new item and print on screen using cursor position
               Input item number to change
          END-DO
          Input record number
     END-DO
     Print program ending message
     End
```

The following is the program:

```
10 REM ***** PROGRAM NAME: F-9-12
20 REM
30 REM ***** ITEM MAINTENANCE - EXERCISE 9 - 12
40 REM
50 FOR I = 1 TO 5
60      READ I$(I),D$(I),Q(I),PD$(I),COST(I)
70 NEXT I
80 FOR I = 1 TO 5
90      READ M$(I),R(I),C(I)            ' MESSAGE,ROW,COLUMN
100 NEXT I
110 REM
120 REM ***** SCREEN DISPLAY
130 REM
140 CLS                                 ' CLEAR THE SCREEN
150 PRINT TAB(10);"INVENTORY MAINTENANCE"
160 PRINT                               ' BLANK LINE
170 PRINT "YOUR OPTIONS ARE:"
180 PRINT                               ' BLANK LINE
190 FOR I = 1 TO 5                       ' PROMPT LOOP
200      PRINT USING "#";I;              ' FIELD NUMBER
210      PRINT ".   ";M$                 ' MESSAGE
220 NEXT I
240 R=23                                ' ROW
250 C=1                                 ' COLUMN
260 GOSUB 5000                          ' CURSOR POSITIONING
270 INPUT "WHAT INVENTORY NUMBER TO CHANGE";I$
280 REM
290 REM ***** VERIFY ITEM
300 REM
305 IF I$="END" THEN 10000              ' END-OF-DATA MARKER
310 FOR I = 1 TO 5                       ' LOCATE LOOP
320      IF I$(I)=I$ THEN 400            ' EXIT LOOP
330 NEXT I
340 M$="INVENTORY NUMBER NOT FOUND.  TRY AGAIN"
350 GOSUB 6000                          ' ERROR ROUTINE
360 GOTO 240                            ' GET INVENTORY NUMBER
370 REM
380 REM ***** DISPLAY RECORD INFORMATION
390 REM
400 R=R(1)
410 C=C(1)
420 GOSUB 5000
430 PRINT I$(I)
440 R=R(2)
450 C=C(2)
460 GOSUB 5000
470 PRINT D$(I)
480 R=R(3)
490 C=C(3)
500 GOSUB 5000
510 PRINT USING "###,###";Q(I)
```

(Program continues)

```
520 R=R(4)
530 C=C(4)
540 GOSUB 5000
550 PRINT D$(I)
560 R=R(5)
570 C=C(5)
580 GOSUB 5000
590 PRINT USING "$###,###.##";C(I)
600 REM
610 REM ***** INPUT ITEM TO CHANGE
620 REM
630 R=23
640 C=1
650 GOSUB 5000                          ' POSITION CURSOR
660 PRINT STRING$(39," ");              ' BLANK LINE
670 GOSUB 5000
680 INPUT "WHAT ITEM TO CHANGE (1-5, 0 TO EXIT)";A
685 IF A=0 THEN 140                     ' REDISPLAY SCREEN
690 IF A>0 AND A<6 THEN 730
700 M$="INCORRECT ENTRY.  TRY AGAIN"
710 GOSUB 6000
720 GOTO 630                            ' REINPUT
730 GOSUB 5000
740 PRINT STRING$(39," ");              ' BLANK LINE
750 GOSUB 5000
760 PRINT "ENTER NEW ";M$(A);          ' PROMPT
770 INPUT A$
780 IF A=1 THEN I$(I)=A$
790 IF A=2 THEN D$(I)=A$
800 IF A=3 THEN Q(I)=VAL(A$)
810 IF A=4 THEN D$(I)=A$
820 IF A=5 THEN COST(I)=VAL(A$)
830 GOTO 400                            ' RETURN TO DISPLAY
9000 DATA 123-BL-BG45/97,HORSE COLLAR,154,10/15/84,15.65
9010 DATA 123-BL-HT32/132,BLUE JEEP,25,10/17/83,1500.00
9020 DATA 135-BL-RD46/2,PETTICOAT,30,12/17/83,12.54
9030 DATA 400-GR-4/2,HAIR PIECE,45,01/15/82,53.45
9040 DATA 542-RE-TF14/35,POOL CUE,156,01/14/82,13.25
9050 DATA INVENTORY ITEM,5,23
9060 DATA ITEM DESCRIPTION,6,25
9070 DATA QUANTITY-ON-HAND,7,30
9080 DATA LAST PURCHASE DATE,8,29
9090 DATA COST AT LAST PURCHASE,9,27
10000 CLS                               ' CLEAR THE SCRREN
10010 PRINT "PROGRAM ENDED...."
10020 END
```

The following is a sample of the way a display screen would look after the item information had been displayed:

```
                   INVENTORY MAINTENANCE

        YOUR OPTIONS ARE:

        1.   INVENTORY ITEM        123-RE-BG45/15
        2.   ITEM DESCRIPTION        HORSE COLLAR
        3.   QUANTITY-ON-HAND                 154
        4.   LAST PURCHASE DATE        10/15/84
        5.   COST AT LAST PURCHASE       $15.65


        WHAT ITEM TO CHANGE (1-5, 0 TO EXIT)?
```

13. There is no pseudocode necessary since this program is simply a series of PRINT statements. The program follows:

```
10 REM ***** PROGRAM NAME: EX-9-13
20 REM
30 REM ***** MENU PROGRAM
40 REM
50 REM ***** WRITTEN BY EDWARD J. COBURN
60 REM
70 REM THIS IS EXERCISE 9-13
80 REM
90 CLS                           ' CLEAR THE SCREEN
100 PRINT TAB(20);"PAYROLL MAIN MENU"
110 PRINT
120 PRINT "*** MAINTENANCE ***          *** REPORT OPTIONS ***"
130 PRINT
140 PRINT "1. ADD A RECORD              8. BY NAME"
150 PRINT
160 PRINT "2. CHANGE A RECORD           9. BY ADDRESS"
170 PRINT
180 PRINT "3. DELETE A RECORD          10. BY SALARY CODE"
190 PRINT
200 PRINT
210 PRINT "*** PAYROLL GENERATION ***   *** MISCELLANEOUS ***"
220 PRINT
230 PRINT "4. WEEKLY INPUT             11. DELETE A FILE"
240 PRINT
250 PRINT "5. EDIT REPORT             12. PRINT W2'S"
260 PRINT
270 PRINT "6. PAYROLL INPUT MAINTENANCE 13. PRINT FICA REPORT"
280 PRINT
290 PRINT "7. PRINT PAYROLL CHECKS
300 END
```

RUN
                    PAYROLL MAIN MENU

*** MAINTENANCE ***   *** REPORT OPTIONS ***

1. ADD A RECORD   8. BY NAME

2. CHANGE A RECORD   9. BY ADDRESS

3. DELETE A RECORD   10. BY SALARY CODE

*** PAYROLL GENERATION ***   *** MISCELLANEOUS ***

4. WEEKLY INPUT   11. DELETE A FILE

5. EDIT REPORT   12. PRINT W2'S

6. PAYROLL INPUT MAINTENANCE   13. PRINT FICA REPORT

7. PRINT PAYROLL CHECKS

14. The pseudocode for the generation program follows:

```
Start
Open the file
Input vehicle ID
DO-WHILE vehicle ID not 0
   Input purchase date and number of maintenance dates
   Initialize counter to 1
   DO-WHILE counter < number of maintenance dates + 1
      Print number of dates into file
      Input the maintenance date
      Print the date into file
      Input mileage check and number of maintenance codes
      Print number of codes into file
      IF number of codes not 0 THEN
         Initialize internal counter to 1
         DO-WHILE internal counter < number of codes + 1
            Input the maintenance code
            Print the code into the file
         END-DO
      (ELSE)
      END-IF
   END-DO
END-DO
Close the file
End
```

The program should look like the following:

```
10 REM ***** PROGRAM NAME: EX-9-141
20 REM
30 REM ***** VEHICLE MAINTENANCE REPORT FILE GENERATION
40 REM
50 REM ***** WRITTEN BY EDWARD J. COBURN
60 REM
70 REM THIS IS EXERCISE 9-14-1
80 REM
90 CLS                              ' CLEAR THE SCREEN
100 OPEN "MAINT" FOR OUTPUT AS #1
110 INPUT "ENTER VEHICLE ID (0 TO END)";ID$
120 IF ID$="0" THEN 290           ' GO PRINT THEN REPORT
130 INPUT "ENTER PURCHASE DATE (MM/DD/YY)";PD$
140 INPUT "HOW MANY DATES ARE THERE";D
150 FOR I=1 TO D
160     PRINT #1,D
170     INPUT "ENTER MAINTENANCE DATE (MM/DD/YY)";MD$
180     PRINT #1,MD$
190     INPUT "WHAT WAS THE MILEAGE CHECK";M
200     INPUT "HOW MANY MAINTENANCE CODES";C
210     PRINT #1,C
220     IF C=0 THEN 270               ' NO CODES
230     FOR J=1 TO C
240         INPUT "WHAT WAS THE MAINTENANCE CODE";MC
250         PRINT #1,MC
260     NEXT J
270 NEXT I
280 GOTO 110
290 CLOSE
300 END
```

The pseudocode for the report program follows:

```
Start
Read maintenance explanations
Print headings
Open the file
DO-UNTIL EOF
   Input vehicle ID, purchase date, and number of maint. dates
   Initialize counter to 1
   DO-WHILE counter < number of maint. dates + 1
      Input maint. date, mileage and number of codes
      Initialize inner counter to 1
      DO-WHILE inner counter < number of codes +
         Input maint. code
         Increment inner counter
      END-DO
      Increment counter
   END-DO
   Initialize counter to 1

(Pseudocode continues)
```

```
      DO-WHILE counter < number of maint. dates + 1
         Print vehicle ID, maintenance date
         Calculate mileage
         IF counter <> last maint. date THEN
            Print mileage
         (ELSE)
         END-IF
         IF number of codes = 0 THEN
            Print message
         ELSE
            Initialize counter to 1
            DO-WHILE counter < number of codes + 1
               Print code and explanation
               Increment counter
            END-DO
         END-IF
      END-DO
   END-DO
END-DO
Close the file
End
```

The program should look like the following:

```
10 REM ***** PROGRAM NAME: EX-9-142
20 REM
30 REM ***** VEHICLE MAINTENANCE REPORT PRINT
40 REM
50 REM ***** WRITTEN BY EDWARD J. COBURN
60 REM
70 REM THIS IS EXERCISE 9-14-2
80 REM
90 CLS                           ' CLEAR THE SCREEN
100 FOR I=1 TO 10
110     READ CODES$(I)           ' READ MAINT. EXPLANATIONS
120 NEXT I
130 LPRINT TAB(20);"VEHICLE MAINTENANCE REPORT"
140 LPRINT
150 LPRINT "                        MILEAGE"
160 LPRINT " ID     MNT. DATE      BETWEEN";
            "    MNT. CODE     EXPLANATION"
170 LPRINT
180 OPEN "#14" FOR INPUT AS #1
190 IF EOF(1) THEN 420           ' END THE PROGRAM
200     INPUT #1,VID,PD$,D        ' INPUT ID, P DATE, # OF M DATES
210     FOR I=1 TO D
220         INPUT #1,MD$(I),MILES(I),C(I) ' DATE, MILES, # CODES
230         FOR J=1 TO C(I)
240             INPUT #1,MC(I,J)' INPUT MAINT. CODE
250         NEXT J
260     NEXT I
270     FOR I=1 TO D
280         LPRINT VID;"  ";MD$(I);"      ";
290         MILES=MILES(I)-MILES(I+1)
```

(Program continues)

```
300          IF I<>D THEN LPRINT USING "###,###";MILES;
                  ELSE LPRINT "UNKNOWN";
310          IF C(I)=0 THEN LPRINT TAB(35);"NONE" : GOTO 350
320          FOR J=1 TO C(I)
330              LPRINT TAB(35);USING "##          &";
                  MC(I,J),CODES$(MC(I,J))
340          NEXT J
350          LPRINT
360      NEXT I
370      LPRINT
380      GOTO 190
390 REM
400 REM ***** END THE PROGRM
410 REM
420 CLOSE
430 END
440 DATA OIL CHANGE, REPLACE FAN BELT, CARBURETOR KIT
450 DATA TUNE UP, REPLACE TIRES, REPAIR AIR CONDITIONING
460 DATA COOLANT SYSTEM, COMPLETE ENGINE OVERHAUL
470 DATA SAFETY STICKER, BODY WORK
RUN
```

```
                    VEHICLE MAINTENANCE REPORT

                 MILEAGE
ID    MNT. DATE   BETWEEN    MNT. CODE    EXPLANATION

134   06/12/85    1,058          6        REPAIR AIR CONDITIONING
                                 7        COOLANT SYSTEM
                                 8        COMPLETE ENGINE OVERHAUL

134   05/15/85    2,821          2        REPLACE FAN BELT
                                 5        REPLACE TIRES

134   03/25/85    6,211          1        OIL CHANGE
                                 2        REPLACE FAN BELT
                                 7        COOLANT SYSTEM

134   01/15/85    5,800          5        REPLACE TIRES
                                 9        SAFETY STICKER
                                10        BODY WORK

134   10/09/84    UNKNOWN         2        REPLACE FAN BELT


1556  07/01/85    3,100          5        REPLACE TIRES

1556  06/05/85    2,900          2        REPLACE FAN BELT
                                 8        COMPLETE ENGINE OVERHAUL
                                10        BODY WORK

1556  04/03/85    3,090          1        OIL CHANGE
                                 2        REPLACE FAN BELT
                                 3        CARBURETOR KIT


(Output continues)
```

1556	01/12/85	356	NONE	
1556	11/29/84	UNKNOWN	5	REPLACE TIRES
			6	REPAIR AIR CONDITIONING
1666	06/18/85	-3,091	2	REPLACE FAN BELT
			4	TUNE UP
			5	REPLACE TIRES
1666	07/22/85	UNKNOWN	NONE	

CHAPTER 10 . . . . . PROMPTS AND ERRORS

10-1 Introduction

1. This chapter reviews the use of the INKEY$ (GET).

2. It also looks at error traps.

10-2 Remember the INKEY$ (GET)

1. Three differences between INPUT and INKEY$:

   A. The INKEY$ does not require RETURN to terminate entry.
      The INKEY$ inputs only one character.

   B. The INKEY$ does not **echo** the character.

   C. The INKEY$ retrieves only string characters.

2. Form of the statement is:

   10 string variable = INKEY$

3. The GET looks like:

   10 GET string variable

4. Need test to determine if key has been pressed:

   10 A$=INKEY$
   20 IF A$="" THEN 10   ' IF EMPTY THEN CHECK AGAIN

5. To echo the character requires PRINT statement.

6. Can test for keys with CHR$ or ASC function:

   30 IF A$=CHR$(13) THEN 10 ' TEST FOR RETURN

   30 IF ASC(A$)=13 THEN 10 ' TEST FOR RETURN

10-3 Using the INKEY$ with Prompts

1. Prompting routine is constructed in this section.

2. The routine begins on page 273.

3. First routine list inputs character and accumulates the
   string.

4. Next we make the length of the input routine flexible

with a FOR-NEXT loop.

5. Next the prompt line is erased to clear off last prompt.

6. The new routine is shown on page 275.

7. The prompt markers are added.

8. Reposition the prompt so it is not next to the message.

9. Add the backspace routine.

   A. The IBM must use the POS(0) command to determine the cursor position.

   B. The Radio Shack and Apple only need to PRINT the backspace character.

10. Finally reduce the length of the accumulated response if backspace is pressed.

11. The completed routine is on page 280.

10-4 Using the New Routine

1. An example should be shown that utilizes the new routine.

2. The book example is on page 281.

10-5 Error Traps

1. **Error traps** are needed to catch errors such as disk drive doors left open.

2. They keep the program from crashing.

The IBM and Radio Shack

1. The error statement is:

   10 ON ERROR GOTO line number

2. Upon error detection, the program will branch to the line number.

3. Some programmers will put error statement at the top of the program.

4. Others prefer to use them in separate areas of the program.

5. The type of error is determined with **ERR** command on the IBM.

6. On the Radio Shack the statement is ERR/2+1.

7. Control must be returned from the error routine with a **RESUME** statement.

8. Three methods are available:

   A. RESUME without a line number returns to the statement that caused the trap.

   B. RESUME with line number branches to that line number.

   C. RESUME NEXT branches to the statement following the one that caused the error.

9. To disable a trap use **ON ERROR GOTO 0**.

The Apple

1. The Apple error trap is

   10 ONERR GOTO line number

2. Some programmers will put error statement at the top of the program.

3. Others prefer to use them in separate areas of the program.

4. To determine the error use the **PEEK (222)** command.

5. The error numbers are shown in Appendix C.

6. The trap keeps a program from crashing upon an error.

7. To disable a previously set trap use **POKE 216,0**.

Answers to Questions to Aid Understanding

1. A. The INKEY$ does not require RETURN to terminate entry. The INKEY$ inputs only one character.

   B. The INKEY$ does not **echo** the character.

   C. The INKEY$ retrieves only string characters.

2. 10 IF A$="" THEN is needed to make the program continue to check the INKEY$ statement since it will not wait for the RETURN to terminate the entry. (Not needed for the Apple IIe and IIc.)

   * 3. The asterisks are there to allow the user to see how many

characters are expected for the answer to the prompt and to guide the user through the entry.

* 4. If you want fancier programs you might choose to use the # symbol for numeric entry, slashes for dates, and maybe $ for money entries. The only problem with such uses is that the prompt routine will be more difficult.

5. Printing the backspace character does not work on the IBM. You get a predefined graphics character instead.

6. CHR$(13) is the RETURN key.

* 7. To do this routine, we will need to use the prompting routine we have already created and patch it. (Therefore, we will not use flowchart or pseudocode.) We will fix the routine so it will check a special prompt code and use the special date routine only when the prompt code is set to "D" for date. On the prompt display, instead of simply displaying 6 asterisks, we will display MM/DD/YY and then we will input using three small loops instead of one large one. The easiest way to do that would be to make the internal loop be a subroutine and call it three times. The following routine will do the job:

```
6970 REM
6980 REM ***** PROMPT AND INPUT ROUTINE
6990 REM
7000 R=24
7010 C=1
7020 GOSUB 5000                  ' POSITION THE CURSOR
7030 PRINT STRING$(39," ");
7040 GOSUB 5000                  ' POSITION THE CURSOR
7050 PRINT P$;                    ' PRINT THE PROMPT
7060 C=LEN(P$)+2                 ' FIND THE COLUMN TO BEGIN
7070 GOSUB 5000                  ' POSITION THE CURSOR
7075 IF PC$="D" THEN PRINT "MM/DD/YY" : GOTO 7110
7080 FOR I=1 TO L
7090     PRINT "*";              ' PRINT PROMPT MARKERS
7100 NEXT I
7110 GOSUB 5000                  ' POSITION THE CURSOR
7112 IF PC$<>"D" THEN 7120
7114 L=2 : GOSUB 7120 : MM$=B$
7115 C=POS(0)+1 : GOSUB 5000
7116 L=2 : GOSUB 7120 : DD$=B$
7117 C=POS(0)+1 : GOSUB 5000
7118 L=2 : GOSUB 7120 : YY$=B$
7119 RETURN
7120 B$=""                       ' NULL THE STRING
7130 FOR I9=1 TO L               ' INPUT LOOP L=PROMPT LENGTH
7140     A$=INKEY$
7150     IF A$="" THEN 7140      ' CHECK FOR CHARACTER
```

(Routine continues)

```
7160       IF A$<>CHR$(8) THEN 7220 ' CHECK FOR BACKSPACE
7170           IF I9=1 THEN 7140 ' NO BACKSPACE WHEN 1ST CHAR.
7180           C=POS(0)-1           ' REDUCE THE COLUMN
7182           GOSUB 5000           ' POSITION THE CURSOR
7184           PRINT "*";           ' PRINT THE MARKER
7186           GOSUB 5000           ' POSITION THE CURSOR
7190           I9=I9-1              ' REDUCE COUNTER
7200           B$=MID$(B$,1,LEN(B$)-1) ' DROP END CHARACTER
7210           GOTO 7140            ' GET CHARACTER AGAIN
7220       IF A$<>CHR$(13) THEN 7260   ' RETURN PRESSED?
7230           I9=L                 ' INCREASE COUNTER TO MAX
7240           PRINT STRING$(L-LEN(B$)," ");
7250           GOTO 7280            ' THIS WILL END LOOP
7260   B$=B$+A$                     ' ACCUMULATE ENTIRE STRING
7270   PRINT A$;                    ' ECHO
7280 NEXT I9
7290 RETURN
```

The changes and additions to the routine are as follows:

1) Line 7075 tests for the PC$ prompt code and if it is D (for date), the MM/DD/YY prompt is printed instead of the asterisks which are skipped with the GOTO.

2) Lines 7112-7119 check for the "D" code again and if it is not, the routine will use the prompt length of 2 (L=2) and the newly created subroutine at line 7120. It then stores the two-digit part of the date (either MM, DD, or YY) so that the date can be kept. The next line then causes a skip over the slash. For the other two machines, you will need to print the character to move the cursor to the right. On the Radio Shack that character is the 9 (CHR$(9)) and on the Apple it is 21 (CHR$(21)).

3) You will also want to note that line 7290 was changed to a RETURN statement to make the input part of the subroutine into its own subroutine.

4) After returning from the subroutine, the program could concatenate the three strings into one 6 digit string.

8.   Since this program is an update of the one in the chapter, we will not show the pseudocode. The program follows (note the new lines for the record add are 65 and 400-470): (on next page)

```
10 REM ***** PROGRAM NAME: EX-10-8
20 REM
30 REM ***** WRITTEN BY EDWARD J. COBURN
40 REM
50 REM THIS PROGRAM WILL INPUT FIELDS AND STORE THEM
60 REM
65 OPEN "DATAOUT" FOR OUTPUT AS #1        ' OPEN THE FILE
70 DATA NAME, 24, ADDRESS, 24, CITY, 15, STATE, 2
80 DATA ZIP CODE, 9, PHONE NUMB. , 12
90 FOR I=1 TO 6
100     READ A$(I),A(I)                   ' DISPLAY INFO, FIELD LENGTH
110 NEXT I
120 CLS                                   ' CLEAR THE SCREEN
130 PRINT TAB(15);"RECORD ENTRY"
140 PRINT
150 FOR I=1 TO 6                          ' DISPLAY LOOP
160     PRINT STR$(I);". ";A$(I)
165 PRINT
170 NEXT I
180 FOR J=1 TO 6                          ' ENTRY LOOP
190     L=A(J)
200     R=3+(J-1)*2                       ' ROW OF ENTRY
210     C=17                              ' COLUMN OF ENTRY
220     GOSUB 7070                        ' PROMPT SUBROUTINE
225     F$(J)=B$
230 NEXT J
240 P$="WHAT FIELD TO CHANGE (0 TO END)?"
250 L=1                                   ' LENGTH OF PROMPT
260 GOSUB 7000                            ' PROMPT SUBROUTINE
270 IF B$="0" THEN 400                    ' ZERO TO END
280 A=VAL(B$)                             ' SHOULD BE NUMBER
290 IF A>0 AND A<7 THEN 330               ' VALID ENTRY BRANCH
300     M$="INVALID ENTRY.  TRY AGAIN"
310     GOSUB 6000                        ' ERROR SUDROUTINE
320     GOTO 240                          ' RETURN FOR NEW INPUT
330 C=17                                  ' COLUMN OF ENTRY
340 R=3+(A-1)*2                           ' OR (A-1) FOR SINGLE SPACING
350 L=A(A)                                ' LENGTH OF FIELD
360 GOSUB 7070                            ' PROMPT ENTRY
365 F$(A)=B$                              ' SAVE CHANGED FIELD
370 GOTO 240                              ' RETURN TO FIELD PROMPT
380 REM
385 REM ***** ADD THE RECORD
390 REM
400 FOR I=1 TO 6                          ' LOOP THROUGH THE FIELDS
410     PRINT #1,F$(I)
420 NEXT I
430 P$="ANY MORE RECORDS TO INPUT (Y OR N)"
440 L=1                                   ' LENGTH OF PROMPT
450 GOSUB 7000                            ' PROMPT SUBROUTINE
460 IF B$="Y" THEN 120                    ' REDO THE SCREEN
470 END
```

9. Since this exercise doesn't specify setting up a menu system for choosing between add and change, we simply attached the change routine to the program, bypassing the add part (the add part was removed from the list for space considerations). The pseudocode for the new part of the program follows:

```
Start
Open the file
Read the display data
Setup entry screen
Initialize the counter to 1
DO-WHILE not EOF
   Input the record putting the fields into an array
   Increment the counter
END-DO
Save the number of record received (the counter)
Input the number of record to change
DO-WHILE number input not 0
   Display record data on the screen
   Input the field number to change
   Edit the input
   DO-WHILE field number not 0
      Input new data
      Input the field number to change
      Edit the input
   END-DO
   Input number of record to change
END-DO
Close the file
Reopen the file for output
Initialize the counter to 1
DO-WHILE counter < number of records + 1
   Print the record into the file
   Increment the counter by 1
END-DO
End
```

The program should look like the following:

```
10 REM ***** PROGRAM NAME: EX-10-9
20 REM
30 REM ***** WRITTEN BY EDWARD J. COBURN
40 REM
50 REM THIS PROGRAM WILL INPUT FIELDS INTO ARRAY AND ALLOW CHANGES
60 REM
62 DIM AR$(25,6)
65 OPEN "DATAOUT" FOR INPUT  AS #1 ' OPEN THE FILE
70 DATA NAME, 24, ADDRESS, 24, CITY, 15, STATE, 2
80 DATA ZIP CODE, 9, PHONE NUMB. , 12
90 FOR I=1 TO 6
100     READ A$(I),A(I)            ' DISPLAY INFO, FIELD LENGTH
110 NEXT I
```

(Program continues)

```
120 CLS                             ' CLEAR THE SCREEN
130 PRINT TAB(15);"RECORD ENTRY"
140 PRINT
150 FOR I=1 TO 6                    ' DISPLAY LOOP
160     PRINT STR$(I);". ";A$(I)
165 PRINT
170 NEXT I
175 GOTO 500                        ' JUMP OUT OF ADD TO CHANGE
176 REM
177 REM ***** JUMP TO CHANGE (DO NOT NEED REST OF ADD)
178 REM
480 REM
490 REM ***** CHANGE ROUTINE
495 REM
500 I=1                             ' INITIALIZE COUNTER
510 IF EOF(1) THEN 570              ' CHECK FOR END OF FILE
520     FOR J=1 TO 6                ' LOOP FOR FIELDS
530         INPUT #1,AR$(I,J)
540     NEXT J
550     I=I+1                       ' INCREMENT COUNTER
560     GOTO 510                    ' END OF LOOP
570 NR=I                            ' SAVE THE NUMBER OF RECORDS
575 P$="WHICH RECORD DO YOU WISH TO CHANGE?"
580 L=2                             ' PROMPT LENGTH
590 GOSUB 7000
595 IF B$="0" THEN 870              ' END OF DATA MARKER
600 RN=VAL(B$)                      ' GET RECORD NUMBER
610 FOR I=1 TO 6                    ' LOOP TO DISPLAY FIELDS
620     C=17                        ' COLUMN OF ENTRY
630     R=3+(I-1)*2                 ' ROW OF ENTRY
640     LOCATE R,C                  ' POSITION CURSOR
645     PRINT STRING$(39," ");      ' ERASE LINE
648     LOCATE R,C                  ' REPOSITION CURSOR
650     PRINT AR$(RN,I)             ' PRINT FIELD
660 NEXT I
670 P$="WHAT FIELD TO CHANGE (0 TO END)?"
680 L=1                             ' LENGTH OF PROMPT
690 GOSUB 7000                      ' PROMPT SUBROUTINE
700 IF B$="0" THEN 575              ' ZERO TO END
710 A=VAL(B$)                       ' SHOULD BE NUMBER
720 IF A>0 AND A<7 THEN 760         ' VALID ENTRY BRANCH
730     M$="INVALID ENTRY.  TRY AGAIN"
740     GOSUB 6000                  ' ERROR SUBROUTINE
750     GOTO 240                    ' RETURN FOR NEW INPUT
760 C=17                            ' COLUMN OF ENTRY
770 R=3+(A-1)*2                     ' OR (A-1) FOR SINGLE SPACING
780 L=A(A)                          ' LENGTH OF FIELD
790 GOSUB 7070                      ' PROMPT ENTRY
800 AR$(RN,A)=B$                    ' SAVE CHANGED FIELD
810 GOTO 670                        ' RETURN TO FIELD PROMPT

(Program continues)
```

```
840 REM
850 REM ***** PUT RECORDS BACK
860 REM
870 CLOSE #1                              ' CLOSE THE INPUT FILE
880 OPEN "DATAOUT" FOR OUTPUT AS #1' REOPEN FOR OUTPUT
890 FOR I=1 TO NR                         ' LOOP TO NUMBER OF RECORDS
900     FOR J=1 TO 6
910         PRINT #1,AR$(I,J)             ' PRINT THE FIELD
920     NEXT J
930 NEXT I
940 END
```

10. The pseudocode for the program follows:

```
Start
Open the file
Print the heading
DO-UNTIL EOF
   Input a record
   Print the record
END-DO
Close the file
End
```

The program would look like the following:

```
10 REM ***** PROGRAM NAME: EX-10-10
20 REM
30 REM ***** WRITTEN BY EDWARD J. COBURN
40 REM
50 REM EXERCISE 10-10 - DATAIN LIST (LIST OF 8 AND 9)
60 REM
70 OPEN "DATAOUT" FOR INPUT AS #1
80 PRINT TAB(30);"DATAIN LIST"
90 PRINT
100 PRINT "NAME               ADDRESS              CITY";
         "          STATE    ZIP         PHONE"
110 IF EOF(1) THEN 180                ' CHECK FOR END OF FILE
120     INPUT #1,N$,A$,C$,S$,Z$,P$
130     PRINT N$;TAB(18);A$;TAB(39);C$;TAB(53);
            S$;TAB(57);Z$;TAB(68);P$
140     GOTO 110
150 REM
160 REM ***** END OF THE PROGRAM
170 REM
180 CLOSE #1                          ' CLOSE THE FILE
190 END
```

(Output on next page)

DATAIN LIST

NAME	ADDRESS	CITY	STATE	ZIP	PHONE
ED COBURN	1400 SOUTH STREET	EL PASO	TX	767080987	498-888-948
TOM SMITH	415 SOUTH STREET	CINCINNATI	OH	987059098	499-049-998
AMY JOHNSON	458 WEST WESTWOOD	NASHVILLE	TN	645789487	938-998-715
HARROLD ROBBINS	896 TERRANCE SQUARE	NEW YORK	NY	100560993	937-287-836

Ok

11. The pseudocode should look like the following:

```
Start
Open the file
RANDOMIZE
Input the name
DO-WHILE name not END
    Print the name into the file
    Generate the 8 grades randomly
    Print the grades into the file
END-DO
Close the file
End
```

The program should look like the following:

```
10 REM ***** PROGRAM NAME: EX-10-11
20 REM
30 REM ***** WRITTEN BY EDWARD J. COBURN
40 REM
50 REM THIS PROGRAM WILL STORE RECORDS WITH NAME AND 8 GRADES
60 REM
65 CLS                                ' CLEAR THE SCREEN
70 OPEN "GRADES" FOR OUTPUT AS #1  ' OPEN THE FILE
75 RANDOMIZE VAL(RIGHT$(TIME$,2))
80 PRINT TAB(20);"NAME AND GRADE FILE CREATION"
90 P$="WHAT IS THE NAME (ENTER 'END' TO QUIT)?"
100 L=20                              ' PROMPT LENGTH
110 GOSUB 7000                        ' PROMPT SUBROUTINE
115 IF B$="END" THEN 240              ' END OF DATA MARKER
120 PRINT #1,B$                       ' WRITE THE NAME IN THE FILE
130 REM
140 REM ***** GENERATE THE NUMBERS
150 REM
160 FOR I=1 TO 8
170     G=INT(RND(1)*50+1)+50         ' GENERATE THE GRADES
180     PRINT #1,G                    ' PUT IT IN THE FILE
190 NEXT I
200 GOTO 90                           ' LOOP BACK
210 REM
220 REM ***** END THE PROGRAM
230 REM
240 CLOSE #1
250 END
```

12. The pseudocode follows:

```
Start
Open the file

Initialize the counter to 1
DO-WHILE not EOF
   Input the record putting the fields into an array
   Increment the counter
END-DO
Save the number of record received (the counter)
Input the number of record to change
DO-WHILE number input not 0
   Display the name and grades on the screen
   Input the field number to change
   Edit the input
   DO-WHILE field number not 0
      Input new data
      Input the field number to change
      Edit the input
   END-DO
   Input number of record to change
END-DO
Close the file
Reopen the file for output
Initialize the counter to 1
DO-WHILE counter < number of records + 1
   Print the record into the file
   Increment the counter by 1
END-DO
End
```

The program should look like the following:

```
10 REM ***** PROGRAM NAME: EX-10-12
20 REM
30 REM ***** WRITTEN BY EDWARD J. COBURN
40 REM
50 REM THIS PROGRAM READS THE STORED RECORDS FOR CHANGES
60 REM
70 DIM AR$(25,9)                    ' DIMENSION THE ARRAY
80 OPEN "GRADES" FOR INPUT AS #1   ' OPEN THE FILE
90 I=1                              ' INITIALIZE COUNTER
100 IF EOF(1) THEN 160             ' END OF FILE
110     FOR J=1 TO 9
120         INPUT #1,AR$(I,J)       ' READ THE FIELD
130     NEXT J
140     I=I+1                       ' INCREMENT COUNTER
150     GOTO 100                    ' END OF LOOP
160 NR=I                            ' SAVE THE NUMBER OF RECORDS
170 CLS                             ' CLEAR THE SCREEN
180 PRINT TAB(30);"GRADE CHANGES"
190 P$="WHAT RECORD DO YOU WANT TO CHANGE (0 TO QUIT)?"
```

(Program continues)

```
200 L=2                               ' PROMPT LENGTH
210 GOSUB 7000                        ' PROMPT SUBROUTINE
220 IF B$="0" THEN 580                ' END OF LOOP
230 RN=VAL(B$)                        ' RECORD NUMBER TO CHANGE
233 REM
235 REM ***** DISPLAY RECORD
237 REM
240 LOCATE 3,20                        ' POSITION CURSOR FOR NAME
250 PRINT "THE NAME IS ";AR$(RN,1) ' PRINT NAME
260 FOR I=1 TO 8
270     IF I<5 THEN LOCATE 6,I*20-19
                ELSE LOCATE 9,(I-4)*20-19
280     PRINT "GRADE";I;"= ";AR$(RN,I+1);  ' DISPLAY GRADE
290 NEXT I
300 REM
310 REM ***** CHANGE FIELDS
320 REM
330 P$="CHANGE NAME (N) OR GRADE (1-8) - (0 WHEN DONE)?"
340 L=1                               ' PROMPT LENGTH
350 GOSUB 7000                        ' PROMPT SUBROUTINE
360 IF B$="N" OR (B$>="0" AND B$<"9") THEN 400
370     M$="ONLY AN N OR 0-8 PLEASE"
380     GOSUB 6000                    ' ERROR ROUTINE
390     GOTO 330                      ' REPROMPT
400 IF B$<>"N" THEN 470               ' BRANCH AROUND NAME
410     C=32                          ' COLUMN POSITION
420     R=3                           ' ROW NUMBER
430     L=20                          ' CURSOR LENGTH
440     GOSUB 7070                    ' PROMPT SUBROUTINE
450     AR$(RN,1)=B$                  ' STORE NEW NAME
460     GOTO 330                      ' RETURN TO PROMPT
470 IF B$="0" THEN 170                ' START A NEW RECORD
480 A=VAL(B$)
490 IF A<5 THEN R=6 ELSE R=9          ' ROW NUMBER
500 IF A<5 THEN C=A*20-9 ELSE C=(A-4)*20-9
510 L=3                               ' PROMPT LENGTH
520 GOSUB 7070                        ' PROMPT ROUTINE
530 AR$(RN,A+1)=B$                    ' STORE NEW GRADE
540 GOTO 330                          ' RETURN TO PROMPT
550 REM
560 REM ***** STORE THE RECORDS BACK INTO THE FILE
570 REM
580 CLOSE #1                          ' CLOSE INPUT FILE
590 OPEN "GRADES" FOR OUTPUT AS #1 ' REOPEN FOR OUTPUT
600 FOR I=1 TO NR                     ' LOOP TO NUMBER OF RECORDS
610     FOR J=1 TO 9                  ' NUMBER OF FIELDS
620         PRINT #1,AR$(I,J)
630     NEXT J
640 NEXT I
650 END
```

13. The pseudocode follows:

Start
Open the file
Print the headings
Initialize student counter
DO-UNTIL EOF
    Increment the student counter
    Zero out grade accumulator
    Input the name and grades from the file
    Print the name and grades
    Total the grades
    Calculate the average grade
    Print the average
    Accumulate the averages
    Print the letter grade (A, B, C, D, or F)
END-DO
Print the final average
Close the file
End

The program follows:

```
10 REM ***** PROGRAM NAME: EX-10-13
20 REM
30 REM ***** WRITTEN BY EDWARD J. COBURN
40 REM
50 REM EXERCISE 10-13 - GRADE LIST
60 REM
70 CLS                                ' CLEAR THE SCREEN
80 OPEN "GRADES" FOR INPUT AS #1
90 PRINT TAB(30);"GRADE FILE LIST"
100 PRINT
110 PRINT TAB(35);"GRADES                          LETTER"
120 PRINT "NAME";TAB(24);"1   2   3   4   5   6   7   8";
        "   AVERAGE      GRADE"
130 PRINT
140 NS=0                              ' INITIALIZE STUDENT COUNTER
150 IF EOF(1) THEN 360                ' CHECK FOR END OF FILE
160     NS=NS+1                       ' INCREMENT STUDENT COUNTER
170     GT=0                          ' ZERO OUT ACCUMULATOR
180     INPUT #1,N$,G(1),G(2),G(3),G(4),G(5),G(6),G(7),G(8)
190     PRINT N$;TAB(21);
200     FOR I=1 TO 8
210         PRINT TAB(22+(I-1)*4);USING "###";G(I);
220         GT=GT+G(I)                ' ACCUMULATE GRADES
230     NEXT I
240     AV=GT/8                       ' FIGURE AVERAGE
250     PRINT USING "     ###.#";AV;
260     TA=TA+AV                      ' ACCUMULATE AVERAGES
270     IF AV>=90 THEN PRINT "          A"
280     IF AV>=80 AND AV<90 THEN PRINT "          B"
290     IF AV>=70 AND AV<80 THEN PRINT "          C"
```

(Program continues)

```
300       IF AV>=60 AND AV<70 THEN PRINT "          D"
310       IF AV<60 THEN PRINT "          F"
320       GOTO 150
330 REM
340 REM ***** END OF THE PROGRAM
350 REM
360 PRINT
370 PRINT TAB(42);USING "FINAL AVERAGE =###.#";TA/NS
380 CLOSE #1                         ' CLOSE THE FILE
390 END
```
RUN

GRADE FILE LIST

NAME	GRADES								AVERAGE	LETTER GRADE
	1	2	3	4	5	6	7	8		
ED COBURN	80	68	76	93	89	96	82	60	80.5	B
TOM SMITH	89	52	63	86	71	86	82	81	76.3	C
JOHN BROWN	95	97	56	95	52	94	77	60	78.3	C
SARA THOMPSON	87	66	91	91	91	71	91	59	80.9	B

FINAL AVERAGE = 79.0

Ok

14. The pseudocode is similar (if not identical) to others
in the chapter. The program follows:

```
10 REM ***** PROGRAM NAME: EX-10-14
20 REM
30 REM ***** WRITTEN BY EDWARD J. COBURN
40 REM
50 REM THIS PROGRAM WILL RECORD PAYROLL INFORMATION AND STORE IT
60 REM
65 OPEN "PAYOUT" FOR OUTPUT AS #1  ' OPEN THE FILE
70 DATA EMP. NUMBER, 5, NAME, 24, PAY RATE, 5, HOURS, 4, DEPENDENTS, 2
90 FOR I=1 TO 5
100       READ A$(I),A(I)            ' DISPLAY INFO, FIELD LENGTH
110 NEXT I
120 CLS                              ' CLEAR THE SCREEN
130 PRINT TAB(15);"PAYROLL RECORD ENTRY"
140 PRINT
150 FOR I=1 TO 5                     ' DISPLAY LOOP
160       PRINT STR$(I);". ";A$(I)
165 PRINT
170 NEXT I
180 FOR J=1 TO 5                     ' ENTRY LOOP
190       L=A(J)
200       R=3+(J-1)*2                 ' ROW OF ENTRY
210       C=17                        ' COLUMN OF ENTRY
220       GOSUB 7070                  ' PROMPT SUBROUTINE
225       F$(J)=B$
230 NEXT J
```

(Program continues)

```
240 P$="WHAT FIELD TO CHANGE (0 TO END)?"
250 L=1                          ' LENGTH OF PROMPT
260 GOSUB 7000                   ' PROMPT SUBROUTINE
270 IF B$="0" THEN 400           ' ZERO TO END
280 A=VAL(B$)                    ' SHOULD BE NUMBER
290 IF A>0 AND A<6 THEN 330      ' VALID ENTRY BRANCH
300     M$="INVALID ENTRY.  TRY AGAIN"
310     GOSUB 6000               ' ERROR SUBROUTINE
320     GOTO 240                 ' RETURN FOR NEW INPUT
330 C=17                         ' COLUMN OF ENTRY
340 R=3+(A-1)*2                  ' OR (A-1) FOR SINGLE SPACING
350 L=A(A)                       ' LENGTH OF FIELD
360 GOSUB 7070                   ' PROMPT ENTRY
365 F$(A)=B$                     ' SAVE CHANGED FIELD
370 GOTO 240                     ' RETURN TO FIELD PROMPT
380 REM
385 REM ***** ADD THE RECORD
390 REM
400 FOR I=1 TO 5                 ' LOOP THROUGH THE FIELDS
410     PRINT #1,F$(I)
420 NEXT I
430 P$="ANY MORE RECORDS TO INPUT (Y OR N)"
440 L=1                          ' LENGTH OF PROMPT
450 GOSUB 7000                   ' PROMPT SUBROUTINE
460 IF B$="Y" THEN 120           ' REDO THE SCREEN
470 END
```

The display will look like:

PAYROLL RECORD ENTRY

1. EMP. NUMBER 22222

2. NAME   *******************

3. PAY RATE   12.3

4. HOURS   34.5

5. DEPENDENTS   3

WHAT FIELD TO CHANGE (0 TO END)? 2

15. The pseudocode for this program is the same as any of the other print programs. The program follows:

```
10 REM ***** PROGRAM NAME: EX-10-15
20 REM
30 REM ***** WRITTEN BY EDWARD J. COBURN
40 REM
50 REM EXERCISE 10-15 - PAYROLL REPORT
60 REM
70 CLS                                ' CLEAR THE SCREEN
80 OPEN "PAYOUT" FOR INPUT AS #1     ' OPEN THE FILE
90 PRINT TAB(30);"PAYROLL FILE LIST"
100 PRINT
110 PRINT "EMP NO  NAME";TAB(32);
        "GROSS PAY    DEPEND.    DEDUCT    NET PAY"
120 TG=0                              ' INITIALIZE TOTAL GROSS
130 TD=0                              ' INITIALIZE TOTAL DEDUCTIONS
140 IF EOF(1) THEN 310                ' CHECK FOR END OF FILE
150     INPUT #1,E$,N$,R,H,D
160     PRINT E$;TAB(9);N$;
170     GP=H*R                        ' CALCULATE GROSS PAY
180     TG=TG+GP                      ' ACCUMULATE TOTAL GROSS
190     F=GP*.0925                    ' FICA
200     TX=GP*.22                     ' FEDERAL TAX
210     IF D=1 THEN DA=50             ' DEDUCTION AMOUNT FOR 1
220     IF D=2 THEN DA=75             ' DEDUCTION AMOUNT FOR 2
230     IF D>2 THEN DA=100            ' DEDUCTION AMOUNT FOR 3 OR MORE
240     NP=GP-F-TX-DA                 ' NET PAY
250     TD=TD+F+TX+DA                 ' ACCUMULATE TOTAL DEDUCTIONS
260     PRINT TAB(33);USING
            "#,###.##      ##      ###.##   #,###.##";
            GP;D;DA+F+TX;NP
270     GOTO 140
280 REM
290 REM ***** END OF THE PROGRAM
300 REM
310 PRINT
320 PRINT "TOTALS";
330 PRINT TAB(32);USING
        "##,###.##               #,###.## ##,###.##";TG;TD;TG-TD
340 CLOSE #1                          ' CLOSE THE FILE
350 END
```

16. The pseudocode for this program would be the same as the previous programs in this chapter. The program follows:

```
10 REM ***** PROGRAM NAME: EX-10-16
20 REM
30 REM ***** WRITTEN BY EDWARD J. COBURN
40 REM
50 REM EXERCISE 10-16 - XYZ PAYROLL
60 REM
70 OPEN "XYZPAY" FOR OUTPUT AS #1   ' OPEN THE FILE
80 DATA NAME, 24, 3, ADDRESS, 20, 5, CITY, 15, 7, STATE, 2, 9
85 DATA ZIP, 5, 9, BIRTH DATE, 8, 11, PAY CODE, 1, 11
90 DATA EMP. DATE, 8, 13, # EXEMPT., 1, 13
100 FOR I=1 TO 9
110      READ A$(I),A(I),R(I)          ' DISPLAY INFO, FIELD LENGTH, ROW
120 NEXT I
130 CLS                               ' CLEAR THE SCREEN
140 PRINT TAB(15);"PAYROLL RECORD ENTRY"
150 PRINT
160 FOR I=1 TO 9                      ' DISPLAY LOOP
170      IF I<4 THEN PRINT STR$(I);". ";A$(I)
                ELSE PRINT STR$(I);". ";A$(I);TAB(35);
                          STR$(I+1);". ";A$(I+1) : I=I+1
180 PRINT
190 NEXT I
200 FOR J=1 TO 9                      ' ENTRY LOOP
210      L=A(J)
220      R=R(J)
230      IF J<5 OR J=6 OR J=8 THEN C=17 ELSE C=50
240      GOSUB 790                    ' PROMPT SUBROUTINE
250      F$(J)=B$
260 NEXT J
270 P$="WHAT FIELD TO CHANGE (0 TO END)?"
280 L=1                               ' LENGTH OF PROMPT
290 GOSUB 730                         ' PROMPT SUBROUTINE
300 IF B$="0" THEN 450                ' ZERO TO END
310 A=VAL(B$)                         ' SHOULD BE NUMBER
320 IF A>0 AND A<10 THEN 360          ' VALID ENTRY BRANCH
330      M$="INVALID ENTRY.  TRY AGAIN"
340      GOSUB 570                    ' ERROR SUBROUTINE
350      GOTO 270                     ' RETURN FOR NEW INPUT
360 IF A<5 OR A=6 OR A=8 THEN C=17 ELSE C=50
370 R=R(A)
380 L=A(A)                            ' LENGTH OF FIELD
390 GOSUB 790                         ' PROMPT ENTRY
400 F$(A)=B$                          ' SAVE CHANGED FIELD
410 GOTO 270                          ' RETURN TO FIELD PROMPT
420 REM
430 REM ***** ADD THE RECORD
440 REM
450 FOR I=1 TO 9                      ' LOOP THROUGH THE FIELDS
```

(Program continues)

```
460      IF I=6 OR I=8 THEN
             F$(I)=LEFT$(F$(I),2)+MID$(F$(I),3,2)+RIGHT$(F$(I),2)
470      PRINT #1,F$(I)
480 NEXT I
490 P$="ANY MORE RECORDS TO INPUT (Y OR N)"
500 L=1                              ' LENGTH OF PROMPT
510 GOSUB 730                        ' PROMPT SUBROUTINE
520 IF B$="Y" THEN 130               ' REDO THE SCREEN
530 CLOSE #1
540 END
```

The input screen should look like:

```
         XYZ CORPORATION
         EMPLOYEE ENTRY

1. NAME      ********************

2. ADDRESS

3. CITY

4. STATE                5. ZIP

6. BIRTH DATE           7. PAY CODE

8. EMP. DATE            9. # EXEMPT.
```

CHAPTER 11 . . . . . RANDOM ACCESS FILE PROCESSING

11-1 Introduction

1. Sequential file processing is fine for some applications.

2. **Random file processing** also known as **direct** is better for many applications.

3. In this chapter we examine the following:

   A. File design

   B. The OPEN statement

   C. The FIELD statement

   D. How to store records on the file

   E. The CLOSE statement

11-2 File Design

1. Sequential records are stored one after another (F-294).

2. Random records are stored in fixed length locations (F-295).

3. The length of a field in a random access file must always be the same length.

4. You should examine how the length of a field is determined.

5. Also show how the length of the record is determined.

11-3 The OPEN Statement

1. The statement is nearly the same as discussed previously.

IBM OPEN Statement

1. The form is:

   10 OPEN "file name" AS #file number LEN=record length

2. An example is:

   10 OPEN "SAMPLE" AS #1 LEN=28

3. The words OPEN, AS, and LEN must be as shown.

4. The file name must be in quotation marks.

5. The LEN is the length of the record.

Radio Shack OPEN Statement

1. The form is:

   10 OPEN "code",file number,"file name",record length

2. A sample is:

   10 OPEN "R",1,"SAMPLE",24

3. The codes were discussed in Chapter 8, the one we need for random files is R.

IBM and Radio Shack Buffer and FIELD statement

1. A **buffer** is set up to accumulate the record to write to the file (F-298).

2. Special variables are used in the buffer and a FIELD statement is necessary to set up these variables.

3. The form of the FIELD statement is:

   10 FIELD #file number, length AS string variable,...

4. A sample statement is:

   10 FIELD #1, 30 AS N$, 20 AS B$, 4 AS A$(1), 4 AS A$(2)

Assigning the IBM and Radio Shack FIELD Statement Variables

1. These special **var**iables require special assignment.

   10 LSET string variable = string, literal or numeric conversion

   10 RSET string variable = string, literal or numeric conversion

2. LSET is left justification and RSET is right justification.

3. For numeric conversion:

   A. MKI$ is for integers and requires 2 bytes to store.

   B. MKS$ is for single precision and 4 bytes to store.

   C. MKD$ is for double precision and 8 bytes to store.

4. A sample statement is:

   10 RSET A$=MKI$(A)

5. To get back from conversion:

   A. CVI is for integers.

   B. CVS is for single precision.

   C. CVD is for double precision.

6. A sample statement is:

   10 A=CVI(A$)

Apple OPEN Statement

1. Don't forget to use the CHR$(4) (or D$).

2. The form of the OPEN statement is:

   10 PRINT D$;"OPEN file name,Lrecord length"

3. A sample statement would be:

   10 PRINT D$;"OPEN SAMPLE,L33"

4. Data is written into random file the same way as sequential file in terms of record length.

11-4 Random I/O

1. We can OPEN the file at the beginning of the program and leave it open throughout the file manipulations.

2. It is not necessary to close the file after each use.

Storing Records on the IBM and Radio Shack

1. We need a PUT # command:

   10 PUT #file number, record number

2. A sample statement would be:

   10 PUT #1,5   ' STORE RECORD NUMBER 5

3. The number on PUT statement can be a variable.

Storing Records on the Apple

1. A **WRITE** statement is needed first:

   10 PRINT D$;"WRITE file name,Rrecord number"

2. A sample statement would be:

   10 PRINT D$;"WRITE SAMPLE,R5"

3. One set for access, the fields are printed into the file the same way as with a sequential file.

Retrieving Records on the IBM and Radio Shack

1. The **GET #** is used to retrieve the records:

   10 GET #file number, record number

2. A sample would be:

   10 GET #1,5   ' GET RECORD NUMBER 5

Retrieving Records on the Apple

1. A **READ** statement is needed:

   10 PRINT D$;"READ file name,Rrecord number"

2. A sample would be:

   10 PRINT D$;"READ SAMPLE,R5"

3. Then INPUT statements can be used as with sequential files.

11-5 The CLOSE Statement

1. The IBM and Radio Shack command is:

   10 CLOSE #file number

   10 CLOSE

2. The Apple command is:

   10 PRINT D$;"CLOSE file name"

   10 PRINT D$;"CLOSE"

11-6 Creating the Program

1. The program has 5 modules, menu, 3 functions, and exit.

The Initial Module

1. This module creates a menu of options on the screen.

2. A dummy record is used to keep track of the number of records in the file (F-302).

3. The dummy means that the record number to access the file will have to be one larger than the record to be accessed.

4. The module is shown on page 304 (F-303).

The Addition Module

1. When the records are added to the file one must be added to the record number (to bypass the dummy record).

2. After a record is added, the dummy record must be updated.

3. The module is shown on page 307 (F-306).

The Change Module

1. Verify that the record number asked for is within the range of the file (use dummy record count).

2. The input fields are displayed on the screen for changes.

3. After the changes are made, the record is dumped back into the file.

4. No changes to the dummy record are needed.

5. Module is shown on page 310 (F-309).

The PRINT Module

1. The records will be printed in numerical order.

2. The dummy record count is used to determine the end of the print loop.

3. The module is shown on page 311 (F-312).

The EXIT Module

    1. This module simply closes the files and ends the program.

    2. The module is shown on page 313 (F-314).

Putting the Program Together

    1. On page 314 are the sample screens for:

        A. The menu

        B. The add screen

        C. The change screen

A Final Note About IBM and Radio Shack

    1. IBM and Radio Shack have the **LOF** statement so the dummy record wasn't needed.

    2. The form is:

        10 numeric variable = LOF(file number)

    3. A sample would be:

        10 R=LOF(1)

    4. Returns the record number of the last record in the file.

    5. If the LOF was used, the rewrite to the dummy upon an add would not be needed.

    6. Other simplification changes are possible also. You may wish to assign this as an exercise if you use IBM or Radio Shack computers in your class. (Exercise 9 on page 317).

****

Answers to Questions to Aid Understanding

    1. Changing records is much more difficult when using sequential files. You can change them by reading all the records into memory, changing the appropriate one and then rewriting them into the file. Alternatively, you can read the records from one file and write them into another, changing the records before they are written out.

* 2. Random file processing, which is also called direct file processing, is the capability of accessing each record stored in a file in any order necessary. That is, if we want access to record 15, we can get to it without needing to access the records in front or behind record 15.

3. On the IBM and Radio Shack the record would require:

```
24 for name
6   for date
9   for social security number
2   for each number (total of 6)
For a total of 45.
```

On the Apple the record would require:

```
24 for name
6   for date
9   for social security number
7   for each number (total of 21)
1   for carriage return
For a total of 61.
```

* 4. In order to find a particular record on the disk, the machine needs to know the length of the records because it has to be able to calculate the total number of bytes to bypass to get to the asked for record. For example, if the records are each 25 bytes long and you want to access the fifth record, 100 bytes need to be skipped to get to the fifth record (4 * 25 = 100).

5. IBM:

10 OPEN "file name" AS #file number LEN=record length

The FOR option is omitted and the LEN is added.

Radio Shack:

10 OPEN "code", file number, "file name", record length

The code would be R and the record length was added.

Apple:

10 PRINT D$;"OPEN file name, Lrecord length"

The L and record length were added.

6. The FIELD statement sets up a buffer area for file access and allows the specification of the variables to be used.

7. Without either the LSET or RSET statement, the assignment to a variable is done in regular storage and the special variables in the FIELD buffer are not assigned.

8. Using file name of SAMPLE.

IBM:

```
10 OPEN "SAMPLE" AS #1 LEN=20
20 FIELD #1, 14 AS NAME$, 6 AS DATE$
30 PUT#1,5                  ' STORE RECORD NUMBER 5
40 GET#1,5                  ' RETRIEVE RECORD NUMBER 5
50 CLOSE #1                 ' CLOSE THE FILE
```

Radio Shack:

```
10 OPEN "R",1,"SAMPLE",20
20 FIELD #1, 14 AS NAME$, 6 AS DATE$
30 PUT#1,5                  ' STORE RECORD NUMBER 5
40 GET#1,5                  ' RETRIEVE RECORD NUMBER 5
50 CLOSE #1                 ' CLOSE THE FILE
```

Apple:

```
10 D$=CHR$(4)
20 PRINT D$;"OPEN SAMPLE,L21"   : REM OPEN THE FILE
30 PRINT D$;"WRITE SAMPLE"      : REM SETUP FOR OUTPUT
40 PRINT NAME$,DATE$            : REM WRITE THE FIELDS
50 PRINT D$;"READ SAMPLE"       : REM SETUP FOR INPUT
60 INPUT NAME$,DATE$            : REM INPUT THE FIELDS
70 PRINT D$;"CLOSE SAMPLE"      : REM CLOSE THE FILE
```

9. The pseudocode for this program would be the same as before. The only changes necessary are to lines:

Lines 80 and 90 are deleted.
Line 100 changed to use LOF.
Lines 650, 660, and 670 deleted.
Line 2050 changed to <= since RECS is exact now.
Line 2080 changed to VAL(B$) since RECS is exact.
Line 3040 changed to FOR I=1 to RECS.

The program should look like the following:

```
10 REM ***** PROGRAM NAME: EX-11-9
20 REM
30 REM ***** WRITTEN BY EDWARD J. COBURN
40 REM
50 REM EXERCISE 11-9 - RANDOM FILES USING LOF COMMAND
60 REM
70 OPEN "CONTDATA" AS #1 LEN=28
100 IF LOF(1)=0 THEN RECS=0 ELSE RECS=LOF(1)/28
110 FIELD #1, 24 AS NF$, 4 AS CF$
120 CLS                          ' CLEAR THE SCREEN
130 PRINT TAB(10);"CONTRIBUTIONS MAINTENANCE"
140 PRINT                        ' BLANK LINE
```

(Program continues)

```
150 PRINT "1. ADD NEW RECORDS"
155 PRINT
160 PRINT "2. CHANGE EXISTING RECORDS"
165 PRINT
170 PRINT "3. PRINT THE FILE"
175 PRINT
180 PRINT "4. EXIT THE PROGRAM"
200 P$="WHAT OPTION (1-4)"          ' PROMPT
210 L=1                             ' LENGTH OF PROMPT
220 GOSUB 7000                      ' PROMPT SUBROUTINE
230 IF B$>"0" AND B$<"5" THEN 270
240    M$="INPUT ERROR. RETRY ENTRY"
250      GOSUB 6000                   ' ERROR SUBROUTINE
260      GOTO 200                     ' REPROMPT
270 ON VAL(B$) GOSUB 500,2000,3000,4000
280 GOTO 120
470 REM
480 REM ***** ADD MODULE
490 REM
500 CLS                             ' CLEAR THE SCREEN
510 PRINT TAB(10);"CONTRIBUTIONS ENTRY"
520 PRINT                           ' BLANK LINE
530 PRINT "1. CONT. NAME"
535 PRINT
540 PRINT "2. CONT. AMOUNT"
550 R=3                             ' ROW NUMBER
560 C=17                            ' COLUMN NUMBER
570 L=24                            ' NAME LENGTH
580 GOSUB 7070                      ' PROMPT SUBROUTINE
590 LSET NF$=B$                     ' ASSIGN NAME
600 R=5                             ' ROW NUMBER
610 L=7                             ' CONTRIBUTION LENGTH
620 GOSUB 7070                      ' PROMPT SUBROUTINE
630 LSET CF$=MKS$(VAL(B$))          ' ASSIGN AMOUNT
635 RECS=RECS+1
640 PUT 1,RECS                      ' PUT THE RECORD
680 P$="DO YOU WANT TO ADD ANY MORE (Y OR N)"
690 L=1                             ' PROMPT LENGTH
700 GOSUB 7000                      ' PROMPT SUBROUTINE
710 IF B$<>"Y" THEN RETURN
720 GOTO 500                        ' GET ANOTHER RECORD
1970 REM
1980 REM ***** CHANGE MODULE
1990 REM
2000 P$="RECORD NUMBER TO CHANGE (0 TO END)"
2020 L=3                            ' PROMPT LENGTH
2030 GOSUB 7000                     ' PROMPT SUBROUTINE
2040 IF VAL(B$)=0 THEN RETURN       ' EXIT SUBROUTINE
2050 IF VAL(B$)<=RECS THEN 2080     ' RECORD OKAY?
2060    M$="RECORD NOT FOUND.  RETRY."
2070      GOSUB 6000                  ' ERROR SUBROUTINE
2075      GOTO 2000                   ' GET INDEX AGAIN
2080 RECORD=VAL(B$)                 ' SAVE THE RECORD NUMBER

(Program continues)
```

```
2082 FIELD #1, 24 AS NF$, 4 AS CF$
2085 GET#1,RECORD                       ' GET THE RECORD
2090 CLS
2100 PRINT TAB(10);"CONTRIBUTIONS CHANGES"
2110 PRINT                              ' BLANK LINE
2120 PRINT "1. CONT. NAME    ";NF$
2130 PRINT
2140 PRINT "2. CONT. AMOUNT ";CVS(CF$)
2150 P$="FIELD TO CHANGE (0 TO END)"
2160 L=1                                ' PROMPT LENGTH
2170 GOSUB 7000                         ' PROMPT SUBROUTINE
2180 IF B$>="0" AND B$<"3" THEN 2220    ' IS ENTRY OKAY?
2190   M$="INVALID ENTRY.  RETRY."' ERROR MESSAGE
2200   GOSUB 6000                       ' ERROR SUBROUTINE
2210   GOTO 2150                        ' REINPUT
2220 IF B$="0" THEN 2290                ' END CHANGES
2230   IF B$="1" THEN L=24 ELSE L=7
2240   IF B$="1" THEN R=3  ELSE R=5
2250   C=17
2260   GOSUB 7070                       ' PROMPT SUBROUTINE
2270   IF R=3 THEN LSET NF$=B$ ELSE LSET CF$=MKS$(VAL(B$))
2280   GOTO 2090                        ' REPROMPT
2290 PUT#1,RECORD                       ' STORE THE RECORD BACK INTO FILE
2300 GOTO 2000                          ' RETURN FOR NEW NUMBER
2970 REM
2980 REM ***** PRINT MODULE
2990 REM
3000 T=0                                ' ZERO OUT TOTAL FIELD
3005 LPRINT TAB(10);"CONTRIBUTIONS LIST"
3010 LPRINT " "                         ' BLANK LINE
3020 LPRINT "NAME";TAB(27);"AMOUNT"
3030 LPRINT " "                         ' BLANK LINE
3040 FOR I=1 TO RECS
3050   GET 1,I                          ' GET THE RECORD
3060   LPRINT NF$;TAB(25);USING "#,###.##";CVS(CF$)
3070   T=T+CVS(CF$)
3080 NEXT I
3090 LPRINT " "                         ' BLANK LINE
3100 LPRINT "TOTAL";TAB(24); USING "##,###.##";T
3110 RETURN
3970 REM
3980 REM ***** EXIT MODULE
3990 REM
4000 CLOSE
4010 END
```

* 10. For this program we will simply modify the program from the chapter a bit. We don't need to flowchart or pseudocode it since it will be virtually the same program. The program will be listed and then we will look at the changes we made:

```
10 REM ***** PROGRAM NAME: F-11-10
20 REM
30 REM ***** PROBLEM 11-10 RANDOM FILE PROCESSING
40 REM
50 REM ***** WRITTEN BY EDWARD J. COBURN
60 REM
70 OPEN "PAYROLL" AS #1 LEN=28
80 FIELD #1, 2 AS RF$      ' DUMMY RECORD
90 GET 1,1                 ' GET THE FIRST RECORD
100 IF CVI(RF$)=0 THEN RECS=1 ELSE RECS=CVI(RF$)
110 FIELD #1, 9 AS SF$, 24 AS NF$, 1 AS CF$, 4 AS PF$
120 CLS                    ' CLEAR THE SCREEN
130 PRINT TAB(10);"PAYROLL MAINTENANCE"
140 PRINT                  ' BLANK LINE
150 PRINT "1.  ADD NEW RECORDS"
155 PRINT
160 PRINT "2.  CHANGE EXISTING RECORD"
165 PRINT
170 PRINT "3.  PRINT THE FILE"
175 PRINT
180 PRINT "4.  EXIT THE PROGRAM"
190 PRINT
200 P$= "WHAT OPTION (1-4)"
210 L=1                    ' LENGTH OF PROMPT
220 GOSUB 7000             ' PROMPT SUBROUTINE
230 IF B$>"0" AND B$<"5" THEN 270
240    M$="INPUT ERROR.  RETRY ENTRY"
250      GOSUB 6000        ' ERROR SUBROUTINE
260      GOTO 200          ' REPROMPT
270 ON VAL(B$) GOSUB 500, 2000, 3000, 4000
280 GOTO 120               ' RETURN FOR ANOTHER INPUT
470 REM
480 REM ***** ADD MODULE
490 REM
500 CLS                    ' CLEAR THE SCREEN
510 PRINT TAB(10);"PAYROLL ENTRY"
520 PRINT                  ' BLANK LINE
530 PRINT "1. SS. NUMBER"
535 PRINT
540 PRINT "2. EMP. NAME"
542 PRINT
544 PRINT "3. SALARY CODE"
546 PRINT
548 PRINT "4. PAY RATE"
550 R=3                    ' ROW NUMBER
552 C=17                   ' COLUMN NUMBER
554 L=9                    ' SS NUMBER LENGTH
556 GOSUB 7070             ' PROMPT SUBROUTINE
558 LSET SF$=B$            ' ASSIGN SS NUMBER
560 R=5                    ' ROW NUMBER
570 L=24                   ' NAME LENGTH
580 GOSUB 7070             ' PROMPT SUBROUTINE
590 LSET NF$=B$            ' ASSIGN NAME
```

(Program continues)

```
600 R=7                     ' ROW NUMBER
610 L=1                     ' SALARY CODE LENGTH
620 GOSUB 7070              ' PROMPT SUBROUTINE
630 LSET SF$=B$             ' ASSIGN SALARY CODE
632 R=9                     ' ROW NUMBER
634 L=8                     ' PAY RATE
636 LSET PF$=MKS$(VAL(B$))     ' ASSIGN AMOUNT
638 RECS=RECS+1             ' INCREMENT RECORD NUMBER
640 PUT 1,RECS             ' PUT THE RECORD
650 FIELD #1, 2 AS RF$     ' FIELD RECORD 1
660 LSET RF$=MKI$(RECS)    ' SET THE FIELD
670 PUT 1,1                ' PUT RECORD 1
680 P$= "DO YOU WANT TO ADD ANY MORE (Y OR N)"
690 L=1                     ' LENGTH OF PROMPT
700 GOSUB 7000             ' PROMPT SUBROUTINE
710 IF B$<>"Y" THEN RETURN
720 GOTO 500               ' GET ANOTHER RECORD
1970 REM
1980 REM ***** CHANGE MODULE
1990 REM
2000 P$="RECORD NUMBER TO CHANGE (0 TO END)"
2020 L=3                    ' PROMPT LENGTH
2030 GOSUB 7000            ' PROMPT SUBROUTINE
2040 IF VAL(B$)=0 THEN RETURN ' EXIT THE SUBROUTINE
2050 IF VAL(B$)<=RECS THEN 2080' RECORD OKAY?
2060      M$="RECORD NOT FOUND.  REENTER."
2070       GOSUB 6000        ' ERROR SUBROUTINE
2075       GOTO 2000         ' GET INDEX AGAIN
2080 RN=VAL(B$)+1          ' RECORD TO ACCESS
2082 FIELD #1, 9 AS SF$, 24 AS NF$, 1 AS CF$, 4 AS PF$
2085 GET #1,RN             ' GET THE RECORD
2090 CLS                   ' CLEAR THE SCREEN
2100 PRINT TAB(10);"PAYROLL CHANGES"
2110 PRINT                 ' BLANK LINE
2120 PRINT "1. SS. NUMBER   ";SF$
2124 PRINT
2128 PRINT "2. EMP. NAME    ";NF$
2132 PRINT
2136 PRINT "3. SALARY CODE  ";SF$
2138 PRINT
2140 PRINT "4. PAY RATE     ";CVS(PF$)
2150 P$="FIELD TO CHANGE (0 TO END)"
2160 L=1                    ' PROMPT LENGTH
2170 GOSUB 7000            ' PROMPT SUBROUTINE
2180 IF B$>="0" AND B$<="4" THEN 2220
2190      M$="INVALID ENTRY.  TRY AGAIN"
2200       GOSUB 6000        ' ERROR SUBROUTINE
2210       GOTO 2150         ' REINPUT
2220 IF B$="0" THEN 2290 ' FIELD ENTRY
2230      IF B$="1" THEN L=9  : R=3
2240      IF B$="2" THEN L=24 : R=5
2242      IF B$="3" THEN L=1  : R=7
2244      IF B$="4" THEN L=8  : R=9
```

(Program continues)

```
2250        C=17            ' COLUMN
2260        GOSUB 7070      ' PROMPT SUBROUTINE
2270        IF R=3 THEN LSET SF$=B$
2272        IF R=5 THEN LSET NF$=B$
2274        IF R=7 THEN LSET SF$=B$
2276        IF R=9 THEN LSET PF$=MKI$(B$)
2280        GOTO 2090       ' REPROMPT
2290 PUT #1,RN              ' STORE THE RECORD BACK INTO FILE
2300 GOTO 2000              ' RETURN FOR NEW NUMBER
2970 REM
2980 REM ***** PRINT MODULE
2990 REM
3000 T=0                    ' ZERO OUT TOTAL FIELD
3002 LPRINT TAB(20);"PAYROLL LIST"
3005 LPRINT " "             ' BLANK LINE
3020 LPRINT " SS. NUMBER  NAME";TAB(39);"PAY CODE   AMOUNT"
3030 LPRINT " "             ' BLANK LINE
3040 FOR I=2 TO RECS        ' TO NUMBER IN FILE
3050        GET #1,I        ' GET RECORD BY NUMBER
3060        LPRINT MID$(SF$,1,3);"/";MID$(SF$,4,3);"/";MID$(SF$,7,4);
3065        LPRINT "  ";NF$;TAB(43);CF$;TAB(50);
3067        LPRINT USING "#,###.##";CVS(PF$)
3070        T=T+CVS(PF$)     ' ACCUMULATE TOTAL
3080 NEXT I
3090 LPRINT TAB(51);"---------"'UNDERLINE
3100 LPRINT "TOTAL";TAB(51);USING "##,###.##";T
3110 RETURN
3970 REM
3980 REM ***** EXIT MODULE
3990 REM
4000 CLOSE #1
4010 END
```

We will not discuss the differences in the versions since this program is simply a rewrite of the program in the chapter. Instead we will discuss the differences in this program with that in the chapter. In the beginning module, we changed the file name to PAYROLL and the file specification was changed (the FIELD statement in the example). Finally, the heading was changed so it said PAYROLL instead of CONTRIBUTIONS. This same change was done in all the modules.

In the add module the changes relate to adding more items for the file. Lines 520-550 needed to list 4 lines on the screen instead of 2. Then, lines 550-640 needed more screen access and more calls to the subroutine.   In the change module, the changes again relate to the fact that we are processing more fields. The FIELD statement (2082) is changed (not for the Apple). Then lines 2100-2140 needed upgrading to reflect the new fields. Lines 2230-2280 needed additional lines in both test groups.

Finally, in the print module, the only changes were to the column heading line and the detail line.

Naturally, don't forget to add the subroutines where appropriate.

11. The pseudocode for this program should be:

```
Start
Open the file
Field the dummy record
Get the dummy record
Calculate the number of records in the file
Field for the records
Initialize counter to 2 (skip dummy record)
DO-WHILE counter < number of records + 1
   Get the record based upon the counter
   IF salary code <> S THEN
      Print the employee's name
      Input the number of hours
   (ELSE)
   END-IF
   Increment counter by 1
END-DO
Print the headings
Initialize the counter to 2
DO-WHILE counter < number of records + 1
   Get the record based upon the counter
   Translate the rate
   Print social security number, name and code
   IF code = S THEN
      Print salary message and blank for hours
   ELSE
      Print rate
      Print hours
      Calculate gross pay
   END-IF
   Print gross pay
   Accumulate total pay
END-DO
Print the total pay
Close the file
End
```

The program should look like the following:

```
10 REM ***** PROGRAM NAME: EX-11-11
20 REM
30 REM ***** SALARY FILE PROGRAM
40 REM
50 REM ***** WRITTEN BY EDWARD J. COBURN
60 REM
70 REM THIS IS EXERCISE 11-11
80 REM
90 DIM H(15)
100 OPEN "PAYROLL" AS #1 LEN=38      ' OPEN THE FILE
110 FIELD #1, 2 AS RF$
120 GET #1,1
```

(Program continues)

```
130 RECS=CVI(RF$)
140 FIELD #1, 9 AS SF$, 24 AS NF$, 1 AS CF$, 4 AS PF$
150 FOR I=2 TO RECS
160     GET #1,I                     ' GET THE RECORD
170     IF CF$="S" THEN 260          ' SKIP IF SALARIED
180     CLS                          ' CLEAR THE SCREEN
190     PRINT TAB(20);"HOURS ENTRY"
200     LOCATE 5,1
210     PRINT "THE EMPLOYEE NAME IS ";NF$
220     P$="HOW MANY HOURS WERE WORKED?"
230     L=5                          ' INPUT LENGTH
240     GOSUB 7000                   ' PROMPT SUBROUTINE
250     H(I)=VAL(B$)                 ' STORE HOURS
260 NEXT I
270 CLS                              ' CLEAR THE SCREEN
280 PRINT TAB(30);"PAYROLL REPORT"
290 PRINT
300 PRINT "SOC. SEC. #    NAME           CODE    RATE    ";
            "HOURS   GROSS PAY"
310 PRINT
320 FOR I=2 TO RECS
330     GET #1,I
340     GP=CVS(PF$)                  ' TRANSLATE RATE
350     PRINT LEFT$(SF$,3);"-";MID$(SF$,4,2);"-";RIGHT$(SF$,4);
            "   ";LEFT$(NF$,15);
360     PRINT TAB(31);CF$;
370     IF CF$="S" THEN PRINT "     SALARY";
            ELSE PRINT USING"     #.##";GP;
380     IF CF$="H" THEN GP=GP*H(I) ' CALCULATE HOURLY
390     IF CF$="H" THEN PRINT TAB(44);USING "##.#";H(I);
            ELSE PRINT "     ";
400     PRINT TAB(52);USING "###.##";GP
420     TP=TP+GP                     ' TOTAL PAY
430 NEXT I
440 REM
450 PRINT TAB(51);"-------"
460 PRINT TAB(51);"-------"
470 PRINT TAB(36);USING "GRAND TOTAL   #,###.##";TP
480 CLOSE #1                         ' CLOSE THE FILE
490 END
```

The report should look like the following:

PAYROLL REPORT

SOC. SEC. #	NAME	CODE	RATE	HOURS	GROSS PAY
289-28-3939	LARRY HAGMAN	S	SALARY		455.00
948-49-4839	ED COBURN	H	4.55	35.0	159.25
928-38-4748	GEORGE TOMAS	S	SALARY		540.00
929-28-3939	SALLY SMITH	H	6.75	40.0	270.00
928-38-4789	HARRISON FORD	H	3.75	45.0	168.75
849-49-8490	FRED JACOBS	H	5.75	40.0	230.00
298-39-4849	BARNEY WILSON	S	SALARY		650.00
987-37-3977	THOMAS RED	H	4.55	30.0	136.50
839-38-4849	JESUS ALVAREZ	H	3.80	35.0	133.00
928-39-3849	GEORGE HARRISON	S	SALARY		390.00

```
                                             -------
                                             -------
                            GRAND TOTAL    3,132.50
```

12. The pseudocode is virtually identical to the previous program. The program follows:

```
10 REM ***** PROGRAM NAME: EX-11-12
20 REM
30 REM ***** SALARY FILE PROGRAM WITH DEDUCTIONS
40 REM
50 REM ***** WRITTEN BY EDWARD J. COBURN
60 REM
70 REM THIS IS EXERCISE 11-12
80 REM
90 DIM H(15)
100 OPEN "PAYROLL" AS #1 LEN=38      ' OPEN THE FILE
110 FIELD #1, 2 AS RF$
120 GET #1,1
130 RECS=CVI(RF$)
140 FIELD #1, 9 AS SF$, 24 AS NF$, 1 AS CF$, 4 AS PF$
150 FOR I=2 TO RECS
160      GET #1,I                    ' GET THE RECORD
170      IF CF$="S" THEN 260         ' SKIP IF SALARIED
180      CLS                         ' CLEAR THE SCREEN
190      PRINT TAB(20);"HOURS ENTRY"
200      LOCATE 5,1
210      PRINT "THE EMPLOYEE NAME IS ";NF$
220      P$="HOW MANY HOURS WERE WORKED?"
230      L=5                         ' INPUT LENGTH
240      GOSUB 7000                  ' PROMPT SUBROUTINE
250      H(I)=VAL(B$)                ' STORE HOURS
260 NEXT I
270 CLS                             ' CLEAR THE SCREEN
280 PRINT TAB(30);"PAYROLL REPORT"
290 PRINT
```

(Program continues)

PAGE 143

```
300 PRINT "SOC. SEC. #   NAME              CODE    RATE    ";
        "HOURS   GROSS PAY  DEDUCT.    NET PAY"
310 PRINT
320 FOR I=2 TO RECS
330     GET #1,I
340     GP=CVS(PF$)                    ' TRANSLATE RATE
350     PRINT LEFT$(SF$,3);"-";MID$(SF$,4,2);"-";RIGHT$(SF$,4);
            "    ";LEFT$(NF$,15);
360     PRINT TAB(31);CF$;
370     IF CF$="S" THEN PRINT "    SALARY";
                ELSE PRINT USING"   #.##";GP;
380     IF CF$="H" THEN GP=GP*H(I) ' CALCULATE HOURLY
390     IF CF$="H" THEN PRINT TAB(44);USING "##.#";H(I);
                ELSE PRINT "   ";
400     PRINT TAB(52);USING "###.##";GP;
410     FICA=GP*.0965                  ' FICA
420     TAX=GP*.22                     ' FED TAX
430     D=FICA+TAX                     ' TOTAL DEDUCTIONS
440     NP=GP-D                        ' NET PAY
450     PRINT USING "      ###.##    ###.##";D;NP
460     TD=TD+D                        ' FINAL TOTAL OF DEDUCTIONS
470     TP=TP+GP                       ' TOTAL PAY
480 NEXT I
490 REM
500 PRINT TAB(51);"-------   ------   ------"
510 PRINT TAB(51);"-------   ------   ------"
520 PRINT TAB(36);USING
        "GRAND TOTAL   #,###.##  #,###.##  #,###.##";TP;TD;TP-TD
530 END
```

The report should appear as:

PAYROLL REPORT

SOC. SEC. #	NAME	CODE	RATE	HOURS	GROSS PAY	DEDUCT.	NET PAY
289-28-3939	LARRY HAGMAN	S	SALARY		455.00	144.01	310.99
948-49-4839	ED COBURN	H	4.55	40.0	182.00	57.60	124.40
928-38-4748	GEORGE TOMAS	S	SALARY		540.00	170.91	369.09
929-28-3939	SALLY SMITH	H	6.75	35.0	236.25	74.77	161.48
928-38-4789	HARRISON FORD	H	3.75	36.0	135.00	42.73	92.27
849-49-8490	FRED JACOBS	H	5.75	40.0	230.00	72.80	157.21
298-39-4849	BARNEY WILSON	S	SALARY		650.00	205.73	444.28
987-37-3977	THOMAS RED	H	4.55	50.0	227.50	72.00	155.50
839-38-4849	JESUS ALVAREZ	H	3.80	40.0	152.00	48.11	103.89
928-39-3849	GEORGE HARRISON	S	SALARY		390.00	123.44	266.57
					-------	------	------
					-------	------	------
			GRAND TOTAL		3,197.75	1,012.09	2,185.66

13. The pseudocode is a duplicate again. There are only
more fields. The program should be similar to:

```
10 REM ***** PROGRAM NAME: EX-11-13
20 REM
30 REM ***** EXERCISE 11-13 - 13 FIELD RANDOM FILE PROCESSING
40 REM
50 REM ***** WRITTEN BY EDWARD J. COBURN
60 REM
65 DIM P$(15),P(15),FD$(13)
70 OPEN "RANDFILE" AS #1 LEN=115
75 DATA DEPT #, 5, SOC. SEC. #, 11, NAME, 20, ADDR, 20
76 DATA CITY, 15, STATE, 2, ZIP CODE, 5, PHONE, 12
77 DATA # DEDUCT., 1, EMERG. PHONE, 12
78 DATA RATE OF PAY, 6, INS. DED., 6, MISC. DED., 6
80 FOR I=1 TO 13
82      READ P$(I),P(I)
83 NEXT I
88 FIELD #1, 2 AS RF$     ' DUMMY RECORD
90 GET 1,1                ' GET THE FIRST RECORD
100 IF CVI(RF$)=0 THEN RECS=1 ELSE RECS=CVI(RF$)
110 FIELD #1,5 AS FD$(1), 11 AS FD$(2), 20 AS FD$(3), 20 AS FD$(4),
             15 AS FD$(5),  2 AS FD$(6),  5 AS FD$(7), 12 AS FD$(8),
              1 AS FD$(9), 12 AS FD$(10), 4 AS FD$(11), 4 AS FD$(12)
              4 AS FD$(13)
120 CLS                    ' CLEAR THE SCREEN
130 PRINT TAB(10);"PAYROLL MAINTENANCE"
140 PRINT                  ' BLANK LINE
150 PRINT "1.  ADD NEW RECORDS"
155 PRINT
160 PRINT "2.  CHANGE EXISTING RECORD"
165 PRINT
170 PRINT "3.  PRINT THE FILE"
175 PRINT
180 PRINT "4.  EXIT THE PROGRAM"
190 PRINT
200 P$= "WHAT OPTION (1-4)"
210 L=1                    ' LENGTH OF PROMPT
220 GOSUB 7000
230 IF B$>"0" AND B$<"5" THEN 270
240    M$="INPUT ERROR.  RETRY ENTRY"
250    GOSUB 6000          ' ERROR SUBROUTINE
260    GOTO 200            ' REPROMPT
270 ON VAL(B$) GOSUB 500, 2000, 3000, 4000
280 GOTO 120               ' RETURN FOR ANOTHER INPUT
470 REM
480 REM ***** ADD MODULE
490 REM
500 CLS                    ' CLEAR THE SCREEN
510 PRINT TAB(20);"PAYROLL ENTRY"
520 PRINT                  ' BLANK LINE
530 FOR I=1 TO 7
535      LOCATE (I+1)*2,1
```

(Program continues)

```
540     IF I<7 THEN PRINT STR$(I);". ";P$(I);TAB(40);
                   USING "##. &";I+7;P$(I+7)
           ELSE PRINT STR$(I);". ";P$(I)
550 NEXT I
560 FOR I=1 TO 13
570     IF I<8 THEN R=(I+1)*2 : C=17
           ELSE R=(I-6)*2 : C=60
580     L=P(I)                ' PROMPT LENGTH
590     GOSUB 7070            ' PROMPT SUBROUTINE
600     IF I<11 THEN LSET FD$(I)=B$ ELSE RSET FD$(I)=MKS$(VAL(B$))
610 NEXT I
638 RECS=RECS+1               ' INCREMENT RECORD NUMBER
640 PUT 1,RECS                ' PUT THE RECORD
650 FIELD #1, 2 AS RF$        ' FIELD RECORD 1
660 LSET RF$=MKI$(RECS)       ' SET THE FIELD
670 PUT 1,1                   ' PUT RECORD 1
675 FIELD #1,5 AS FD$(1), 11 AS FD$(2), 20 AS FD$(3), 20 AS FD$(4),
           15 AS FD$(5),  2 AS FD$(6),  5 AS FD$(7), 12 AS FD$(8),
            1 AS FD$(9), 12 AS FD$(10), 4 AS FD$(11), 4 AS FD$(12)
            4 AS FD$(13)
680 P$= "DO YOU WANT TO ADD ANY MORE (Y OR N)"
690 L=1                       ' LENGTH OF PROMPT
700 GOSUB 7000               ' PROMPT SUBROUTINE
710 IF B$<>"Y" THEN RETURN
720 GOTO 500                  ' GET ANOTHER RECORD
1970 REM
1980 REM ***** CHANGE MODULE
1990 REM
2000 P$="RECORD NUMBER TO CHANGE (0 TO END)"
2020 L=3                      ' PROMPT LENGTH
2030 GOSUB 7000               ' PROMPT SUBROUTINE
2040 IF VAL(B$)=0 THEN RETURN ' EXIT THE SUBROUTINE
2050 IF VAL(B$)<=RECS THEN 2080' RECORD OKAY?
2060     M$="RECORD NOT FOUND.  REENTER."
2070     GOSUB 6000          ' ERROR SUBROUTINE
2075     GOTO 2000           ' GET INDEX AGAIN
2080 RN=VAL(B$)+1            ' RECORD TO ACCESS
2082 FIELD #1,5 AS FD$(1), 11 AS FD$(2), 20 AS FD$(3), 20 AS FD$(4)
           15 AS FD$(5),  2 AS FD$(6),  5 AS FD$(7), 12 AS FD$(8)
            1 AS FD$(9), 12 AS FD$(10), 4 AS FD$(11), 4 AS FD$(12
            4 AS FD$(13)
2085 GET #1,RN               ' GET THE RECORD
2090 CLS                     ' CLEAR THE SCREEN
2100 PRINT TAB(20);"PAYROLL CHANGES"
2110 PRINT                   ' BLANK LINE
2120 FOR I=1 TO 7
2124     LOCATE (I+1)*2,1
```

```
2128    IF I<4 THEN PRINT STR$(I);". ";P$(I);TAB(17);FD$(I);
                TAB(40);USING "##. &        &";I+7;P$(I+7);FD$(I)
                ELSE IF I<7 THEN PRINT
                STR$(I);". ";P$(I);TAB(17);FD$(I);
2129 REM LOCATE (I+1)*2,1
2132 REM IF I<4 THEN PRINT TAB(17);FD$(I);TAB(60);FD$(I+6)
                ELSE IF I<7 THEN
            PRINT TAB(17);FD$(I);TAB(60);USING "###.##";CVS(FD$(I));
                            ELSE PRINT TAB(17);FD$(I)
2136 NEXT I
2150 P$="FIELD TO CHANGE (0 TO END)"
2160 L=1                ' PROMPT LENGTH
2170 GOSUB 7000         ' PROMPT SUBROUTINE
2180 IF B$>="0" AND B$<="4" THEN 2220
2190     M$="INVALID ENTRY.  TRY AGAIN"
2200     GOSUB 6000     ' ERROR SUBROUTINE
2210     GOTO 2150      ' REINPUT
2220 IF B$="0" THEN 2290 ' FIELD ENTRY
2230     IF B$="1" THEN L=9  : R=3
2240     IF B$="2" THEN L=24 : R=5
2242     IF B$="3" THEN L=1  : R=7
2244     IF B$="4" THEN L=8  : R=9
2250     C=17               ' COLUMN
2260     GOSUB 7070         ' PROMPT SUBROUTINE
2270     IF R=3 THEN LSET SF$=B$
2272     IF R=5 THEN LSET NF$=B$
2274     IF R=7 THEN LSET CF$=B$
2276     IF R=9 THEN RSET PF$=MKS$(VAL(B$))
2280     GOTO 2090          ' REPROMPT
2290 PUT #1,RN              ' STORE THE RECORD BACK INTO FILE
2300 GOTO 2000             ' RETURN FOR NEW NUMBER
2970 REM
2980 REM ***** PRINT MODULE
2990 REM
3000 LPRINT TAB(20);"PAYROLL LIST"
3005 LPRINT " "            ' BLANK LINE
3020 LPRINT " SS. NUMBER  NAME";TAB(39);"PAY CODE      AMOUNT"
3030 LPRINT " "            ' BLANK LINE
3040 FOR I=2 TO RECS       ' TO NUMBER IN FILE
3050     GET #1,I          ' GET RECORD BY NUMBER
3060     LPRINT MID$(SF$,1,3);"-";MID$(SF$,4,3);"-";MID$(SF$,7,4);
3065     LPRINT " ";NF$;TAB(43);CF$;TAB(50);
3067     LPRINT USING "#,###.##";CVS(PF$)
3070     T=T+CVS(PF$)      ' ACCUMULATE TOTAL
3080 NEXT I
3090 LPRINT TAB(51);"---------"'UNDERLINE
3100 LPRINT "TOTAL";TAB(51);USING "##,###.##";T
3110 RETURN

(Program continues)
```

```
3970 REM
3980 REM ***** EXIT MODULE
3990 REM
4000 CLOSE #1
4010 END
```

The screen display will look like the following:

PAYROLL ENTRY

1. EMP. ID   8. PHONE

2. SOC. SEC. #   9. # DEDUCT.

3. NAME   10. EMERG. PHONE

4. ADDR   11. RATE OF PAY

5. CITY   12. INS. DED.

6. STATE   13. MISC. DED.

7. ZIP CODE

The printed report should look like the following:

PAYROLL LIST

DEPT #	NAME	PHONE	# DED	RATE	INS.DED.	MISC.DED
11111	JOHN SMITH	939-959-9484	1	11.56	75.00	51.0
11111	HOWARD SMITH	194-947-7346	1	3.95	45.50	111.0
33333	ED COBURN	129-698-5698	3	3.65	63.00	23.0
33333	ROBERT SMITH	125-859-6935	2	8.97	110.00	135.0
55555	TOM JONES	458-959-8652	5	6.36	90.30	50.0
TOTAL					383.80	370.0

14. The pseudocode is the same as any of the other control break programs we have written. The program looks like the following:

```
10 REM ***** PROGRAM NAME: EX-11-14
20 REM
30 REM ***** CONTROL BREAK PROGRAM
40 REM
50 REM ***** WRITTEN BY EDWARD J. COBURN
60 REM
70 REM THIS IS EXERCISE 11-14
80 REM
90 DIM FD$(13)
100 OPEN "RANDFILE" AS #1 LEN=115      ' OPEN THE FILE
```

(Program continues)

```
110 FIELD #1, 2 AS RF$      ' DUMMY RECORD
120 GET 1,1                 ' GET THE FIRST RECORD
130 RECS=CVI(RF$)
140 FIELD #1,5 AS FD$(1), 11 AS FD$(2), 20 AS FD$(3), 20 AS FD$(4),
            15 AS FD$(5),  2 AS FD$(6),  5 AS FD$(7), 12 AS FD$(8),
             1 AS FD$(9), 12 AS FD$(10), 4 AS FD$(11), 4 AS FD$(12),
             4 AS FD$(13)
150 PRINT TAB(30);"PAYROLL REPORT"
160 PRINT
170 PRINT "DEPT #    NAME";TAB(33);"PHONE       # DED      RATE";
          "   INS.DED.  MISC.DED."
180 PRINT
190 FOR I=2 TO RECS         ' TO NUMBER IN FILE
200     GET #1,I            ' GET RECORD BY NUMBER
210     IF T$<>"" AND T$<>FD$(1) THEN GOSUB 390 ' CONTROL BREAK
220     PRINT FD$(1);"   ";FD$(3);" ";FD$(8);"      ";FD$(9);
230     PRINT USING "  #,###.##    #,###.##    #,###.##";
                    CVS(FD$(11));CVS(FD$(12));CVS(FD$(13))
240     TI=TI+CVS(FD$(12))     ' ACCUMULATE INSURANCE
250     SI=SI+CVS(FD$(12))     ' ACCUMULATE INSURANCE SUBTOTAL
260     TM=TM+CVS(FD$(13))     ' ACCUMULATE MISCELLANEOUS
270     SM=SM+CVS(FD$(13))     ' ACCUMULATE MISCELLANEOUS SUBTOTAL
280     T$=FD$(1)             ' ASSIGN BREAK FIELD
290 NEXT I
300 REM
310 GOSUB 390                          ' CONTROL SUBROUTINE
320 PRINT TAB(61);"--------- ---------"
330 PRINT TAB(61);"--------- ---------"
340 PRINT "GRAND TOTALS";TAB(61);USING "##,###.##  ##,###.##";TI,TM
345 CLOSE #1
350 GOTO 460                           ' BRANCH AROUND SUBROUTINE
360 REM
370 REM ***** CONTROL SUBROUTINE
380 REM
390 PRINT TAB(61);"--------- ---------"
400 PRINT "SUBTOTALS FOR DEPARTMENT # ";T$;TAB(61);USING
          "##,###.##  ##,###.##";SI,SM
410 PRINT
420 SI=0                               ' ZERO OUT SUBTOTAL
430 SM=0                               ' ZERO OUT SUBTOTAL
440 T$=FD$(I)                          ' BREAK FIELD
450 RETURN
460 END
```

The report should look like the following:

PAYROLL REPORT

DEPT #	NAME	PHONE	# DED	RATE	INS.DED.	MISC.DE
11111	JOHN SMITH	939-959-9484	1	11.56	75.00	51.
11111	HOWARD SMITH	194-947-7346	1	3.95	45.50	111.
					---------	-------
SUBTOTALS FOR DEPARTMENT # 11111					120.50	1162
33333	ED COBURN	129-698-5698	3	3.65	63.00	23.
33333	ROBERT SMITH	125-859-6935	2	8.97	110.00	135.
					---------	-------
SUBTOTALS FOR DEPARTMENT # 33333					173.00	158.
55555	TOM JONES	458-959-8652	5	6.36	90.30	50.
					---------	-------
SUBTOTALS FOR DEPARTMENT # 55555					90.30	50.
					---------	-------
					---------	-------
GRAND TOTALS					383.80	370.

15. Once again, the pseudocode would merely be a copy of
that at the beginning of the chapter. The program should look
like the following:

```
10 REM ***** PROGRAM NAME: EX-11-15
20 REM
30 REM ***** EXERCISE 11-15 - XYZ CORPORATION EMPLOYEE FILE
40 REM
50 REM ***** WRITTEN BY EDWARD J. COBURN
60 REM
65 DIM A$(15),A(15),FD$(9)
70 OPEN "XYZPAYRD" AS #1 LEN=76      ' OPEN THE FILE
75 DATA NAME, 24, 3, ADDRESS, 20, 5, CITY, 15, 7, STATE, 2, 9
76 DATA ZIP, 5, 9, BIRTH DATE, 8, 11, PAY CODE, 1, 11
77 DATA EMP. DATE, 8, 13, # EXEMPT., 1, 13
80 FOR I=1 TO 9
82       READ A$(I),A(I),R(I)
83 NEXT I
88 FIELD #1, 2 AS RF$     ' DUMMY RECORD
90 GET 1,1                ' GET THE FIRST RECORD
100 IF CVI(RF$)=0 THEN RECS=1 ELSE RECS=CVI(RF$)
110 FIELD #1,20 AS FD$(1), 20 AS FD$(2), 15 AS FD$(3), 2 AS FD$(4),
             5 AS FD$(5),  6 AS FD$(6),  1 AS FD$(7), 6 AS FD$(8),
             1 AS FD$(9)
120 CLS                   ' CLEAR THE SCREEN
130 PRINT TAB(10);"PAYROLL MAINTENANCE"
```

(Program continues)

```
140 PRINT                    ' BLANK LINE
150 PRINT "1.  ADD NEW RECORDS"
155 PRINT
160 PRINT "2.  CHANGE EXISTING RECORD"
165 PRINT
170 PRINT "3.  PRINT THE FILE"
175 PRINT
180 PRINT "4.  EXIT THE PROGRAM"
190 PRINT
200 P$= "WHAT OPTION (1-4)"
210 L=1                      ' LENGTH OF PROMPT
220 GOSUB 7000
230 IF B$>"0" AND B$<"5" THEN 270
240    M$="INPUT ERROR.  RETRY ENTRY"
250      GOSUB 6000          ' ERROR SUBROUTINE
260      GOTO 200            ' REPROMPT
270 ON VAL(B$) GOSUB 500, 2000, 3000, 4000
280 GOTO 120                 ' RETURN FOR ANOTHER INPUT
470 REM
480 REM ***** ADD MODULE
490 REM
500 CLS                      ' CLEAR THE SCREEN
510 PRINT TAB(20);"PAYROLL ENTRY"
520 PRINT                    ' BLANK LINE
530 FOR I=1 TO 9             ' DISPLAY LOOP
532    IF I<4 THEN PRINT STR$(I);". ";A$(I)
              ELSE PRINT STR$(I);". ";A$(I);TAB(35);'
                        STR$(I+1);". ";A$(I+1) : I=I+1
534 PRINT
536 NEXT I
538 FOR J=1 TO 9                     ' ENTRY LOOP
540    L=A(J)
542    R=R(J)
544    IF J<5 OR J=6 OR J-8 THEN C-17 ELSE C=50
546      GOSUB 7070                  ' PROMPT SUBROUTINE
547      IF J=7 AND B$<>"S" AND B$<>"H" THEN 546 ' ERROR
548      LSET FD$(J)=B$
550 NEXT J
560 P$="WHAT FIELD TO CHANGE (0 TO END)?"
562 L=1                              ' LENGTH OF PROMPT
564 GOSUB 7000                       ' PROMPT SUBROUTINE
566 IF B$="0" THEN 638               ' ZERO TO END
568 A=VAL(B$)                        ' SHOULD BE NUMBER
570 IF A>0 AND A<10 THEN 10350       ' VALID ENTRY BRANCH
572    M$="INVALID ENTRY.  TRY AGAIN"
574      GOSUB 10560                 ' ERROR SUBROUTINE
576      GOTO 10260                  ' RETURN FOR NEW INPUT
578 IF A<5 OR A=6 OR A=8 THEN C=17 ELSE C=50
580 R=R(A)
582 L=A(A)                           ' LENGTH OF FIELD
584 GOSUB 10780                      ' PROMPT ENTRY
586 FD$(A)=B$                        ' SAVE CHANGED FIELD
588 GOTO 560                         ' RETURN TO FIELD PROMPT

(Program continues)
```

PAGE 151

```
638 RECS=RECS+1                        ' INCREMENT RECORD NUMBER
640 PUT 1,RECS                         ' PUT THE RECORD
650 FIELD #1, 2 AS RF$                 ' FIELD RECORD 1
660 LSET RF$=MKI$(RECS)                ' SET THE FIELD
670 PUT 1,1                            ' PUT RECORD 1
675 FIELD #1,20 AS FD$(1), 20 AS FD$(2), 15 AS FD$(3), 2 AS FD$(4),
            5 AS FD$(5),  6 AS FD$(6),  1 AS FD$(7), 6 AS FD$(8),
            1 AS FD$(9)
680 P$= "DO YOU WANT TO ADD ANY MORE (Y OR N)"
690 L=1                          ' LENGTH OF PROMPT
700 GOSUB 7000                   ' PROMPT SUBROUTINE
710 IF B$<>"Y" THEN RETURN
720 GOTO 500                     ' GET ANOTHER RECORD
1970 REM
1980 REM ***** CHANGE MODULE
1990 REM
2000 P$="RECORD NUMBER TO CHANGE (0 TO END)"
2020 L=3                         ' PROMPT LENGTH
2030 GOSUB 7000                  ' PROMPT SUBROUTINE
2040 IF VAL(B$)=0 THEN RETURN ' EXIT THE SUBROUTINE
2050 IF VAL(B$)<=RECS THEN 2080' RECORD OKAY?
2060     M$="RECORD NOT FOUND.  REENTER."
2070        GOSUB 6000          ' ERROR SUBROUTINE
2075        GOTO 2000           ' GET INDEX AGAIN
2080 RN=VAL(B$)+1               ' RECORD TO ACCESS
2082 FIELD #1,20 AS FD$(1), 20 AS FD$(2), 15 AS FD$(3), 2 AS FD$(4),
            5 AS FD$(5),  6 AS FD$(6),  1 AS FD$(7), 6 AS FD$(8),
            1 AS FD$(9)
2085 GET #1,RN                  ' GET THE RECORD
2090 CLS                        ' CLEAR THE SCREEN
2100 PRINT TAB(20);"XYZ EMPLOYEE CHANGES"
2110 PRINT                      ' BLANK LINE
2120 FOR I=1 TO 9                      ' DISPLAY LOOP
2130   IF I<4 THEN PRINT STR$(I);". ";A$(I);TAB(17);FD$(I)
            ELSE IF I=4 THEN PRINT STR$(I);". ";A$(I);TAB(17);
            FD$(I);TAB(35);STR$(I+1);". ";A$(I+1);TAB(50);FD$(I+1)
            : I=I+1
2135   IF I=6 OR I=8 THEN PRINT STR$(I);". ";A$(I);TAB(17);
            LEFT$(FD$(I),2);"/";MID$(FD$(I),3,2);"/";
            RIGHT$(FD$(I),2);TAB(35);STR$(I+1);". ";A$(I+1);
            TAB(50);FD$(I+1) : I=I+1
2140 PRINT
2145 NEXT I
2150 P$="FIELD TO CHANGE (0 TO END)"
2160 L=2                         ' PROMPT LENGTH
2170 GOSUB 7000                  ' PROMPT SUBROUTINE
2175 ITEM=VAL(B$)                ' MAKE INTO NUMERIC
2180 IF ITEM>=0 AND ITEM<=13 THEN 2220
2190     M$="INVALID ENTRY.  TRY AGAIN"
2200        GOSUB 6000           ' ERROR SUBROUTINE
2210        GOTO 2150            ' REINPUT
2220 IF ITEM=0 THEN 2290 ' FIELD ENTRY
2225 R=R(ITEM)
2230 IF ITEM<5 OR ITEM=6 OR ITEM=8 THEN C=17 ELSE C=50
2240     L=A(ITEM)               ' PROMPT LENGTH
```

```
2242       GOSUB 7070      ' PROMPT SUBROUTINE
2243       IF ITEM=7 AND B$<>"S" AND B$<>"H" THEN 2242' ERROR
2244    IF ITEM=6 OR ITEM=8 THEN
             B$=LEFT$(B$,2)+MID$(B$,4,2)+RIGHT$(B$,2)
2250       LSET FD$(ITEM)=B$
2280       GOTO 2090       ' REPROMPT
2290 PUT #1,RN             ' STORE THE RECORD BACK INTO FILE
2300 GOTO 2000             ' RETURN FOR NEW NUMBER
2970 REM
2980 REM ***** PRINT MODULE
2990 REM
3000 LPRINT TAB(20);"XYZ CORPORATION"
3002 LPRINT TAB(21);"EMPLOYEE LIST"
3005 LPRINT " "           ' BLANK LINE
3020 LPRINT "NAME";TAB(21);"BIRTH DATE  CODE   EMP. DATE    # EXEMPT."
3030 LPRINT " "           ' BLANK LINE
3040 FOR I=2 TO RECS      ' TO NUMBER IN FILE
3050      GET #1,I        ' GET RECORD BY NUMBER
3060      LPRINT FD$(1);" ";
3067      LPRINT LEFT$(FD$(6),2);"/";MID$(FD$(6),3,2);"/";
             RIGHT$(FD$(6),2);
3070      LPRINT TAB(36);FD$(7);"     ";
3075      LPRINT LEFT$(FD$(8),2);"/";MID$(FD$(8),3,2);"/";
             RIGHT$(FD$(8),2);
3080      LPRINT "          ";FD$(9)
3090 NEXT I
3110 RETURN
3970 REM
3980 REM ***** EXIT MODULE
3990 REM
4000 CLOSE #1
4010 END
```

Tho output chould look like tho following

```
                   XYZ CORPORATION
                   EMPLOYEE LIST

NAME                  BIRTH DATE   CODE   EMP. DATE    # EXEMPT.

ED COBURN             05/16/43      H     12/15/84        3
SARA SMITH            03/22/50      S     05/18/80        1
TOM JONES             02/02/65      H     06/16/84        5
HAROLD HARRIS         03/15/44      S     05/15/76        3
EVERITT JOHNSON       04/18/22      H     04/16/53        2
```

CHAPTER 12 . . . . . INDEXED FILE PROCESSING

12-1 Introduction

1. Random files have the flaw of having to know what record to access.

2. **Indexed files** allow access by use of an index field.

3. In this chapter we shall examine:

    A. How to create and use indexed files.

    B. How to do a binary search.

12-2 Indexed Files

1. The file must contain a unique field called the **index.**

2. Indexed files actually use two - main and index files (F-323).

3. The index file will contain only the index field and the random record number of the record in the main file.

12-3 Binary search

1. The index file must be in sequence.

2. To search the index file we will use a **binary search.**

3. The search requires the following steps:

    A. Find the middle item.

    B. Compare that item to the item being searched for.

    C. If the item searched for is less, the search drops down to the lower half and compares again.

    D. If the item searched for is greater, the search jumps to the middle of the upper half and compares again.

    E. The process continues until either the list is exhausted or the item is found.

4. Illustrations of the techniques are shown on pages 324-326.

5. Sample program is on page 328 (F-327).

12-4 Sequencing the Index File

1. The index file must be kept in sequence while records are added.

2. We use a **bubble insert** to add the records.

3. The insert requires the following steps:

   A. The new item is placed at the top of the list.

   B. The new item is compared with the next item in the list.

   C. If the current item is less, the two are switched.

   D. The comparison and switching continues until the next item is less than the current item. At that point, the new item is in the proper position.

   E. Figure 12-6 on page 330 shows the technique.

4. A sample program can be found on page 331 (F-332).

12-5 Additional Considerations

1. There can be no duplicate entries in the index file.

   A. The bubble technique would add duplicate records.

   B. A check must be made before the record is added.

   C. If the index is a duplicate but still needs to be added you can modify the new index slightly (use an initial).

2. If disk space is short, the main file can be built without the index field. This is not a good technique.

3. The bubble insert techniques works fine up to about 500 entries; after that it becomes too slow.

4. Speed can be increased by putting the index into memory.

12-6 Creating an Indexed File Program

1. To create this program, the program from the previous chapter may be used though some of the changes needed are substantial.

2. The modules are basically the same as the last chapter except we now need a binary search module. The bubble insert is put in the add module.

The Initial Module

1. This module needs to open both the index file and the main file.

2. The module is on page 335 (F-336).

The Binary Search Subroutine

1. The routine is the same as before but it needs to access the index file rather than use an array.

2. The subroutine is on page 338.

The Addition Module

1. This module adds two more fields to the display and input.

2. The routine to add the records will have to use the index file:

   A. First we check the index file for a duplicate.

   B. If so, reprompt the user for a new entry.

   C. The rest of the fields are input and the record is put in the main file.

   D. The index file is bubbled.

   E. The dummy record is used to keep track of the number of records again.

3. The module is on page 340 (F-339).

The Change Module

1. The index is input from the user and then searched for.

2. If it is not found, an error is flashed and reinput.

3. When found, the index is used to get the record number from the index file and then used to retrieve the record from the main file.

4. When the record is retrieved, four fields may be changed instead of the two in the last chapter.

5. The module is shown on page 344 (F-343).

A Note About the Change Routine

1. The constructed routine allows the index field to be changed.

2. This should not be allowed. Instead the routine should:

   A. The index should be checked to see if the new one is a duplicate.

   B. If not a duplicate, the old one needs to be deleted from the index and the new one added.

   C. This is left as an exercise for the student.

   D. Figure 12-11 on page 346 shows index deletion.

The PRINT Module

1. This module will print the list in sequence by accessing the index file first.

2. The module is on page 346 (F-347).

The EXIT Module

1. This module is exactly the same as the previous chapter.

Putting the Program Together

1. Don't forget all the subroutine needed for prompting, etc.

2. An example of a generated report is on page 349.

****

Answers to Questions to Aid Understanding

*   1. An indexed file is easier for the user because the records are accessed by name index rather than by number. That is a record is not retrieved because it is record 4 but because it is the JONES record. Of course, to the programmer, it works about the same way since indexed processing is simply an extension of random processing, but to the user, indexed is much easier.

    2.   There must be a file for the main information and another file for the index field and the record number of the record in the main file.

* 3. In order to search through an index file it must be in sequence; otherwise, the program would not be able to determine if the searched for index is in the file without searching each index, until the one looked for is either found, or the end of the index is found. Obviously, such a search would be extremely slow.

4. The binary search begins looking at the middle item in the list and compares that item to the item being searched for. If the searched for item is smaller, then the next test is on the lower half of the list. If the searched for item is larger, the next search begins in the middle of the upper half. The splitting of the list continues until either the item is found or there are no more records to search.

5. The bubble insert begins by putting the new record at the end of the list. The new item is then compared with the next item in the list and if the new one is smaller, the items are switched. This process continues until the new item is larger than the next item. When this occurs, the item is in the proper location.

* 6. If we do not search the index, duplicate records can be added since the bubble routine to add the index does not check for duplicates.

* 7. The changes to the BINARY program are really pretty simple. The first thing is to change the data statements to contain strings (in order, of course), which also entails changing the array references in lines 80, 100, 170, 200, 230, and 270. Finally, the INPUT statement (line 140) needs to ask for a name. The changed program should look like the following: (The changes are so slight we will not pseudocode the program. Check the chapter for them if needed.)

```
10 REM ***** PROGRAM NAME: F-7-7
20 REM
30 REM ***** WRITTEN BY EDWARD J. COBURN
40 REM
50 REM THIS PROGRAM SEARCH FOR A STRING INDEX
60 REM
70 CLS                        ' CLEAR THE SCREEN
80 DIM B$(20)                 ' ARRAY FOR THE LIST
90 FOR I=1 TO 20
100      READ B$(I)           ' READ IN THE LIST
110 NEXT I
120 H=21                      ' HIGH POINT = NUMBER ITEMS + 1
130 L=0                       ' LOW POINT ALWAYS STARTS AT ZERO
140 INPUT "SEARCH FOR WHAT NAME";N$
150 C=INT(H/2)                ' C=CURRENT ITEM NUMBER
160 PRINT "* ";               ' JUST A MARKER TO INDICATE LOOPS
170 IF N$<>B$(C) THEN 230' IS CURRENT = SEARCHED ITEM
```

(Program continues)

```
180     PRINT "THERE IS A MATCH"
190     PRINT "SEARCHED FOR ";N$
200     PRINT "FOUND        ";B$(C)
210     GOTO 280
220 REM
230 IF N$<B$(C) THEN H=C : C=INT((L+C)/2)
             ELSE L=C : C=C+INT((H-C)/2)
240 IF H<>C AND L<>C THEN 160      ' NOT LOW OR HIGH
250     PRINT "THERE IS NO MATCH"
260     PRINT "SEARCHED FOR    ";N$
270     PRINT "ENDED SEARCH AT ";B$(C)
280 END
290 DATA AL, BETTY, BOB, BOBBY, CALVIN
300 DATA CARL, DAN, DOUG, ED, ERVIN
310 DATA FRANK, FRED, GEORGE, HARRY, INGA
320 DATA MARY, NORMAN, PAUL, ROBERT, SAM
RUN
SEARCH FOR WHAT NAME? AL
* * * * THERE IS A MATCH
SEARCHED FOR AL
FOUND        AL
Ok
RUN
SEARCH FOR WHAT NAME? TOM
* * * * THERE IS NO MATCH
SEARCHED FOR    TOM
ENDED SEARCH AT SAM
Ok
RUN
SEARCH FOR WHAT NAME? ED
* * * * THERE IS A MATCH
SEARCHED FOR ED
FOUND        ED
Ok
```

8. This program uses the regular program shown in the
chapter with the addition of the name change routine. We added
line 2405 to the program so that when the name field was changed,
the change name subroutine was called. The pseudocode for the
subroutine follows:

```
Start change name subroutine
DO-UNTIL new name entered
   Assign the search field
   Search the file (use search subroutine)
   IF name is found THEN
      Print error message
   (ELSE)
   END-IF
END-DO
Initialize counter to current record number

(Pseudocode continues)
```

```
DO-WHILE counter < number of records +1 (remove index loop)
   Get the record from the file
   Put it back with counter - 1
END-DO
Set high to number of records - 2
Get the index
DO-WHILE name to insert >= current index
   Put the old record at high + 1
   Decrease the high counter
   Get the index
END-DO
Assign the fields and put the record into the file at high + 1
End subroutine
```

The program segment should look like the following:

```
4470 REM
4480 REM ***** CHANGE NAME ROUTINE
4490 REM
4500 S$=B$                          ' ASSIGN THE SEARCH FIELD
4510 GOSUB 9000                      ' SEARCH SUBROUTINE
4520 IF SC=0 THEN 4620               ' SKIP IF SEARCH OKAY
4530    M$="DUPLICATE INDEX.  REENTER."
4540    GOSUB 6000                   ' ERROR SUBROUTINE
4550    R=R(1)                       ' ROW
4560    C=16                         ' COLUMN
4570    L=L(1)                       ' PROMPT LENGTH
4580    GOSUB 7070                   ' PROMPT SUBROUTINE
4585 GOTO 4500
4590 REM
4600 REM ***** REMOVE OLD NAME FROM INDEX
4610 REM
4620 FOR I=SVE+1 TO RECS             ' USE SAVED INDEX NUMBER
4630    GET #2,I                     ' TO MOVE THE INDEXES
4640    PUT #2,I-1                   ' DOWN BY 1
4650 NEXT I
4660 REM
4670 REM ***** PUT NEW NAME IN INDEX
4680 REM
4690 H=RECS-2                        ' NUMBER OF RECORDS
4710 GET 2,H                         ' GET THE INDEX
4720 IF B$>=ID$ THEN 4760            ' EXIT THE LOOP
4730    PUT 2,H+1                    ' PUT THE OLD RECORD
4740    H=H-1                        ' REDUCE THE HIGH
4750    IF H>0 THEN 4710             ' GET THE NEXT INDEX
4760 LSET ID$=B$                     ' ASSIGN THE INDEX
4770 RSET IN$=MKS$(RECORD)           ' ASSIGN THE RECORD NUMBER
4780 PUT 2,H+1                       ' PUT THE NEW INDEX
4790 RETURN                          ' RETURN FROM SUBROUTINE
```

9. This program is virtually identical to the one in the chapter except we changed the lines that access the index file. Upon exiting the program, the index file is dumped back out.

```
10 REM ***** PROGRAM NAME: EX-12-9
20 REM
30 REM ***** WRITTEN BY EDWARD J. COBURN
40 REM
50 REM THE INDEXED FILE PROGRAM WITH INDEXES IN ARRAY
60 REM
65 DIM IDX$(25),REC(25)                ' DIMENSION THE INDEXES
70 OPEN "INDXDATA" AS #1 LEN=44        ' OPEN DATA FILE
75 OPEN "CINDEX" AS #2 LEN=28          ' OPEN INDEX FILE
80 FIELD #1, 2 AS RF$
90 GET 1,1                             ' GET THE FIRST RECORD
100 IF CVI(RF$)=0 THEN RECS=1 ELSE RECS=CVI(RF$)
110 FIELD #1, 24 AS F$(1), 4 AS F$(2), 6 AS F$(3), 10 AS F$(4)
112 FIELD #2, 24 AS ID$, 4 AS IN$
114 FOR I=1 TO RECS-1
115     GET #2,I                       ' GET RECORD
116     IDX$(I)=ID$                     ' STORE ID
117     REC(I)=CVS(IN$)                 ' STORE RECORD NUMBER
118 NEXT I
119 REC(I)=CVS(IN$)                     ' STORE RECORD NUMBER
120 CLS                                 ' CLEAR THE SCREEN
130 PRINT TAB(10);"CONTRIBUTIONS MAINTENANCE"
140 PRINT                               ' BLANK LINE
150 PRINT "1. ADD NEW RECORDS"
155 PRINT
160 PRINT "2. CHANGE EXISTING RECORDS"
165 PRINT
170 PRINT "3. PRINT THE FILE"
175 PRINT
180 PRINT "4. EXIT THE PROGRAM"
200 P$="WHAT OPTION (1-4)"             ' PROMPT
210 L=1                                 ' LENGTH OF PROMPT
220 GOSUB 7000                          ' PROMPT SUBROUTINE
230 IF B$>"0" AND B$<"5" THEN 270
240     M$="INPUT ERROR. RETRY ENTRY"
250     GOSUB 6000                      ' ERROR SUBROUTINE
260     GOTO 200                        ' REPROMPT
270 ON VAL(B$) GOSUB 1000 , 2000 , 3000 , 4000
280 GOTO 120
970 REM
980 REM ***** ADD MODULE
990 REM
1000 DATA CONT. NAME, 24, 3, CONT. AMT., 7, 5
1010 DATA DATE , 8, 7, PHONE NUMB. , 12, 9
1020 CLS                                ' CLEAR THE SCREEN
1030 RESTORE                            ' RESET DATA POINTER
1040 FIELD #1, 24 AS F$(1), 4 AS F$(2), 6 AS F$(3), 10 AS F$(4)
1050 PRINT TAB(10);"CONTRIBUTIONS ENTRY"
```

(Program continues)

```
1060 PRINT                                   ' BLANK LINE
1070 FOR I=1 TO 4
1080     READ D$(I),L(I),R(I)               ' THE PROMPT, LENGTH, ROW
1090     PRINT MID$(STR$(I),2,1);". ";D$(I) ' DISPLAY THE PROMPT IN
1100     PRINT                               ' BLANK LINE
1110 NEXT I
1120 FOR I=1 TO 4
1130     L=L(I)                              ' PROMPT LENGTH
1140     R=R(I)                              ' ROW NUMBER
1150     C=16                                ' COLUMN NUMBER
1160     GOSUB 7070                          ' PROMPT SUBROUTINE
1170     IF I<>1 THEN 1260                   ' SKIP THE SEARCH
1180             S$=B$                       ' ASSIGN THE SEARCH FIELD
1190             GOSUB 9000                  ' SEARCH SUBROUTINE
1200             IF SC=0 THEN 1260           ' SKIP IF SEARCH OKAY
1210                 M$="DUPLICATE INDEX.  REENTER."
1220                 GOSUB 6000 ' ERROR SUBROUTINE
1230                 R=3        ' ROW
1240                 C=16       ' COLUMN
1250                 GOTO 1130  ' REDO THE PROMPT
1260             G$(I)=B$                    ' STORE THE FIELD
1270 NEXT I
1280 LSET F$(1)=G$(1)                        ' ASSIGN THE FIELDS
1290 LSET F$(3)=MID$(G$(3),1,2)+MID$(G$(3),4,2)+MID$(G$(3),7,2)
1300 LSET F$(4)=MID$(G$(4),1,3)+MID$(G$(4),5,3)+MID$(G$(4),9,4)
1310 RSET F$(2)=MKS$(VAL(G$(2)))
1320 PUT 1,RECS+1                            ' PUT THE RECORD
1330 FIELD #1, 2 AS RF$                      ' FIELD RECORD 1
1340 RECS=RECS+1                             ' INCREASE RECORD COUNT
1350 LSET RF$=MKI$(RECS)                     ' SET THE FIELD
1360 PUT 1,1                                 ' PUT RECORD 1
1365 FIELD #2, 24 AS ID$, 4 AS IN$
1370 H=RECS-2                                ' NUMBER OF RECORDS
1380 IF H=0 THEN 1440                        ' BYPASS IF NO RECORDS
1400 IF G$(1)>=IDX$(H) THEN 1440             ' EXIT THE LOOP
1410     IDX$(H+1)=IDX$(H)                   ' MOVE THE INDEX
1415     REC(H+1)=REC(H)                     ' MOVE RECORD NUMBER
1420     H=H-1                               ' REDUCE THE HIGH
1430     IF H>0 THEN 1400                    ' GET THE NEXT INDEX
1440 IDX$(H+1)=G$(1)                         ' ASSIGN THE INDEX
1450 REC(H+1)=RECS                           ' USE THE ACTUAL NUMBER
1470 P$="DO YOU WANT TO ADD ANY MORE (Y OR N)"
1480 L=1                                     ' PROMPT LENGTH
1490 GOSUB 7000                              ' PROMPT SUBROUTINE
1500 IF B$<>"Y" THEN RETURN
1510 GOTO 1020                               ' GET ANOTHER RECORD
1970 REM
1980 REM ***** CHANGE MODULE
1990 REM
2000 P$="NAME (0=END)"
2010 L=24                                    ' PROMPT LENGTH
2020 GOSUB 7000                              ' PROMPT SUBROUTINE
2030 IF B$="0" THEN RETURN                   ' EXIT SUBROUTINE

(Program continues)
```

```
2040 S$=B$                          ' ASSIGN SEARCH INDEX
2050 GOSUB 9000
2060 IF SC=1 THEN 2095              ' SKIP IF SEARCH FOUND
2070    M$="RECORD NOT FOUND.  RETRY."
2080    GOSUB 6000                  ' ERROR SUBROUTINE
2090    GOTO 2000                   ' GET INDEX AGAIN
2095 RECORD=REC(C)                  ' ASSIGN RECORD NUMBER
2100 FIELD #1, 24 AS F$(1), 4 AS F$(2), 6 AS F$(3), 10 AS F$(4)
2110 GET 1,RECORD                   ' GET THE MAIN RECORD
2120 CLS
2130 PRINT TAB(10);"CONTRIBUTIONS CHANGES"
2140 PRINT                          ' BLANK LINE
2150 RESTORE                        ' RESET DATA POINTER
2160 FOR I=1 TO 4
2170    READ D$(I),L(I),R(I)        ' PROMPT, LENGTH, ROW
2180    PRINT MID$(STR$(I),2,1);". ";D$(I);
2190    R=R(I)                      ' ROW
2200    C=16                        ' COLUMN
2210    GOSUB 5000                  ' CURSOR POSITIONING
2220    IF I=1 THEN PRINT F$(1)     ' NAME
2230    IF I=3 THEN PRINT MID$(F$(3),1,2);"/";MID$(F$(3),3,2);
                        "/";MID$(F$(3),5,2)
2240    IF I=4 THEN PRINT MID$(F$(4),1,3);"-";MID$(F$(4),4,3);
                        "-";MID$(F$(4),7,4)
2250    IF I=2 THEN PRINT USING "####.##";CVS(F$(2))
2260    PRINT                       ' BLANK LINE
2270 NEXT I
2280 P$="WHAT FIELD TO CHANGE (1-4, 0 TO END)"
2290 L=1                            ' PROMPT LENGTH
2300 GOSUB 7000                     ' PROMPT SUBROUTINE
2310 IF B$>="0" AND B$<"5" THEN 2350    ' IS ENTRY OKAY?
2320    M$="INVALID ENTRY.  RETRY."' ERROR MESSAGE
2330    GOSUB 6000                  ' ERROR SUBROUTINE
2340    GOTO 2280
2350 IF B$="0" THEN 2460            ' END CHANGES
2360 B=VAL(B$)                      ' CONVERT INPUT
2370 R=R(B)                         ' ROW
2380 C=16                           ' COLUMN
2390 L=L(B)                         ' PROMPT LENGTH
2400 GOSUB 7070                     ' PROMPT SUBROUTINE
2410 IF B=1 THEN LSET F$(1)=B$      ' ASSIGN FIELDS
2420 IF B=2 THEN RSET F$(2)=MKS$(VAL(B$))
2430 IF B=3 THEN LSET F$(3)=MID$(B$,1,2)+MID$(B$,4,2)+MID$(B$,7,2)
2440 IF B=4 THEN LSET F$(4)=MID$(B$,1,3)+MID$(B$,5,3)+MID$(B$,9,4)
2450 GOTO 2120
2460 PUT 1,RECORD                   ' STORE THE RECORD BACK INTO FILE
2470 GOTO 2000                      ' RETURN FOR NEW NUMBER
2970 REM
2980 REM ***** PRINT MODULE
2990 REM
3000 T=0                            ' ZERO OUT TOTAL FIELD
3005 LPRINT TAB(25);"CONTRIBUTIONS LIST"
3010 LPRINT " "                     ' BLANK LINE
```

(Program continues)

```
3020 LPRINT "NAME";TAB(28);"AMOUNT        DATE         PHONE NUMBER"
3030 LPRINT " "                         ' BLANK LINE
3040 FOR I=1 TO RECS-1
3050    GET 2,I                         ' GET THE INDEX
3060    GET 1,CVS(IN$)                  ' GET THE RECORD
3070    LPRINT F$(1);TAB(27);
3080    LPRINT USING "####.##";CVS(F$(2));
3090    LPRINT "      ";MID$(F$(3),1,2);"/";MID$(F$(3),3,2);
             "/";MID$(F$(3),5,2);
3100    LPRINT "      ";MID$(F$(4),1,3);"-";MID$(F$(4),4,3);
             "-";MID$(F$(4),7,4)
3110    T=T+CVS(F$(2))
3120 NEXT I
3130 LPRINT TAB(25);"---------"
3140 LPRINT "TOTAL";TAB(25); USING "######.##";T
3150 RETURN
3970 REM
3980 REM ***** EXIT MODULE
3990 REM
4000 FOR I=1 TO RECS-1
4010    LSET ID$=IDX$(I)                ' MOVE FIELD INTO BUFFER
4020    RSET IN$=MKS$(REC(I))
4030    PUT #2,I
4040 NEXT I
4050 CLOSE
4060 END
```

10.   This program would be designed the same as the one in the chapter. The output would be the same as in the previous chapter and will not be shown. The following is the program listing:

```
10 REM ***** PROGRAM NAME: EX-12-10
20 REM
30 REM ***** EXERCISE 12-10 PAYROLL INDEXED PROCESSING
40 REM
50 REM ***** WRITTEN BY EDWARD J. COBURN
60 REM
70 OPEN "PAYINDX" AS #1 LEN=38
72 OPEN "PINDEX" AS #2 LEN=13
80 FIELD #1, 2 AS RF$              ' DUMMY RECORD
90 GET 1,1                         ' GET THE FIRST RECORD
100 IF CVI(RF$)=0 THEN RECS=1 ELSE RECS=CVI(RF$)
110 FIELD #1,9 AS SF$, 24 AS NF$, 1 AS CF$, 4 AS PF$
115 FIELD #2, 9 AS ID$, 4 AS IN$
120 CLS                           ' CLEAR THE SCREEN
130 PRINT TAB(10);"PAYROLL MAINTENANCE"
140 PRINT                         ' BLANK LINE
150 PRINT "1.  ADD NEW RECORDS"
155 PRINT
160 PRINT "2.  CHANGE EXISTING RECORD"
```

(Program continues)

```
165 PRINT
170 PRINT "3.  PRINT THE FILE"
175 PRINT
180 PRINT "4.  EXIT THE PROGRAM"
190 PRINT
200 P$= "WHAT OPTION (1-4)"
210 L=1                         ' LENGTH OF PROMPT
220 GOSUB 7000
230 IF B$>"0" AND B$<"5" THEN 270
240    M$="INPUT ERROR.  RETRY ENTRY"
250      GOSUB 6000             ' ERROR SUBROUTINE
260      GOTO 200               ' REPROMPT
270 ON VAL(B$) GOSUB 500, 2000, 3000, 4000
280 GOTO 120                    ' RETURN FOR ANOTHER INPUT
470 REM
480 REM ***** ADD MODULE
490 REM
500 CLS                         ' CLEAR THE SCREEN
510 PRINT TAB(10);"PAYROLL ENTRY"
520 PRINT                       ' BLANK LINE
530 PRINT "1. SS. NUMBER"
540 PRINT
550 PRINT "2. EMP. NAME"
560 PRINT
570 PRINT "3. SALARY CODE"
580 PRINT
590 PRINT "4. PAY RATE"
600 R=3                         ' ROW NUMBER
610 C=17                        ' COLUMN NUMBER
620 L=9                         ' SS NUMBER LENGTH
630 GOSUB 7070                  ' PROMPT SUBROUTINE
640 S$=B$                       ' ASSIGN THE SEARCH FIELD
650 GOSUB 9000                  ' SEARCH SUBROUTINE
660 IF SC=0 THEN 700            ' SKIP IF SEARCH OKAY
670    M$="DUPLICATE INDEX.  REENTER."
680      GOSUB 6000             ' ERROR SUBROUTINE
690      GOTO 600               ' REDO THE INPUT
700 LSET SF$=B$                 ' ASSIGN SS NUMBER
710 SVE$=B$                     ' SAVE SS# FOR LATER
720 R=5                         ' ROW NUMBER
730 L=24                        ' NAME LENGTH
740 GOSUB 7070                  ' PROMPT SUBROUTINE
750 LSET NF$=B$                 ' ASSIGN NAME
760 R=7                         ' ROW NUMBER
770 L=1                         ' SALARY CODE LENGTH
780 GOSUB 7070                  ' PROMPT SUBROUTINE
790 LSET CF$=B$                 ' ASSIGN SALARY CODE
800 R=9                         ' ROW NUMBER
810 L=8                         ' PAY RATE
820 GOSUB 7070
830 LSET PF$=MKS$(VAL(B$))      ' ASSIGN AMOUNT
840 RECS=RECS+1                 ' INCREMENT RECORD NUMBER
850 PUT 1,RECS                  ' PUT THE RECORD
```

(Program continues)

```
860 FIELD #1, 2 AS RF$          ' FIELD RECORD 1
870 LSET RF$=MKI$(RECS)         ' SET THE FIELD
880 PUT 1,1                     ' PUT RECORD 1
890 FIELD #2, 9  AS ID$, 4 AS IN$
900 H=RECS-2                    ' NUMBER OF RECORDS
910 IF H=0 THEN 970             ' BYPASS IF NO RECORDS
920 GET 2,H                     ' GET THE INDEX
930 IF SVE$>=ID$ THEN 970       ' EXIT THE LOOP
940     PUT 2,H+1               ' PUT THE OLD RECORD
950     H=H-1                   ' REDUCE THE HIGH
960     IF H>0 THEN 920         ' GET THE NEXT INDEX
970 LSET ID$=SVE$               ' ASSIGN THE INDEX
980 RSET IN$=MKS$(RECS)         ' USE THE ACTUAL NUMBER
990 PUT 2,H+1                   ' STORE THE INDEX
1000 P$= "DO YOU WANT TO ADD ANY MORE (Y OR N)"
1010 L=1                        ' LENGTH OF PROMPT
1020 GOSUB 7000                 ' PROMPT SUBROUTINE
1030 IF B$<>"Y" THEN RETURN
1040 GOTO 500                   ' GET ANOTHER RECORD
1970 REM
1980 REM ***** CHANGE MODULE
1990 REM
2000 P$="SOCIAL SECURITY NUMBER (0 TO END)"
2010 L=9                        ' PROMPT LENGTH
2020 GOSUB 7000                 ' PROMPT SUBROUTINE
2030 IF B$="0" THEN RETURN      ' EXIT THE SUBROUTINE
2040 S$=B$                      ' ASSIGN SEARCH INDEX
2050 GOSUB 9000                 ' SEARCH SUBROUTINE
2060 IF SC=1 THEN 2100          ' SKIP IF SEARCH FOUND
2070     M$="RECORD NOT FOUND.  REENTER."
2080       GOSUB 6000           ' ERROR SUBROUTINE
2090       GOTO 2000            ' GET INDEX AGAIN
2100 RN=CVS(IN$)                ' RECORD TO ACCESS
2110 FIELD #1,9 AS SF$, 24 AS NF$,1 AS CF$, 4 AS PF$
2120 GET #1,RN                  ' GET THE RECORD
2130 CLS                        ' CLEAR THE SCREEN
2140 PRINT TAB(10);"PAYROLL CHANGES"
2150 PRINT                      ' BLANK LINE
2160 PRINT "1. SS. NUMBER    ";SF$
2170 PRINT
2180 PRINT "2. EMP. NAME     ";NF$
2190 PRINT
2200 PRINT "3. SALARY CODE   ";CF$
2210 PRINT
2220 PRINT "4. PAY RATE      ";CVS(PF$)
2230 P$="FIELD TO CHANGE (0 TO END)"
2240 L=1                        ' PROMPT LENGTH
2250 GOSUB 7000                 ' PROMPT SUBROUTINE
2260 IF B$>="0" AND B$<="4" THEN 2300
2270     M$="INVALID ENTRY.  TRY AGAIN"
2280       GOSUB 6000           ' ERROR SUBROUTINE
2290       GOTO 2230            ' REINPUT
2300 IF B$="0" THEN 2420        ' FIELD ENTRY

(Program continues)
```

```
2310        IF B$="1" THEN L=9  : R=3
2320        IF B$="2" THEN L=24 : R=5
2330        IF B$="3" THEN L=1  : R=7
2340        IF B$="4" THEN L=8  : R=9
2350        C=17                ' COLUMN
2360        GOSUB 7070          ' PROMPT SUBROUTINE
2370        IF R=3 THEN LSET SF$=B$
2380        IF R=5 THEN LSET NF$=B$
2390        IF R=7 THEN LSET CF$=B$
2400        IF R=9 THEN RSET PF$=B$
2410        GOTO 2130           ' REPROMPT
2420 PUT #1,RN                  'STORE THE RECORD
2430 GOTO 2000                  ' RETURN FOR NEW NUMBER
2970 REM
2980 REM ***** PRINT MODULE
2990 REM
3000 LPRINT TAB(20);"PAYROLL LIST"
3010 LPRINT " "                 ' BLANK LINE
3020 LPRINT " SS. NUMBER  NAME";TAB(39);"PAY CODE      AMOUNT"
3030 LPRINT " "                 ' BLANK LINE
3040 FOR I=2 TO RECS            ' TO NUMBER IN FILE
3050     GET #1,I               ' GET RECORD BY NUMBER
3060     LPRINT MID$(SF$,1,3);"-";MID$(SF$,4,3);"-";MID$(SF$,7,4);
3070     LPRINT "  ";NF$;TAB(43);CF$;TAB(50);
3080     LPRINT USING "#,###.##";CVS(PF$)
3090     T=T+CVS(PF$)           ' ACCUMULATE TOTAL
3100 NEXT I
3110 LPRINT TAB(51);"---------"'UNDERLINE
3120 LPRINT "TOTAL";TAB(49);USING "##,###.##";T
3130 RETURN
3970 REM
3980 REM ***** EXIT MODULE
3990 REM
4000 CLOSE #1
4010 END
```

11. The pseudocode for this report would be the same as any
of the other reports. The program follows:

```
10 REM ***** PROGRAM NAME: EX-12-11
20 REM
30 REM ***** INDEXED PAYROLL FILE PRINT PROGRAM
40 REM
50 REM ***** WRITTEN BY EDWARD J. COBURN
60 REM
70 REM THIS IS EXERCISE 12-11
80 REM
90 DIM H(15)
100 OPEN "PAYINDX" AS #1 LEN=38    ' OPEN THE FILE
105 OPEN "PINDEX" AS #2 LEN=13' OPEN INDEX FILE
110 FIELD #1, 2 AS RF$
120 GET #1,1
```

(Program continues)

```
130 RECS=CVI(RF$)
140 FIELD #1, 9 AS SF$, 24 AS NF$, 1 AS CF$, 4 AS PF$
145 FIELD #2, 9 AS ID$, 4 AS IN$
150 FOR I=1 TO RECS-1
160     GET #2,I                     ' GET THE INDEX RECORD
163     REC=CVS(IN$)                 ' GET THE RECORD NUMBER
166     GET #1,REC                   ' GET THE FILE RECORD
170     IF CF$="S" THEN 260          ' SKIP IF SALARIED
180     CLS                          ' CLEAR THE SCREEN
190     PRINT TAB(20);"HOURS ENTRY"
200     LOCATE 5,1
210     PRINT "THE EMPLOYEE NAME IS ";NF$
220     P$="HOW MANY HOURS WERE WORKED?"
230     L=5                          ' INPUT LENGTH
240     GOSUB 7000                   ' PROMPT SUBROUTINE
250     H(I)=VAL(B$)                 ' STORE HOURS
260 NEXT I
270 CLS                              ' CLEAR THE SCREEN
280 PRINT TAB(30);"PAYROLL REPORT"
290 PRINT
300 PRINT "SOC. SEC. #    NAME            CODE    RATE    ";
          "HOURS   GROSS PAY"
310 PRINT
320 FOR I=1 TO RECS-1
330     GET #2,I                     ' GET THE INDEX RECORD
334     REC=CVS(IN$)                 ' GET THE RECORD NUMBER
336     GET #1,REC                   ' GET THE FILE RECORD
340     GP=CVS(PF$)                  ' TRANSLATE RATE
350     PRINT LEFT$(SF$,3);"-";MID$(SF$,4,2);"-";RIGHT$(SF$,4);
          "    ";LEFT$(NF$,15);
360     PRINT TAB(31);CF$;
370     IF CF$="S" THEN PRINT "     SALARY";
          ELSE PRINT USING"   #.##";GP;
380     IF CF$="H" THEN GP=GP*H(I)   ' CALCULATE HOURLY
390     IF CF$="H" THEN PRINT TAB(44);USING "##.#";H(I);
          ELSE PRINT "     ";
400     PRINT TAB(52);USING "###.##";GP
410     TD=TD+D                      ' FINAL TOTAL OF DEDUCTIONS
420     TP=TP+GP                     ' TOTAL PAY
430 NEXT I
440 REM
450 PRINT TAB(51);"-------"
460 PRINT TAB(51);"-------"
470 PRINT TAB(36);USING "GRAND TOTAL   #,###.##";TP
480 GOTO 490                         ' BRANCH AROUND SUBROUTINE
490 END
```

The report should look like the following:

PAYROLL REPORT

SOC. SEC. #	NAME	CODE	RATE	HOURS	GROSS PAY
289-28-3939	LARRY HAGMAN	S	SALARY		455.00
948-49-4839	ED COBURN	H	4.55	35.0	159.25
928-38-4748	GEORGE TOMAS	S	SALARY		540.00
929-28-3939	SALLY SMITH	H	6.75	40.0	270.00
928-38-4789	HARRISON FORD	H	3.75	45.0	168.75
849-49-8490	FRED JACOBS	H	5.75	40.0	230.00
298-39-4849	BARNEY WILSON	S	SALARY		650.00
987-37-3977	THOMAS RED	H	4.55	30.0	136.50
839-38-4849	JESUS ALVAREZ	H	3.80	35.0	133.00
928-39-3849	GEORGE HARRISON	S	SALARY		390.00

```
                                       -------
                                       -------
                          GRAND TOTAL  3,132.50
```

12. This is the same as the last program with the addition of the deductions. The program follows:

```
10 REM ***** PROGRAM NAME: EX-12-12
20 REM
30 REM ***** INDEXED SALARY FILE PROGRAM WITH DEDUCTIONS
40 REM
50 REM ***** WRITTEN BY EDWARD J. COBURN
60 REM
70 REM THIS IS EXERCISE 12-12
80 REM
90 DIM H(15)
100 OPEN "PAYINDX" AS #1 LEN=38     ' OPEN THE FILE
105 OPEN "PINDEX" AS #2 LEN=13      ' OPEN INDEX FILE
110 FIELD #1, 2 AS RF$
120 GET #1,1
130 RECS=CVI(RF$)
140 FIELD #1, 9 AS SF$, 24 AS NF$, 1 AS CF$, 4 AS PF$
145 FIELD #2, 9 AS ID$, 4 AS IN$
150 FOR I=1 TO RECS-1
160     GET #2,I                    ' GET THE INDEX RECORD
163     REC=CVS(IN$)                ' GET THE RECORD NUMBER
166     GET #1,REC                  ' GET THE FILE RECORD
170     IF CF$="S" THEN 260         ' SKIP IF SALARIED
180     CLS                         ' CLEAR THE SCREEN
190     PRINT TAB(20);"HOURS ENTRY"
200     LOCATE 5,1
210     PRINT "THE EMPLOYEE NAME IS ";NF$
220     P$="HOW MANY HOURS WERE WORKED?"
230     L=5                         ' INPUT LENGTH
240     GOSUB 7000                  ' PROMPT SUBROUTINE
250     H(I)=VAL(B$)                ' STORE HOURS
```

```basic
260 NEXT I
270 CLS                          ' CLEAR THE SCREEN
280 PRINT TAB(30);"PAYROLL REPORT"
290 PRINT
300 PRINT "SOC. SEC. #   NAME              CODE    RATE     ";
          "HOURS   GROSS PAY  DEDUCT.    NET PAY"
310 PRINT
320 FOR I=1 TO RECS-1
330     GET #2,I                 ' GET THE INDEX RECORD
334     REC=CVS(IN$)             ' GET THE RECORD NUMBER
336     GET #1,REC               ' GET THE FILE RECORD
340     GP=CVS(PF$)              ' TRANSLATE RATE
350     PRINT LEFT$(SF$,3);"-";MID$(SF$,4,2);"-";RIGHT$(SF$,4);
          "  ";LEFT$(NF$,15);
360     PRINT TAB(31);CF$;
370     IF CF$="S" THEN PRINT "   SALARY";
             ELSE PRINT USING"     #.##";GP;
380     IF CF$="H" THEN GP=GP*H(I) ' CALCULATE HOURLY
390     IF CF$="H" THEN PRINT TAB(44);USING "##.#";H(I);
                ELSE PRINT "      ";
400     PRINT TAB(52);USING "###.##";GP;
410     FICA=GP*.0965            ' FICA
420     TAX=GP*.22               ' FED TAX
430     D=FICA+TAX               ' TOTAL DEDUCTIONS
440     NP=GP-D                  ' NET PAY
450     PRINT USING "     ###.##     ###.##";D;NP
460     TD=TD+D                  ' FINAL TOTAL OF DEDUCTIONS
470     TP=TP+GP                 ' TOTAL PAY
480 NEXT I
490 REM
500 PRINT TAB(51);"-------    ------    ------"
510 PRINT TAB(51);"-------    ------    ------"
520 PRINT TAB(36);USING
          "GRAND TOTAL    #,###.##   #,###.##   #,###.##";TP;TD;TP-TD
530 END
```

The report will look like the following:

```
                          PAYROLL REPORT

SOC. SEC. #    NAME             CODE    RATE    HOURS    GROSS PAY    DEDUCT.    NET PAY
289-28-3939    LARRY HAGMAN      S      SALARY              455.00     144.01     310.99
948-49-4839    ED COBURN         H      4.55    40.0        182.00      57.60     124.40
928-38-4748    GEORGE TOMAS      S      SALARY              540.00     170.91     369.09
929-28-3939    SALLY SMITH       H      6.75    35.0        236.25      74.77     161.48
928-38-4789    HARRISON FORD     H      3.75    36.0        135.00      42.73      92.27
849-49-8490    FRED JACOBS       H      5.75    40.0        230.00      72.80     157.21
298-39-4849    BARNEY WILSON     S      SALARY              650.00     205.73     444.28
987-37-3977    THOMAS RED        H      4.55    50.0        227.50      72.00     155.50
839-38-4849    JESUS ALVAREZ     H      3.80    40.0        152.00      48.11     103.89
928-39-3849    GEORGE HARRISON   S      SALARY              390.00     123.44     266.57
                                                          -------    ------    ------
                                                          -------    ------    ------
                                            GRAND TOTAL  3,197.75  1,012.09  2,185.66
```

13. This program would be designed like the other indexed programs except that it would use more fields. The program would look like the following:

```
10 REM ***** PROGRAM NAME: EX-12-13
20 REM
30 REM ***** EXERCISE 12-13 - 13 FIELD INDEXED FILE PROCESSING
40 REM
50 REM ***** WRITTEN BY EDWARD J. COBURN
60 REM
65 DIM P$(15),P(15),FD$(13)
70 OPEN "INDXFILE" AS #1 LEN=115
72 OPEN "FINDEX" AS #2 LEN=15
75 DATA SOC. SEC. #, 11, DEPT #, 5, NAME, 20, ADDR, 20
76 DATA CITY, 15, STATE, 2, ZIP CODE, 5, PHONE, 12
77 DATA # DEDUCT., 1, EMERG. PHONE, 12
78 DATA RATE OF PAY, 6, INS. DED., 6, MISC. DED., 6
80 FOR I=1 TO 13
82     READ P$(I),P(I)
83 NEXT I
88 FIELD #1, 2 AS RF$      ' DUMMY RECORD
90 GET 1,1                 ' GET THE FIRST RECORD
100 IF CVI(RF$)=0 THEN RECS=1 ELSE RECS=CVI(RF$)
110 FIELD #1,11 AS FD$(1), 5 AS FD$(2), 20 AS FD$(3), 20 AS FD$(4),
            15 AS FD$(5),  2 AS FD$(6),  5 AS FD$(7), 12 AS FD$(8),
             1 AS FD$(9), 12 AS FD$(10), 4 AS FD$(11), 4 AS FD$(12),
             4 AS FD$(13)
115 FIELD #2, 11 AS ID$, 4 AS IN$
120 CLS                    ' CLEAR THE SCREEN
130 PRINT TAB(10);"PAYROLL MAINTENANCE"
140 PRINT                  ' BLANK LINE
150 PRINT "1.  ADD NEW RECORDS"
155 PRINT
160 PRINT "2.  CHANGE EXISTING RECORD"
165 PRINT
170 PRINT "3.  PRINT THE FILE"
175 PRINT
180 PRINT "4.  EXIT THE PROGRAM"
190 PRINT
200 P$= "WHAT OPTION (1-4)"
210 L=1                    ' LENGTH OF PROMPT
220 GOSUB 7000
230 IF B$>"0" AND B$<"5" THEN 270
240    M$="INPUT ERROR.  RETRY ENTRY"
250    GOSUB 6000          ' ERROR SUBROUTINE
260    GOTO 200            ' REPROMPT
270 ON VAL(B$) GOSUB 500, 2000, 3000, 4000
280 GOTO 120               ' RETURN FOR ANOTHER INPUT
470 REM
480 REM ***** ADD MODULE
490 REM
500 CLS                    ' CLEAR THE SCREEN
```

(Program continues)

```
510 PRINT TAB(20);"PAYROLL ENTRY"
520 PRINT                      ' BLANK LINE
530 FOR I=1 TO 7
535     LOCATE (I+1)*2,1
540     IF I<7 THEN PRINT STR$(I);". ";P$(I);TAB(40);
                           USING "##. &";I+7;P$(I+7)
              ELSE PRINT STR$(I);". ";P$(I)
550 NEXT I
560 FOR I=1 TO 13
570     IF I<8 THEN R=(I+1)*2 : C=17
              ELSE R=(I-6)*2 : C=60
580     L=P(I)                 ' PROMPT LENGTH
590     GOSUB 7070             ' PROMPT SUBROUTINE
591     IF I<>1 THEN 600       ' SKIP THE SEARCH
592         S$=B$              ' ASSIGN THE SEARCH FIELD
593         GOSUB 9000         ' SEARCH SUBROUTINE
594         IF SC=0 THEN 600' SKIP IF SEARCH OKAY
595             M$="DUPLICATE INDEX.  REENTER."
596             GOSUB 6000     ' ERROR SUBROUTINE
599             GOTO 570       ' REDO THE PROMPT
600     IF I<11 THEN LSET FD$(I)=B$ ELSE RSET FD$(I)=MKS$(VAL(B$))
605     IF I=1 THEN SVE$=B$    ' SAVE SS# FOR LATER USE
610 NEXT I
638 RECS=RECS+1               ' INCREMENT RECORD NUMBER
640 PUT 1,RECS                ' PUT THE RECORD
650 FIELD #1, 2 AS RF$        ' FIELD RECORD 1
660 LSET RF$=MKI$(RECS)       ' SET THE FIELD
670 PUT 1,1                   ' PUT RECORD 1
671 FIELD #1,11 AS FD$(1), 5 AS FD$(2), 20 AS FD$(3), 20 AS FD$(4),
            15 AS FD$(5),  2 AS FD$(6),  5 AS FD$(7), 12 AS FD$(8)
             1 AS FD$(9), 12 AS FD$(10), 4 AS FD$(11), 4 AS FD$(12
             4 AS FD$(13)
672 H=RECS-2                  ' NUMBER OF RECORDS
673 IF H=0 THEN 679           ' BYPASS IF NO RECORDS
674 GET 2,H                   ' GET THE INDEX
675 IF SVE$>=ID$ THEN 679' EXIT THE LOOP
676     PUT 2,H+1             ' PUT THE OLD RECORD
677     H=H-1                 ' REDUCE THE HIGH
678     IF H>0 THEN 674       ' GET THE NEXT INDEX
679 LSET ID$=SVE$             ' ASSIGN THE INDEX
680 RSET IN$=MKS$(RECS)       ' USE THE ACTUAL NUMBER
681 PUT 2,H+1                 ' STORE THE INDEX
689 P$= "DO YOU WANT TO ADD ANY MORE (Y OR N)"
690 L=1                       ' LENGTH OF PROMPT
700 GOSUB 7000                ' PROMPT SUBROUTINE
710 IF B$<>"Y" THEN RETURN
720 GOTO 500                  ' GET ANOTHER RECORD
1970 REM
1980 REM ***** CHANGE MODULE
1990 REM
2000 P$="SOCIAL SECURITY NUMBER (0 TO END)"
2020 L=11                     ' PROMPT LENGTH
2030 GOSUB 7000               ' PROMPT SUBROUTINE

(Program continues)
```

```
2040 IF B$="0" THEN RETURN      ' EXIT THE SUBROUTINE
2050 S$=B$                      ' ASSIGN SEARCH INDEX
2053 GOSUB 9000                 ' SEARCH SUBROUTINE
2055 IF SC=1 THEN 2080          ' SKIP IF SEARCH FOUND
2060     M$="RECORD NOT FOUND.  REENTER."
2070       GOSUB 6000           ' ERROR SUBROUTINE
2075       GOTO 2000            ' GET INDEX AGAIN
2080 RN=CVS(IN$)                ' RECORD TO ACCESS
2082 FIELD #1,11 AS FD$(1), 5 AS FD$(2), 20 AS FD$(3), 20 AS FD$(4),
               15 AS FD$(5),  2 AS FD$(6),  5 AS FD$(7), 12 AS FD$(8),
                1 AS FD$(9), 12 AS FD$(10), 4 AS FD$(11), 4 AS FD$(12),
                4 AS FD$(13)
2085 GET #1,RN                  ' GET THE RECORD
2090 CLS                        ' CLEAR THE SCREEN
2100 PRINT TAB(20);"PAYROLL CHANGES"
2110 PRINT                      ' BLANK LINE
2120 FOR I=1 TO 7
2124     LOCATE (I+1)*2,1
2128     IF I<7 THEN PRINT STR$(I);". ";P$(I);TAB(40);
                         USING "##. &";I+7;P$(I+7)
               ELSE PRINT STR$(I);". ";P$(I)
2129     LOCATE (I+1)*2,17
2132     PRINT FD$(I);
2134     LOCATE (I+1)*2,60
2135     IF I<4 THEN PRINT FD$(I+7);
2136     IF I>3 AND I<7 THEN PRINT TAB(60);USING
                              "###.##";CVS(FD$(I+7));
2145 NEXT I
2150 P$="FIELD TO CHANGE (0 TO END)"
2160 L=2                        ' PROMPT LENGTH
2170 GOSUB 7000                 ' PROMPT SUBROUTINE
2175 ITEM=VAL(B$)               ' MAKE INTO NUMERIC
2180 IF ITEM>=0 AND ITEM<=13 THEN 2220
2190     M$="INVALID ENTRY.  TRY AGAIN"
2200       GOSUB 6000           ' ERROR SUBROUTINE
2210       GOTO 2150            ' REINPUT
2220 IF ITEM=0 THEN 2290 ' FIELD ENTRY
2230       IF ITEM<8 THEN R=(ITEM+1)*2 : C=17 ELSE R=(ITEM-6)*2 : C=60
2240       L=P(ITEM)            ' PROMPT LENGTH
2242       GOSUB 7070           ' PROMPT SUBROUTINE
2244       IF ITEM<11 THEN LSET FD$(ITEM)=B$
                     ELSE RSET FD$(ITEM)=MKS$(VAL(B$))
2280       GOTO 2090            ' REPROMPT
2290 PUT #1,RN                  ' STORE THE RECORD BACK INTO FILE
2300 GOTO 2000                  ' RETURN FOR NEW NUMBER
2970 REM
2980 REM ***** PRINT MODULE
2990 REM
3000 LPRINT TAB(20);"PAYROLL LIST"
3005 LPRINT " "                 ' BLANK LINE
3020 LPRINT "SOC. SEC #  NAME";TAB(36);"PHONE      # DED     RATE";
            " INS.DED.  MISC.DED."
3030 LPRINT " "                 ' BLANK LINE

(Program continues)
```

```
3040 FOR I=1 TO RECS-1      ' TO NUMBER IN FILE
3045      GET #2,I          ' GET INDEX RECORD
3047      REC=CVS(IN$)      ' GET RECORD NUMBER
3050      GET #1,REC        ' GET RECORD BY NUMBER
3060      LPRINT FD$(1);" ";FD$(3);" ";FD$(8);"    ";FD$(9);
3067      LPRINT USING "  #,###.##   #,###.##    #,###.##";
               CVS(FD$(11));CVS(FD$(12));CVS(FD$(13))
3070      TI=TI+CVS(FD$(12))      ' ACCUMULATE INSURANCE
3075      TM=TM+CVS(FD$(13))      ' ACCUMULATE MISCELLANEOUS
3080 NEXT I
3090 LPRINT TAB(61);"---------  ---------"
3100 LPRINT "TOTAL";TAB(61);USING "##,###.##   ##,###.##";TI,TM
3110 RETURN
3970 REM
3980 REM ***** EXIT MODULE
3990 REM
4000 CLOSE #1
4010 END
```

The output would look like the following:

PAYROLL LIST

DEPT #	NAME	PHONE	# DED	RATE	INS.DED.	MISC.DED.
11111	JOHN SMITH	939-959-9484	1	11.56	75.00	51.00
11111	HOWARD SMITH	194-947-7346	1	3.95	45.50	111.00
33333	ED COBURN	129-698-5698	3	3.65	63.00	23.00
33333	ROBERT SMITH	125-859-6935	2	8.97	110.00	135.00
55555	TOM JONES	458-959-8652	5	6.36	90.30	50.00
					---------	---------
TOTAL					383.80	370.00

14. This program would be designed as the others in the chapter. The program follows:

```
10 REM ***** PROGRAM NAME: EX-12-14
20 REM
30 REM ***** EXERCISE 12-14 - XYZ CORPORATION EMPLOYEE FILE
40 REM
50 REM ***** WRITTEN BY EDWARD J. COBURN
60 REM
70 DIM A$(15),A(15),FD$(9)
80 OPEN "XYZPAYIN" AS #1 LEN=76         ' OPEN THE FILE
90 OPEN "XYZINDEX" AS #2 LEN=24         ' OPEN THE FILE
100 DATA NAME, 20, 3, ADDRESS, 20, 5, CITY, 15, 7, STATE, 2, 9
105 DATA ZIP, 5, 9, BIRTH DATE, 8, 11, PAY CODE, 1, 11
110 DATA EMP. DATE, 8, 13, # EXEMPT., 1, 13
120 FOR I=1 TO 9
130      READ A$(I),A(I),R(I)
140 NEXT I
```

(Program continues)

```
150 FIELD #1, 2 AS RF$              ' DUMMY RECORD
160 GET 1,1                         ' GET THE FIRST RECORD
170 IF CVI(RF$)=0 THEN RECS=1 ELSE RECS=CVI(RF$)
180 FIELD #1,20 AS FD$(1), 20 AS FD$(2), 15 AS FD$(3), 2 AS FD$(4),
            5 AS FD$(5),  6 AS FD$(6),  1 AS FD$(7), 6 AS FD$(8),
            1 AS FD$(9)
190 FIELD #2, 20 AS ID$, 4 AS IN$
200 CLS                             ' CLEAR THE SCREEN
210 PRINT TAB(10);"PAYROLL MAINTENANCE"
220 PRINT                           ' BLANK LINE
230 PRINT "1.  ADD NEW RECORDS"
240 PRINT
250 PRINT "2.  CHANGE EXISTING RECORD"
260 PRINT
270 PRINT "3.  PRINT THE FILE"
280 PRINT
290 PRINT "4.  EXIT THE PROGRAM"
300 PRINT
310 P$= "WHAT OPTION (1-4)"
320 L=1                             ' LENGTH OF PROMPT
330 GOSUB 7000
340 IF B$>"0" AND B$<"5" THEN 380
350    M$="INPUT ERROR.  RETRY ENTRY"
360    GOSUB 6000                   ' ERROR SUBROUTINE
370    GOTO 310                     ' REPROMPT
380 ON VAL(B$) GOSUB 500, 2000, 3000, 4000
390 GOTO 200                        ' RETURN FOR ANOTHER INPUT
470 REM
480 REM ***** ADD MODULE
490 REM
500 CLS                             ' CLEAR THE SCREEN
510 PRINT TAB(20);"PAYROLL ENTRY"
520 PRINT                           ' BLANK LINE
530 FOR I=1 TO 9                        ' DISPLAY LOOP
540    IF I<4 THEN PRINT STR$(I);". ";A$(I)
            ELSE PRINT STR$(I);". ";A$(I);TAB(35);
                      STR$(I+1);". ";A$(I+1) : I=I+1
550 PRINT
560 NEXT I
570 FOR J=1 TO 9                        ' ENTRY LOOP
580    L=A(J)
590    R=R(J)
600    IF J<5 OR J=6 OR J=8 THEN C=17 ELSE C=50
610    GOSUB 7070                       ' PROMPT SUBROUTINE
620    IF J<>1 THEN 690                  ' SKIP THE SEARCH
630       S$=B$                          ' ASSIGN THE SEARCH FIELD
640       GOSUB 9000                     ' SEARCH SUBROUTINE
650       IF SC=0 THEN 690               ' SKIP IF SEARCH OKAY
660          M$="DUPLICATE INDEX.  REENTER."
670          GOSUB 6000                  ' ERROR SUBROUTINE
680          GOTO 580                    ' REDO THE PROMPT
690    IF J=7 AND B$<>"S" AND B$<>"H" THEN 610 ' ERROR
700    LSET FD$(J)=B$
```

(Program continues)

```
710 NEXT J
720 P$="WHAT FIELD TO CHANGE (0 TO END)?"
730 L=1                               ' LENGTH OF PROMPT
740 GOSUB 7000                        ' PROMPT SUBROUTINE
750 IF B$="0" THEN 950                ' ZERO TO END
760 A=VAL(B$)                         ' SHOULD BE NUMBER
770 IF A>0 AND A<10 THEN 810          ' VALID ENTRY BRANCH
780     M$="INVALID ENTRY.  TRY AGAIN"
790       GOSUB 6000                  ' ERROR SUBROUTINE
800       GOTO 720                    ' RETURN FOR NEW INPUT
810 IF A<5 OR A=6 OR A=8 THEN C=17 ELSE C=50
820 R=R(A)
830 L=A(A)                            ' LENGTH OF FIELD
840 GOSUB 7070                        ' PROMPT ENTRY
850     IF A<>1 THEN 930              ' SKIP THE SEARCH
860       S$=B$                       ' ASSIGN THE SEARCH FIELD
870       GOSUB 9000                  ' SEARCH SUBROUTINE
880       IF SC=0 THEN 930            ' SKIP IF SEARCH OKAY
890         M$="DUPLICATE INDEX.  REENTER."
900           GOSUB 6000              ' ERROR SUBROUTINE
910           GOTO 820                ' REDO THE PROMPT
920     IF A=7 AND B$<>"S" AND B$<>"H" THEN 840 ' ERROR
930 LSET FD$(A)=B$                    ' SAVE CHANGED FIELD
940 GOTO 720                          ' RETURN TO FIELD PROMPT
950 RECS=RECS+1                       ' INCREMENT RECORD NUMBER
960 PUT 1,RECS                        ' PUT THE RECORD
965 SV$=FD$(1)                        ' TEMPORARILY STORE INDEX
970 FIELD #1, 2 AS RF$                ' FIELD RECORD 1
980 LSET RF$=MKI$(RECS)               ' SET THE FIELD
990 PUT 1,1                           ' PUT RECORD 1
1000 FIELD #1,20 AS FD$(1), 20 AS FD$(2), 15 AS FD$(3), 2 AS FD$(4)
               5 AS FD$(5),  6 AS FD$(6),  1 AS FD$(7), 6 AS FD$(8)
               1 AS FD$(9)
1010 FIELD #2, 20 AS ID$, 4 AS IN$
1020 H=RECS-2                         ' NUMBER OF RECORDS
1030 IF H=0 THEN 1090                 ' BYPASS IF NO RECORDS
1040 GET 2,H                          ' GET THE INDEX
1050 IF SV$>=ID$ THEN 1090            ' EXIT THE LOOP
1060     PUT 2,H+1                    ' PUT THE OLD RECORD
1070     H=H-1                        ' REDUCE THE HIGH
1080       IF H>0 THEN 1040           ' GET THE NEXT INDEX
1090 LSET ID$=SV$                     ' ASSIGN THE INDEX
1100 RSET IN$=MKS$(RECS)              ' USE THE ACTUAL NUMBER
1110 PUT 2,H+1                        ' STORE THE INDEX
1120 P$="DO YOU WANT TO ADD ANY MORE (Y or N)?"
1130 L=1                              ' LENGTH OF PROMPT
1140 GOSUB 7000                  ' PROMPT SUBROUTINE
1150 IF B$<>"Y" THEN RETURN
1160 GOTO 500                    ' GET ANOTHER RECORD
1970 REM
1980 REM ***** CHANGE MODULE
1990 REM
2000 P$="ENTER NAME TO CHANGE (0 TO END)"
```

(Program continues)

```
2010 L=20                        ' PROMPT LENGTH
2020 GOSUB 7000                  ' PROMPT SUBROUTINE
2030 IF B$="0" THEN RETURN       ' EXIT THE SUBROUTINE
2040 S$=B$                       ' ASSIGN SEARCH INDEX
2050 GOSUB 9000
2060 IF SC=1 THEN 2100           ' SKIP IF SEARCH FOUND
2070      M$="RECORD NOT FOUND.  REENTER."
2080        GOSUB 6000           ' ERROR SUBROUTINE
2090        GOTO 2000            ' GET INDEX AGAIN
2100 RN=CVS(IN$)                 ' RECORD TO ACCESS
2110 FIELD #1,20 AS FD$(1), 20 AS FD$(2), 15 AS FD$(3), 2 AS FD$(4)
             5 AS FD$(5),  6 AS FD$(6),  1 AS FD$(7), 6 AS FD$(8)
             1 AS FD$(9)
2120 GET #1,RN                   ' GET THE RECORD
2130 CLS                         ' CLEAR THE SCREEN
2140 PRINT TAB(20);"XYZ EMPLOYEE CHANGES"
2150 PRINT                       ' BLANK LINE
2160 FOR I=1 TO 9                         ' DISPLAY LOOP
2170   IF I<4 THEN PRINT STR$(I);". ";A$(I);TAB(17);FD$(I)
             ELSE IF I=4 THEN PRINT STR$(I);". ";A$(I);TAB(17);
                 FD$(I);TAB(35);STR$(I+1);". ";A$(I+1);TAB(50);
                 FD$(I+1) : I=I+1
2180   IF I=6 OR I=8 THEN PRINT STR$(I);". ";A$(I);TAB(17);
         LEFT$(FD$(I),2);"/";MID$(FD$(I),3,2);"/";RIGHT$(FD$(I),2)
         TAB(35);STR$(I+1);". ";A$(I+1);TAB(50);FD$(I+1) : I=I+1
2190 PRINT
2200 NEXT I
2210 P$="FIELD TO CHANGE (0 TO END)"
2220 L=2                         ' PROMPT LENGTH
2230 GOSUB 7000                  ' PROMPT SUBROUTINE
2240 ITEM=VAL(B$)                ' MAKE INTO NUMERIC
2250 IF ITEM>=0 AND ITEM<=13 THEN 2290
2260      M$="INVALID ENTRY.  TRY AGAIN"
2270        GOSUB 6000           ' ERROR SUBROUTINE
2280        GOTO 2210            ' REINPUT
2290 IF ITEM=0 THEN 2380         ' FIELD ENTRY
2300 R=R(ITEM)
2310 IF ITEM<5 OR ITEM=6 OR ITEM=8 THEN C=17 ELSE C=50
2320      L=A(ITEM)                 ' PROMPT LENGTH
2330        GOSUB 7070           ' PROMPT SUBROUTINE
2340      IF ITEM=7 AND B$<>"S" AND B$<>"H" THEN 2330' ERROR
2350   IF ITEM=6 OR ITEM=8 THEN
                 B$=LEFT$(B$,2)+MID$(B$,4,2)+RIGHT$(B$,2)
2360      LSET FD$(ITEM)=B$
2370        GOTO 2130            ' REPROMPT
2380 PUT #1,RN                   ' STORE THE RECORD BACK INTO FILE
2390 GOTO 2000                   ' RETURN FOR NEW NUMBER
2970 REM
2980 REM ***** PRINT MODULE
2990 REM
3000 LPRINT TAB(20);"XYZ CORPORATION"
3002 LPRINT TAB(21);"EMPLOYEE LIST"
3005 LPRINT " "                  ' BLANK LINE
```

(Program continues)

```
3020 LPRINT "NAME";TAB(21);"BIRTH DATE   CODE   ";
          "EMP. DATE    # EXEMPT."
3030 LPRINT " "              ' BLANK LINE
3040 FOR I=2 TO RECS         ' TO NUMBER IN FILE
3050     GET #1,I            ' GET RECORD BY NUMBER
3060     LPRINT FD$(1);" ";
3067     LPRINT LEFT$(FD$(6),2);"/";MID$(FD$(6),3,2);"/";
              RIGHT$(FD$(6),2);
3070     LPRINT TAB(36);FD$(7);"    ";
3075     LPRINT LEFT$(FD$(8),2);"/";MID$(FD$(8),3,2);"/";
              RIGHT$(FD$(8),2);
3080     LPRINT "          ";FD$(9)
3090 NEXT I
3110 RETURN
3970 REM
3980 REM ***** EXIT MODULE
3990 REM
4000 CLOSE #1
4010 END
```

The report is:

```
               XYZ CORPORATION
               EMPLOYEE LIST

NAME                BIRTH DATE   CODE   EMP. DATE    # EXEMPT.

ED COBURN            05/16/43     H     12/15/84        3
SARA SMITH           03/22/50     S     05/18/80        1
TOM JONES            02/02/65     H     06/16/84        5
HAROLD HARRIS        03/15/44     S     05/15/76        3
EVERITT JOHNSON      04/18/22     H     04/16/53        2
```

CHAPTER 13 . . . . . TREE STRUCTURES

13-1 Introduction

1. This chapter shows **tree structures.**

2. How to create an index process without an index file.

3. Accessing records is not **necessarily** any faster but adding records is faster **than** using the bubble insert.

13-2 Developing the Tree Structure

1. A **tree** is an index without cycles. The index is examined in sequence without jumping back and forth like the binary search.

2. The first entry is called the **root.**

3. All the other entries are called **nodes.**

4. The connections to the nodes are called **branches.**

5. When we search a branch we are **traversing** the tree.

6. The tree is created and searched as follows:

   A. The first element is used as the root.

   B. Each node element is moved down the right branch if it is larger than the root and down the left if smaller.

   C. This movement continues until the end of a branch is found. Then the node is added at that point.

7. Examples are shown in Figures 13-8 and 13-9 pages 356-357.

13-3 Utilizing the tree structure

1. To use a tree, each record needs to keep track of its next lower and next higher node record numbers.

2. The lower and higher node numbers of the root node (and any newly added node) begin as zero.

3. When a node is added, its immediately preceding node is updated with its lower or higher record number depending upon whether the new node is lower or higher.

13-4 A Sample Program

1. The program must first input the root node.

2. Each subsequent entry will traverse the tree until there is a match or no more branches in the indicated direction.

3. The number of entries in the file must be kept and updated every time a new node is added.

4. The program uses a two dimensional array:

    A. The first dimension is for the number of possible nodes.

    B. The second dimension is for:

       1) The value of the node.

       2) The next lower node.

       3) The next higher node.

5. The original code is on page 361 (F-360).

6. The program is then updated with DATA statements to set up an original tree that can be checked for duplicates and added to.

7. The update program is shown on page 363.

13-5 Creating a Tree Structure Program

1. The book continues to use the contributions program.

2. Few changes are needed to the main body of the program.

3. The tree search routine will need to be used, however.

Tree Search Module

1. The array access in the sample is changed to file access.

2. The routine is shown on pages 368-369 (F-366-367).

The Initial Module

1. Only one OPEN statement is needed for this program.

2. The file length changes (as do the FIELD statements) to include room for the two node record numbers.

The Addition Module

1. The lines to add to the index file need to be deleted.

2. Values of zero need to be put in for the node values of the new records.

3. The module is shown on pages 370-371.

The Change Module

1. The module must allow no changes to the index field.

2. The module is shown on pages 372-373.

The PRINT Module

1. The file access in this module needs to be the main file again rather than the index file.

2. This will cause the file to print items in the order they were entered into the file.

3. To print them in sequential order requires traversing the tree for every record.

4. The only practical way to print the file sequentially is to sort it. Chapter 14 is about sorts.

5. The PRINT module is not shown in this chapter. Look back to the previous chapter for the list.

The EXIT Module

1. This is identical to the last two chapters and is not shown here.

Testing the Program

1. The program in the book has a line that shows the nodes that have been added.

2. The students should compare their results with the table shown in the book on page 374.

13-6 Additional Considerations about Trees

1. To change an index in the tree, the original index needs to be deleted and the new one added.

2. Indexes can be deleted by marking a field of the record so that the program will recognize the deletion.

3. Trees can become unbalanced and a balancing program needs to be used occasionally.

4. Self-balancing tree programs are complicated. It is much easier to write a balancing routine.

5. When the tree is balanced, deleted records can be removed.

6. To balance the file:

   A. It needs to be sorted.

   B. Then the middle item is used as the root.

   C. The lower node will be the middle of the bottom half.

   D. The higher node will be the middle of the upper half.

   E. This continues until all the records are nodes.

   F. Figure 13-14 on page 376 shows this process.

13-7 Another Useful Technique

1. To save bytes of storage, each byte can be used to store a number up to 256 by using the decimal equivalent.

2. Larger numbers (up to 65,535) can be stored in two bytes by using the highest byte as the place value (in base 256).

3. To calculate, we divide the number to store by 256 and that number is stored in the highest byte. The remainder is stored in the low byte.

4. To reconstruct the number simply multiply the high byte value by 256 and add the low byte value to it.

5. This technique can be used for larger numbers by using more bytes.

****

Answers to Questions to Aid Understanding

1. A. The tree structure does not require an extra file like the index file does.

   B. Adding records to the tree file is generally faster.

2. A tree is preferable when disk space is at a premium since it does not require an index file.

3. An indexed file is preferable when you will need to
print the file in sequential order most of the time.

* 4. Because each entry in the tree structure points to the
next item and the item is checked by value, if that value were
changed, the order of the tree would no longer be able to be
followed.

5. One method is to mark some part of the record (other
than the index) with a special code that the program will
recognize as a deletion symbol.
   Another method (not discussed in the book) is to keep an
additional pointer in each record back to the previous node.
Then when the record is deleted, the previous record is accessed,
and the forward pointers changed to reflect what was in the
deleted record.

* 6. See Figure F-13.

7. The output should look like the following (Note that the
end-of-data marker in the program must be changed to -1 because
one of the entries is 0):

```
WHAT NUMBER 150
WHAT NUMBER 10
WHAT NUMBER 35
WHAT NUMBER 165
WHAT NUMBER 80
WHAT NUMBER 195
WHAT NUMBER 195
FOUND
WHAT NUMBER 11
WHAT NUMBER 0
WHAT NUMBER 45
WHAT NUMBER 155
WHAT NUMBER 152
WHAT NUMBER 88
WHAT NUMBER 171
WHAT NUMBER 90
WHAT NUMBER 122
WHAT NUMBER 149
WHAT NUMBER 205
WHAT NUMBER 196
WHAT NUMBER-1
ITEM= 1   VALUE= 150   LOW= 2   HIGH= 4
ITEM= 2   VALUE= 10   LOW= 8   HIGH= 3
ITEM= 3   VALUE= 35   LOW= 7   HIGH= 5
ITEM= 4   VALUE= 165   LOW= 10   HIGH= 6
ITEM= 5   VALUE= 80   LOW= 9   HIGH= 12
ITEM= 6   VALUE= 195   LOW= 13   HIGH= 17
ITEM= 7   VALUE= 11   LOW= 0   HIGH= 0
ITEM= 8   VALUE= 0   LOW= 0   HIGH= 0
```

(Output continues)

```
ITEM= 9   VALUE= 45   LOW= 0   HIGH= 0
ITEM= 10   VALUE= 155   LOW= 11   HIGH= 0
ITEM= 11   VALUE= 152   LOW= 0   HIGH= 0
ITEM= 12   VALUE= 88   LOW= 0   HIGH= 14
ITEM= 13   VALUE= 171   LOW= 0   HIGH= 0
ITEM= 14   VALUE= 90   LOW= 0   HIGH= 15
ITEM= 15   VALUE= 122   LOW= 0   HIGH= 16
ITEM= 16   VALUE= 149   LOW= 0   HIGH= 0
ITEM= 17   VALUE= 205   LOW= 18   HIGH= 0
ITEM= 18   VALUE= 196   LOW= 0   HIGH= 0
Ok
```

    * 8. To do this program we will merely use the program out of the chapter and modify it a bit. The few changes will be to first add the statement to RANDOMIZE (line 80). Then line 120 will be used to generate a random number instead of INPUT it. Line 130 is deleted since we won't use the end-of-data marker. Finally, line 165 is added to check for the 50th number. When it is reached the program exits the loop and prints the items from the tree. (We will not show the output, tree, flowchart, or pseudocode since they would be virtually the same as we demonstrated in the chapter.)

```
10 REM ***** PROGRAM NAME: F-8-10
20 REM
30 REM ***** WRITTEN BY EDWARD J. COBURN
40 REM
50 REM THIS PROGRAM WILL RANDOMLY INSERT IN THE TREE
60 REM
65 CLS                                ' CLEAR THE SCREEN
70 DIM B(100,3)                       ' ARRAY FOR THE LIST
80 RANDOMIZE(RIGHT$(TIME$,2))
120 X=INT(RND(0)*100)+1               ' GENERATE RANDOM NUMBER
140 IF B<>0 THEN 190
150     B(1,1)=X                      ' ASSIGN ROOT NODE
160     B=B+1                         ' COUNT THAT NODE
170     GOTO 120                      ' GET NEW INDEX
180                                   '
190 I=1                               ' BEGIN SEARCH LOOP
200     IF X=B(I,1) THEN PRINT "FOUND" : GOTO 120
210     IF X>B(I,1) THEN C=3 ELSE C=2 ' SET LOW OR HIGH CODE
220                                   ' CHECK NODE
230         IF B(I,C)<>0 THEN 320
240                                   ' AREA FOR NO NEXT NODE
270             B(I,C)=B+1            ' ASSIGN NEXT NODE
280             B(B+1,1)=X            ' ASSIGN VALUE
290             B=B+1                 ' INCREASE # OF NODES
295             IF B=50 THEN 360      ' EXIT LOOP
300             GOTO 120              ' GET NEW INDEX
310             ' NEXT NODE FOUND - NEED TO CHECK AGAIN
320             I=B(I,C)              ' SET NEW NODE CHECK
330             GOTO 200              ' CHECK NEW NODE
```

(Program continues)

```
340                                         '
350                                         '
360 FOR I=1 TO B
370    PRINT "ITEM=";I;"  VALUE=";B(I,1);
380    PRINT "  LOW=";B(I,2);"  HIGH=";B(I,3)
390 NEXT I
400 END
```

9. The pseudocode is simple:

```
Start
Input the number
Divide the number by 256
Subtract that number from the original number
Assign the two numbers to strings
Print the numbers
Recombine the numbers
Print the numbers
End
```

The program would look like the following:

```
10 REM ***** PROGRAM NAME: EX-13-9
20 REM
30 REM ***** EXERCISE 13-9 - TWO CHARACTER ASSIGNMENT
40 REM
50 REM ***** WRITTEN BY EDWARD J. COBURN
60 REM
70 CLS
80 INPUT "GIVE ME A NUMBER BETWEEN 0 AND 65,000";I
90 A=INT(I/256)
100 B=I-A*256
110 A$=CHR$(A)
120 B$=CHR$(B)
130 PRINT "THE HIGH PORTION IS";A;"AND THE LOW PORTION IS";B
140 C=ASC(A$)*256+ASC(B$)
150 PRINT
160 PRINT "THE RECONSTRUCTED NUMBER IS";C
170 END
```

10. Since most of the program is the same, we will only
pseudocode the deletion module:

```
Start delete module
Input name to delete
DO-WHILE name <> 0
   Assign search index
   Search the tree
   IF record not found THEN
      Print error message
      Input name to delete
   ELSE
      Input fields from file
      Display the fields on the screen
      Input choice from user about deletion
      IF choice is Y to delete THEN
         Assign "DELETED" to one of the fields
         Put the record back into the file
      (ELSE)
      END-IF
   END-IF
END-DO
End module
```

The entire program would look like:

```
10 REM ***** PROGRAM NAME: EX-13-10
20 REM
30 REM ***** WRITTEN BY EDWARD J. COBURN
40 REM
50 REM EXERCISE 13-10 - TREE FILE PROGRAM WITH DELETED RECORDS
60 REM
70 OPEN "TREEDATA" AS #1 LEN=48
80 FIELD #1, 2 AS RF$
90 GET 1,1                                ' GET THE FIRST RECORD
100 IF CVI(RF$)=0 THEN RECS=1 ELSE RECS=CVI(RF$)
110 FIELD #1, 24 AS F$(1), 4 AS F$(2), 6 AS F$(3), 10 AS F$(4),
              2 AS F$(5), 2 AS F$(6)
120 CLS                                   ' CLEAR THE SCREEN
130 PRINT TAB(10);"CONTRIBUTIONS MAINTENANCE"
140 PRINT                                 ' BLANK LINE
150 PRINT "1. ADD NEW RECORDS"
155 PRINT
160 PRINT "2. CHANGE EXISTING RECORDS"
165 PRINT
170 PRINT "3. DELETE EXISTING RECORDS"
175 PRINT
177 PRINT "4. PRINT THE FILE"
178 PRINT
180 PRINT "5. EXIT THE PROGRAM"
200 P$="WHAT OPTION (1-4)"                ' PROMPT
210 L=1                                   ' LENGTH OF PROMPT
```

(Program continues)

```
220 GOSUB 7000                                  ' PROMPT SUBROUTINE
230 IF B$>"0" AND B$<"6" THEN 270
240    M$="INPUT ERROR. RETRY ENTRY"
250    GOSUB 6000                               ' ERROR SUBROUTINE
260    GOTO 200                                 ' REPROMPT
270 ON VAL(B$) GOSUB 1000, 2000, 4500, 3000, 4000
280 GOTO 120
970 REM
980 REM ***** ADD MODULE
990 REM
1000 DATA CONT. NAME, 24, 3, CONT. AMT., 7, 5
1010 DATA DATE , 8, 7, PHONE NUMB., 12, 9
1020 CLS                                        ' CLEAR THE SCREEN
1030 RESTORE                                    ' RESET DATA POINTER
1040 FIELD #1, 24 AS F$(1), 4 AS F$(2), 6 AS F$(3), 10 AS F$(4),
                2 AS F$(5), 2 AS F$(6)
1050 PRINT TAB(10);"CONTRIBUTIONS ENTRY"
1060 PRINT                                      ' BLANK LINE
1070 FOR I=1 TO 4
1080    READ D$(I),L(I),R(I)                    ' THE PROMPT, LENGTH, ROW
1090    PRINT MID$(STR$(I),2,1);". ";D$(I)' DISPLAY THE PROMPT INF
1100    PRINT                                   ' BLANK LINE
1110 NEXT I
1120 FOR I=1 TO 4
1130    L=L(I)                                  ' FIELD LENGTH
1140    R=R(I)                                  ' ROW NUMBER
1150    C=16                                    ' COLUMN NUMBER
1160    GOSUB 7070                              ' PROMPT SUBROUTINE
1170    IF I<>1 THEN 1260                       ' SKIP THE SEARCH
1180       S$=B$                                ' ASSIGN THE SEARCH FIELD
1185       IC=1                                 ' ADD CODE FOR SEARCH
1190       GOSUB 8000                           ' SEARCH SUBROUTINE
1200       IF SC=0 THEN 1260                    ' SKIP IF SEARCH OKAY
1201          IF F$(3)<>"DELETE" THEN 1212
1202          P$="THIS RECORD WAS DELETED. ADD BACK (Y OR N)?"
1203          L=1                               ' PROMPT LENGTH
1204          GOSUB 7000                        ' PROMPT SUBROUTINE
1205          IF B$<>"Y" THEN GOTO 1130
1206          LSET F$(3)=""                     ' WIPE OUT DELETE MARK
1207          M$="RESTORED.  EDIT TO REENTER SS NUMBER"
1208          GOSUB 6000
1209          PUT 1,TR                          ' DUMP OUT THE RECORD
1210          GOTO 1130                         ' GET NEW RECORD
1212          M$="DUPLICATE INDEX.  REENTER."
1220          GOSUB 6000                        ' ERROR SUBROUTINE
1230          R=3                               ' ROW
1240          C=16                              ' COLUMN
1250          GOTO 1130                         ' REDO THE PROMPT
1260       G$(I)=B$                             ' STORE THE FIELD
1270 NEXT I
1280 LSET F$(1)=G$(1)                           ' ASSIGN THE FIELDS
1290 LSET F$(3)=MID$(G$(3),1,2)+MID$(G$(3),4,2)+MID$(G$(3),7,2)
1300 LSET F$(4)=MID$(G$(4),1,3)+MID$(G$(4),5,3)+MID$(G$(4),9,4)

(Program continues)
```

```
1310 RSET F$(2)=MKS$(VAL(G$(2)))
1315 RSET F$(5)=MKI$(0)
1317 RSET F$(6)=MKI$(0)
1320 PUT 1,RECS+1                        ' PUT THE RECORD
1330 FIELD #1, 2 AS RF$                   ' FIELD RECORD 1
1340 RECS=RECS+1                          ' INCREASE RECORD COUNT
1350 LSET RF$=MKI$(RECS)                  ' SET THE FIELD
1360 PUT 1,1                              ' PUT RECORD 1
1470 P$="DO YOU WANT TO ADD ANY MORE (Y OR N)"
1480 L=1                                  ' PROMPT LENGTH
1490 GOSUB 7000                           ' PROMPT SUBROUTINE
1500 IF B$<>"Y" THEN RETURN
1510 GOTO 1020                            ' GET ANOTHER RECORD
1970 REM
1980 REM ***** CHANGE MODULE
1990 REM
2000 P$="NAME (0=END)"
2005 FIELD #1, 24 AS F$(1), 4 AS F$(2), 6 AS F$(3), 10 AS F$(4),
                2 AS F$(5), 2 AS F$(6)
2010 L=24                                 ' PROMPT LENGTH
2020 GOSUB 7000                           ' PROMPT SUBROUTINE
2030 IF B$="0" THEN RETURN                ' EXIT SUBROUTINE
2040 S$=B$                                ' ASSIGN SEARCH INDEX
2045 IC=0                                 ' ADD CODE MUST BE 0
2050 GOSUB 9000
2060 IF SC=1 THEN 2100                    ' SKIP IF SEARCH FOUND
2070    M$="RECORD NOT FOUND.  RETRY."
2080    GOSUB 6000                        ' ERROR SUBROUTINE
2090    GOTO 2000                         ' GET INDEX AGAIN
2100 IF F$(3)<>"DELETE" THEN 2120         ' IS IT DELETED
2105    M$="RECORD HAS BEEN DELETED"      ' MESSAGE
2110    GOSUB 6000                        ' ERROR SUBROUTINE
2115    GOTO 2000                         ' RETURN FOR NEW NAME
2120 CLS
2130 PRINT TAB(10);"CONTRIBUTIONS CHANGES"
2140 PRINT                                ' BLANK LINE
2150 RESTORE                              ' RESET DATA POINTER
2160 FOR I=1 TO 4
2170    READ D$(I),L(I),R(I)              ' PROMPT, LENGTH, ROW
2180    PRINT MID$(STR$(I),2,1);". ";D$(I);
2190    R=R(I)                            ' ROW
2200    C=16                              ' COLUMN
2210    GOSUB 5000                        ' CURSOR POSITIONING
2220    IF I=1 THEN PRINT F$(1)           ' NAME
2230    IF I=3 THEN PRINT MID$(F$(3),1,2);"/";
                        MID$(F$(3),3,2);"/";MID$(F$(3),5,2)
2240    IF I=4 THEN PRINT MID$(F$(4),1,3);"-";
                        MID$(F$(4),4,3);"-";MID$(F$(4),7,4)
2250    IF I=2 THEN PRINT USING "####.##";CVS(F$(2))
2260    PRINT                             ' BLANK LINE
2270 NEXT I
2275 PRINT"LOW = ";CVI(F$(5));"   HIGH =";CVI(F$(6))
2280 P$="WHAT FIELD TO CHANGE (2-4, 0 TO END)"

(Program continues)
```

```
2290 L=1                                    ' PROMPT LENGTH
2300 GOSUB 7000                             ' PROMPT SUBROUTINE
2310 IF B$>="0" AND B$<>"1" AND B$<"5" THEN 2350    ' IS ENTRY OKAY?
2320   M$="INVALID ENTRY.  RETRY."          ' ERROR MESSAGE
2330   GOSUB 6000                           ' ERROR SUBROUTINE
2340   GOTO 2280
2350 IF B$="0" THEN 2460                     ' END CHANGES
2360 B=VAL(B$)                               ' CONVERT INPUT
2370 R=R(B)                                  ' ROW
2380 C=16                                    ' COLUMN
2390 L=L(B)                                  ' PROMPT LENGTH
2400 GOSUB 7070                              ' PROMPT SUBROUTINE
2410 IF B=1 THEN LSET F$(1)=B$               ' ASSIGN FIELDS
2420 IF B=2 THEN RSET F$(2)=MKS$(VAL(B$))
2430 IF B=3 THEN LSET F$(3)=MID$(B$,1,2)+MID$(B$,4,2)+MID$(B$,7,2)
2440 IF B=4 THEN LSET F$(4)=MID$(B$,1,3)+MID$(B$,5,3)+MID$(B$,9,4)
2450 GOTO 2120
2460 PUT 1,TR                                ' STORE RECORD INTO FILE
2470 GOTO 2000                               ' RETURN FOR NEW NUMBER
2970 REM
2980 REM ***** PRINT MODULE
2990 REM
3000 T=0                                     ' ZERO OUT TOTAL FIELD
3005 LPRINT TAB(25);"CONTRIBUTIONS LIST"
3010 LPRINT " "                              ' BLANK LINE
3020 LPRINT "NAME";TAB(28);"AMOUNT        DATE        PHONE NUMBER"
3030 LPRINT " "                              ' BLANK LINE
3040 FOR I=2 TO RECS
3060    GET 1,I                              ' GET THE RECORD
3070    LPRINT F$(1);TAB(27);
3080    LPRINT USING "####.##";CVS(F$(2));
3090    LPRINT "       ";MID$(F$(3),1,2);"/";MID$(F$(3),3,2);
           "/";MID$(F$(3),5,2);
3100    LPRINT "        ";MID$(F$(4),1,3);"-";MID$(F$(4),4,3);
           "-";MID$(F$(4),7,4)
3110    T=T+CVS(F$(2))
3120 NEXT I
3130 LPRINT TAB(25);"---------"
3140 LPRINT "TOTAL";TAB(25); USING "######.##";T
3150 RETURN
3970 REM
3980 REM ***** EXIT MODULE
3990 REM
4000 CLOSE
4010 END
4470 REM
4480 REM ***** DELETE MODULE
4490 REM
4500 P$="NAME OF RECORD TO DELETE (0=END)"
4510 L=24                                    ' PROMPT LENGTH
4520 GOSUB 7000                              ' PROMPT SUBROUTINE
4530 IF B$="0" THEN RETURN                   ' EXIT SUBROUTINE
4540 S$=B$                                   ' ASSIGN SEARCH INDEX
```

(Program continues)

```
4550 IC=0                                      ' ADD CODE MUST BE 0
4560 GOSUB 9000
4570 IF SC=1 THEN 4610                          ' SKIP IF SEARCH FOUND
4580    M$="RECORD NOT FOUND.  RETRY."
4590      GOSUB 6000                            ' ERROR SUBROUTINE
4600      GOTO 4500                             ' GET INDEX AGAIN
4610 CLS
4620 PRINT TAB(10);"CONTRIBUTIONS CHANGES"
4630 PRINT                                      ' BLANK LINE
4640 RESTORE                                    ' RESET DATA POINTER
4650 FOR I=1 TO 4
4660    READ D$(I),L(I),R(I)                    ' PROMPT, LENGTH, ROW
4670    PRINT MID$(STR$(I),2,1);". ";D$(I);
4680    R=R(I)                                  ' ROW
4690    C=16                                    ' COLUMN
4700    GOSUB 5000                              ' CURSOR POSITIONING
4710    IF I=1 THEN PRINT F$(1)                 ' NAME
4720    IF I=3 THEN PRINT MID$(F$(3),1,2);"/";MID$(F$(3),3,2);
                     "/";MID$(F$(3),5,2)
4730    IF I=4 THEN PRINT MID$(F$(4),1,3);"-";MID$(F$(4),4,3);
                     "-";MID$(F$(4),7,4)
4740    IF I=2 THEN PRINT USING "####.##";CVS(F$(2))
4750    PRINT                                   ' BLANK LINE
4760 NEXT I
4780 P$="IS THIS THE RECORD YOU WISH TO DELETE (Y OR N)?"
4790 L=1                                        ' PROMPT LENGTH
4800 GOSUB 7000                                 ' PROMPT SUBROUTINE
4810 IF B$<>"Y" THEN 4840                       ' DO NOT DELETE
4820 LSET F$(3)="DELETED"                       ' MARK AS DELETED
4830 PUT 1,TR                                   ' STORE THE RECORD
4840 GOTO 4500                                  ' GET NEW RECORD TO DELETE
```

11. The change module is virtually the only thing changed so we will pseudocode it:

```
Start change module
Prompt for index of record to change
DO-WHILE index <> 0
   Assign search field
   Search for the record (search subroutine)
   DO-WHILE search code <> 1 and record not deleted
      Print error message
      Prompt for index of record to change
      Search for the record (search subroutine)
   END-DO
   Get the record
   Display the data on the screen
   Prompt for field to change
   DO-WHILE field <> 0
      IF field is invalid THEN
         Print error message
      ELSE
```

(Pseudocode continues)

PAGE 190

```
            IF field = 1 (name) THEN
                Save old record number
                Assign search field
                Search for the record
                DO-WHILE search code <> 0
                    IF record marked deleted THEN
                        Ask user to replace
                        IF user responds yes THEN
                            Erase delete mark
                            Display message to user to edit ss no.
                            Store the record back out
                            Increase the number of records in dummy
                            Get old record
                            Mark for deletion
                            Store the old record
                            Get the new record again
                        (ELSE)
                        END-IF
                    ELSE
                        Print duplicate message
                        Assign search field
                        Search for the record
                    END-IF
                END-DO
                Assign new name and 0 out nodes
                Store the record
                Increase the dummy record count
                Get the old record back
                Mark it for deletion
                Store the old record back
                Get the new record again
            (ELSE)
            END-IF
            Input new field
            Assign new field
        END-IF
        Prompt for field to change
    END-DO
    Put the changed record back in the file
END-DO
End module
```

The entire module will look like the following:

```
10 REM ***** PROGRAM NAME: EX-13-11
20 REM
30 REM ***** WRITTEN BY EDWARD J. COBURN
40 REM
50 REM EXERCISE 13-11 - TREE FILE PROGRAM WITH NAME CHANGE
60 REM
70 OPEN "TREEDATA" AS #1 LEN=48
80 FIELD #1, 2 AS RF$
```

(Program continues)

```
90 GET 1,1                              ' GET THE FIRST RECORD
100 IF CVI(RF$)=0 THEN RECS=1 ELSE RECS=CVI(RF$)
110 FIELD #1, 24 AS F$(1), 4 AS F$(2), 6 AS F$(3), 10 AS F$(4),
            2 AS F$(5), 2 AS F$(6)
120 CLS                                 ' CLEAR THE SCREEN
130 PRINT TAB(10);"CONTRIBUTIONS MAINTENANCE"
140 PRINT                               ' BLANK LINE
150 PRINT "1. ADD NEW RECORDS"
155 PRINT
160 PRINT "2. CHANGE EXISTING RECORDS"
165 PRINT
170 PRINT "3. DELETE EXISTING RECORDS"
175 PRINT
177 PRINT "4. PRINT THE FILE"
178 PRINT
180 PRINT "5. EXIT THE PROGRAM"
200 P$="WHAT OPTION (1-4)"              ' PROMPT
210 L=1                                 ' LENGTH OF PROMPT
220 GOSUB 7000                          ' PROMPT SUBROUTINE
230 IF B$>"0" AND B$<"6" THEN 270
240    M$="INPUT ERROR. RETRY ENTRY"
250    GOSUB 6000                       ' ERROR SUBROUTINE
260    GOTO 200                         ' REPROMPT
270 ON VAL(B$) GOSUB 1000, 2000, 4500, 3000, 4000
280 GOTO 120
970 REM
980 REM ***** ADD MODULE
990 REM
1000 DATA CONT. NAME, 24, 3, CONT. AMT., 7, 5
1010 DATA DATE , 8, 7, PHONE NUMB., 12, 9
1020 CLS                                ' CLEAR THE SCREEN
1030 RESTORE                            ' RESET DATA POINTER
1040 FIELD #1, 24 AS F$(1), 4 AS F$(2), 6 AS F$(3), 10 AS F$(4),
             2 AS F$(5), 2 AS F$(6)
1050 PRINT TAB(10);"CONTRIBUTIONS ENTRY"
1060 PRINT                              ' BLANK LINE
1070 FOR I=1 TO 4
1080    READ D$(I),L(I),R(I)            ' THE PROMPT, LENGTH, ROW
1090    PRINT MID$(STR$(I),2,1);". ";D$(I)' DISPLAY THE PROMPT INF
1100    PRINT                           ' BLANK LINE
1110 NEXT I
1120 FOR I=1 TO 4
1130    L=L(I)                          ' FIELD LENGTH
1140    R=R(I)                          ' ROW NUMBER
1150    C=16                            ' COLUMN NUMBER
1160    GOSUB 7070                      ' PROMPT SUBROUTINE
1170    IF I<>1 THEN 1260               ' SKIP THE SEARCH
1180        S$=B$                       ' ASSIGN THE SEARCH FIELD
1185        IC=1                        ' ADD CODE FOR SEARCH
1190        GOSUB 9000                  ' SEARCH SUBROUTINE
1200        IF SC=0 THEN 1260           ' SKIP IF SEARCH OKAY
1201            IF F$(3)<>"DELETE" THEN 1212
1202            P$="THIS RECORD WAS DELETED. ADD BACK (Y OR N)?"

(Program continues)
```

```
1203               L=1                    ' PROMPT LENGTH
1204               GOSUB 7000             ' PROMPT SUBROUTINE
1205               IF B$<>"Y" THEN GOTO 1130
1206               LSET F$(3)=""          ' WIPE OUT DELETE MARK
1207               M$="RESTORED.  EDIT TO REENTER SS NUMBER"
1208               GOSUB 6000
1209               PUT 1,TR               ' DUMP OUT THE RECORD
1210               GOTO 1130              ' GET NEW RECORD
1212               M$="DUPLICATE INDEX.  REENTER."
1220               GOSUB 6000             ' ERROR SUBROUTINE
1230               R=3                    ' ROW
1240               C=16                   ' COLUMN
1250               GOTO 1130              ' REDO THE PROMPT
1260          G$(I)=B$                    ' STORE THE FIELD
1270 NEXT I
1280 LSET F$(1)=G$(1)                     ' ASSIGN THE FIELDS
1290 LSET F$(3)=MID$(G$(3),1,2)+MID$(G$(3),4,2)+MID$(G$(3),7,2)
1300 LSET F$(4)=MID$(G$(4),1,3)+MID$(G$(4),5,3)+MID$(G$(4),9,4)
1310 RSET F$(2)=MKS$(VAL(G$(2)))
1315 RSET F$(5)=MKI$(0)
1317 RSET F$(6)=MKI$(0)
1320 PUT 1,RECS+1                         ' PUT THE RECORD
1330 FIELD #1, 2 AS RF$                   ' FIELD RECORD 1
1340 RECS=RECS+1                          ' INCREASE RECORD COUNT
1350 LSET RF$=MKI$(RECS)                  ' SET THE FIELD
1360 PUT 1,1                              ' PUT RECORD 1
1470 P$="DO YOU WANT TO ADD ANY MORE (Y OR N)"
1480 L=1                                  ' PROMPT LENGTH
1490 GOSUB 7000                           ' PROMPT SUBROUTINE
1500 IF B$<>"Y" THEN RETURN
1510 GOTO 1020                            ' GET ANOTHER RECORD
1970 REM
1980 REM ***** CHANGE MODULE
1990 REM
2000 P$="NAME (0=END)"
2010 FIELD #1, 24 AS F$(1), 4 AS F$(2), 6 AS F$(3), 10 AS F$(4),
                2 AS F$(5), 2 AS F$(6)
2020 L=24                                 ' PROMPT LENGTH
2030 GOSUB 7000                           ' PROMPT SUBROUTINE
2040 IF B$="0" THEN RETURN                ' EXIT SUBROUTINE
2050 S$=B$                                ' ASSIGN SEARCH INDEX
2060 IC=0                                 ' ADD CODE MUST BE 0
2070 GOSUB 9000
2080 IF SC=1 THEN 2120                    ' SKIP IF SEARCH FOUND
2090    M$="RECORD NOT FOUND.  RETRY."
2100    GOSUB 6000                        ' ERROR SUBROUTINE
2110    GOTO 2000                         ' GET INDEX AGAIN
2120 IF F$(3)<>"DELETE" THEN 2160         ' IS IT DELETED
2130    M$="RECORD HAS BEEN DELETED"      ' MESSAGE
2140    GOSUB 6000                        ' ERROR SUBROUTINE
2150    GOTO 2000                         ' RETURN FOR NEW NAME
2160 CLS
2170 PRINT TAB(10);"CONTRIBUTIONS CHANGES"
```

(Program continues)

```
2180 PRINT                              ' BLANK LINE
2190 RESTORE                            ' RESET DATA POINTER
2200 FOR I=1 TO 4
2210   READ D$(I),L(I),R(I)            ' PROMPT, LENGTH, ROW
2220   PRINT MID$(STR$(I),2,1);". ";D$(I);
2230   R=R(I)                          ' ROW
2240   C=16                            ' COLUMN
2250   GOSUB 5000                      ' CURSOR POSITIONING
2260   IF I=1 THEN PRINT F$(1)         ' NAME
2270   IF I=3 THEN PRINT MID$(F$(3),1,2);"/";MID$(F$(3),3,2);
                     "/";MID$(F$(3),5,2)
2280   IF I=4 THEN PRINT MID$(F$(4),1,3);"-";MID$(F$(4),4,3);
                     "-";MID$(F$(4),7,4)
2290   IF I=2 THEN PRINT USING "####.##";CVS(F$(2))
2300   PRINT                           ' BLANK LINE
2310 NEXT I
2320 PRINT"LOW = ";CVI(F$(5));"   HIGH =";CVI(F$(6))
2330 P$="WHAT FIELD TO CHANGE (1-4, 0 TO END)"
2340 L=1                               ' PROMPT LENGTH
2350 GOSUB 7000                        ' PROMPT SUBROUTINE
2360 IF B$>="0" AND B$<"5" THEN 2400   ' IS ENTRY OKAY?
2370   M$="INVALID ENTRY.  RETRY."     ' ERROR MESSAGE
2380   GOSUB 6000                      ' ERROR SUBROUTINE
2390   GOTO 2330
2400 IF B$="0" THEN 2840               ' END CHANGES
2410 B=VAL(B$)                         ' CONVERT INPUT
2420 R=R(B)                            ' ROW
2430 C=16                              ' COLUMN
2440 L=L(B)                            ' PROMPT LENGTH
2450 GOSUB 7070                        ' PROMPT SUBROUTINE
2460 SR=TR                             ' SAVE OLD RECORD NUMBER
2470 S$=B$                             ' ASSIGN THE SEARCH FIELD
2480 IC=1                              ' ADD CODE FOR SEARCH
2490 GOSUB 9000                        ' SEARCH SUBROUTINE
2500 IF SC=0 THEN 2650                 ' SKIP IF SEARCH OKAY
2510     IF F$(3)<>"DELETE" THEN 2610
2520        P$="THIS RECORD WAS DELETED. ADD BACK (Y OR N)?"
2530        L=1                        ' PROMPT LENGTH
2540        GOSUB 7000                 ' PROMPT SUBROUTINE
2550     IF B$<>"Y" THEN GOTO 2410
2560        LSET F$(3)=""              ' WIPE OUT DELETE MARK
2570        M$="RESTORED.  EDIT TO REENTER SS NUMBER"
2580        GOSUB 6000
2590        PUT 1,TR                   ' DUMP OUT THE RECORD
2600        GOTO 2700                  ' GO DELETE OLD RECORD
2610     M$="DUPLICATE INDEX.  REENTER."
2620     GOSUB 6000                    ' ERROR SUBROUTINE
2630     B=1                           ' FIELD NUMBER
2640     GOTO 2420                     ' REDO THE PROMPT
2650 IF B<>1 THEN 2800                 ' AROUND CHANGE ROUTINE
2660   LSET F$(1)=B$                   ' ASSIGN NEW NAME
2670   RSET F$(5)=MKI$(0)              ' LOW NODE
2680   RSET F$(6)=MKI$(0)              ' HIGH NODE

(Program continues)
```

```
2690     PUT 1,RECS+1                    ' PUT THE RECORD
2700     FIELD #1, 2 AS RF$              ' FIELD RECORD 1
2710     RECS=RECS+1                     ' INCREASE RECORD COUNT
2720     LSET RF$=MKI$(RECS)             ' SET THE FIELD
2730     PUT 1,1                         ' PUT RECORD 1
2740 FIELD #1, 24 AS F$(1), 4 AS F$(2), 6 AS F$(3), 10 AS F$(4),
             2 AS F$(5), 2 AS F$(6)
2750     GET 1,SR                        ' GET OLD RECORD
2760     LSET F$(3)="DELETE"             ' DELETE RECORD
2770     PUT 1,SR                        ' PUT OLD RECORD BACK OUT
2780     TR=RECS                         ' NEW RECORD NUMBER
2790     GET 1,TR                        ' GET NEW RECORD AGAIN
2800 IF B=2 THEN RSET F$(2)=MKS$(VAL(B$))
2810 IF B=3 THEN LSET F$(3)=MID$(B$,1,2)+MID$(B$,4,2)+MID$(B$,7,2)
2820 IF B=4 THEN LSET F$(4)=MID$(B$,1,3)+MID$(B$,5,3)+MID$(B$,9,4)
2830 GOTO 2160
2840 PUT 1,TR                            ' STORE RECORD INTO FILE
2850 GOTO 2000                           ' RETURN FOR NEW NUMBER
2970 REM
2980 REM ***** PRINT MODULE
2990 REM
3000 T=0                                 ' ZERO OUT TOTAL FIELD
3005 LPRINT TAB(25);"CONTRIBUTIONS LIST"
3010 LPRINT " "                          ' BLANK LINE
3020 LPRINT "NAME";TAB(28);"AMOUNT        DATE          PHONE NUMBER"
3030 LPRINT " "                          ' BLANK LINE
3040 FOR I=2 TO RECS
3060     GET 1,I                         ' GET THE RECORD
3070     LPRINT F$(1);TAB(27);
3080     LPRINT USING "####.##";CVS(F$(2));
3090     LPRINT "    ";MID$(F$(3),1,2);"/";MID$(F$(3),3,2);
             "/";MID$(F$(3),5,2);
3100     LPRINT "    ";MID$(F$(4),1,3);"-";MID$(F$(4),4,3);
             "-";MID$(F$(4),7,4)
3110     T=T+CVS(F$(2))
3120 NEXT I
3130 LPRINT TAB(25);"---------"
3140 LPRINT "TOTAL";TAB(25); USING "######.##";T
3150 RETURN
3970 REM
3980 REM ***** EXIT MODULE
3990 REM
4000 CLOSE
4010 END
4470 REM
4480 REM ***** DELETE MODULE
4490 REM
4500 P$="NAME OF RECORD TO DELETE (0=END)"
4510 L=24                                ' PROMPT LENGTH
4520 GOSUB 7000                          ' PROMPT SUBROUTINE
4530 IF B$="0" THEN RETURN               ' EXIT SUBROUTINE
4540 S$=B$                               ' ASSIGN SEARCH INDEX
4550 IC=0                                ' ADD CODE MUST BE 0

(Program continues)
```

```
4560 GOSUB 9000
4570 IF SC=1 THEN 4610                        ' SKIP IF SEARCH FOUND
4580    M$="RECORD NOT FOUND.  RETRY."
4590      GOSUB 6000                          ' ERROR SUBROUTINE
4600      GOTO 4500                           ' GET INDEX AGAIN
4610 CLS
4620 PRINT TAB(10);"CONTRIBUTIONS CHANGES"
4630 PRINT                                    ' BLANK LINE
4640 RESTORE                                  ' RESET DATA POINTER
4650 FOR I=1 TO 4
4660    READ D$(I),L(I),R(I)                  ' PROMPT, LENGTH, ROW
4670    PRINT MID$(STR$(I),2,1);". ";D$(I);
4680    R=R(I)                                ' ROW
4690    C=16                                  ' COLUMN
4700    GOSUB 5000                            ' CURSOR POSITIONING
4710    IF I=1 THEN PRINT F$(1)              ' NAME
4720    IF I=3 THEN PRINT MID$(F$(3),1,2);"/";MID$(F$(3),3,2);
                       "/";MID$(F$(3),5,2)
4730    IF I=4 THEN PRINT MID$(F$(4),1,3);"-";MID$(F$(4),4,3);
                       "-";MID$(F$(4),7,4)
4740    IF I=2 THEN PRINT USING "####.##";CVS(F$(2))
4750    PRINT                                 ' BLANK LINE
4760 NEXT I
4780 P$="IS THIS THE RECORD YOU WISH TO DELETE (Y OR N)?"
4790 L=1                                      ' PROMPT LENGTH
4800 GOSUB 7000                               ' PROMPT SUBROUTINE
4810 IF B$<>"Y" THEN 4840                     ' DO NOT DELETE
4820 LSET F$(3)="DELETED"                     ' MARK AS DELETED
4830 PUT 1,TR                                 ' STORE THE RECORD
4840 GOTO 4500                                ' GET NEW RECORD TO DELETE
```

12. The changes are virtually the same as those performed in the chapter. The new program should look like the following:

```
10 REM ***** PROGRAM NAME: EX-13-12
20 REM
30 REM *****  EXERCISE 13-12 PAYROLL TREE PROCESSING
40 REM
50 REM ***** WRITTEN BY EDWARD J. COBURN
60 REM
70 OPEN "TREEINDX" AS #1 LEN=42
80 FIELD #1, 2 AS RF$            ' DUMMY RECORD
90 GET 1,1                       ' GET THE FIRST RECORD
100 IF CVI(RF$)=0 THEN RECS=1 ELSE RECS=CVI(RF$)
110 FIELD #1,9 AS SF$, 24 AS NF$, 1 AS CF$, 4 AS PF$,
            2 AS T1$, 2 AS T2$
120 CLS                          ' CLEAR THE SCREEN
130 PRINT TAB(10);"PAYROLL MAINTENANCE"
140 PRINT                        ' BLANK LINE
150 PRINT "1.  ADD NEW RECORDS"
155 PRINT
```

(Program continues)

```
160 PRINT "2.   CHANGE EXISTING RECORD"
165 PRINT
170 PRINT "3.   PRINT THE FILE"
175 PRINT
180 PRINT "4.   EXIT THE PROGRAM"
190 PRINT
200 P$= "WHAT OPTION (1-4)"
210 L=1                            ' LENGTH OF PROMPT
220 GOSUB 7000
230 IF B$>"0" AND B$<"5" THEN 270
240    M$="INPUT ERROR.   RETRY ENTRY"
250     GOSUB 6000                 ' ERROR SUBROUTINE
260     GOTO 200                   ' REPROMPT
270 ON VAL(B$) GOSUB 500, 2000, 3000, 4000
280 GOTO 120                       ' RETURN FOR ANOTHER INPUT
470 REM
480 REM ***** ADD MODULE
490 REM
500 CLS                            ' CLEAR THE SCREEN
510 PRINT TAB(10);"PAYROLL ENTRY"
520 PRINT                          ' BLANK LINE
530 PRINT "1. SS. NUMBER"
540 PRINT
550 PRINT "2. EMP. NAME"
560 PRINT
570 PRINT "3. SALARY CODE"
580 PRINT
590 PRINT "4. PAY RATE"
600 R=3                            ' ROW NUMBER
610 C=17                           ' COLUMN NUMBER
620 L=9                            ' SS NUMBER LENGTH
630 GOSUB 7070                     ' PROMPT SUBROUTINE
640 S$=B$                          ' ASSIGN THE SEARCH FIELD
645 IC=1                           ' ADD CODE FOR SEARCH
650 GOSUB 9000                     ' SEARCH SUBROUTINE
660 IF SC=0 THEN 700               ' SKIP IF SEARCH OKAY
670    M$="DUPLICATE INDEX.   REENTER."
680     GOSUB 6000                 ' ERROR SUBROUTINE
690     GOTO 600                   ' REDO THE INPUT
700 LSET SF$=B$                    ' ASSIGN SS NUMBER
710 SVE$=B$                        ' SAVE SS# FOR LATER
720 R=5                            ' ROW NUMBER
730 L=24                           ' NAME LENGTH
740 GOSUB 7070                     ' PROMPT SUBROUTINE
750 LSET NF$=B$                    ' ASSIGN NAME
760 R=7                            ' ROW NUMBER
770 L=1                            ' SALARY CODE LENGTH
780 GOSUB 7070                     ' PROMPT SUBROUTINE
790 LSET CF$=B$                    ' ASSIGN SALARY CODE
800 R=9                            ' ROW NUMBER
810 L=8                            ' PAY RATE
820 GOSUB 7070
830 LSET PF$=MKS$(VAL(B$))         ' ASSIGN AMOUNT
```

(Program continues)

```
835 LSET T1$=MKI$(0)              ' ASSIGN LOW NODE
837 LSET T2$=MKI$(0)              ' ASSIGN HIGH NODE
840 RECS=RECS+1                   ' INCREMENT RECORD NUMBER
850 PUT 1,RECS                    ' PUT THE RECORD
860 FIELD #1, 2 AS RF$            ' FIELD RECORD 1
870 LSET RF$=MKI$(RECS)           ' SET THE FIELD
880 PUT 1,1                       ' PUT RECORD 1
1000 P$= "DO YOU WANT TO ADD ANY MORE (Y OR N)"
1010 L=1                          ' LENGTH OF PROMPT
1020 GOSUB 7000                   ' PROMPT SUBROUTINE
1030 IF B$<>"Y" THEN RETURN
1040 GOTO 500                     ' GET ANOTHER RECORD
1970 REM
1980 REM ***** CHANGE MODULE
1990 REM
2000 P$="SOCIAL SECURITY NUMBER (0 TO END)"
2010 L=9                          ' PROMPT LENGTH
2020 GOSUB 7000                   ' PROMPT SUBROUTINE
2030 IF B$="0" THEN RETURN        ' EXIT THE SUBROUTINE
2040 S$=B$                        ' ASSIGN SEARCH INDEX
2045 IC=0                         ' ADD CODE MUST BE 0
2050 GOSUB 9000                   ' SEARCH SUBROUTINE
2060 IF SC=1 THEN 2120            ' SKIP IF SEARCH FOUND
2070     M$="RECORD NOT FOUND.  REENTER."
2080       GOSUB 6000             ' ERROR SUBROUTINE
2090       GOTO 2000              ' GET INDEX AGAIN
2120 RN=TR                        ' ASSIGN RECORD NUMBER
2130 CLS                          ' CLEAR THE SCREEN
2140 PRINT TAB(10);"PAYROLL CHANGES"
2150 PRINT                        ' BLANK LINE
2160 PRINT "1. SS. NUMBER    ";SF$
2170 PRINT
2180 PRINT "2. EMP. NAME     ";NF$
2190 PRINT
2200 PRINT "3. SALARY CODE   ";CF$
2210 PRINT
2220 PRINT "4. PAY RATE      ";CVS(PF$)
2222 PRINT
2225 PRINT "LOW =";CVI(T1$);"   HIGH =";CVI(T2$)
2230 P$="FIELD TO CHANGE (2-4,0 TO END)"
2240 L=1                          ' PROMPT LENGTH
2250 GOSUB 7000                   ' PROMPT SUBROUTINE
2260 IF B$>="0" AND B$<>"1" AND B$<="4" THEN 2300
2270     M$="INVALID ENTRY.  TRY AGAIN"
2280       GOSUB 6000             ' ERROR SUBROUTINE
2290       GOTO 2230              ' REINPUT
2300 IF B$="0" THEN 2420          ' FIELD ENTRY
2320     IF B$="2" THEN L=24 : R=5
2330     IF B$="3" THEN L=1  : R=7
2340     IF B$="4" THEN L=8  : R=9
2350     C=17                     ' COLUMN
2360     GOSUB 7070               ' PROMPT SUBROUTINE
2380     IF R=5 THEN LSET NF$=B$
```

(Program continues)

```
2390        IF R=7 THEN LSET CF$=B$
2400        IF R=9 THEN RSET PF$=MKS$(VAL(B$))
2410        GOTO 2130            ' REPROMPT
2420 PUT #1,RN                   '       STOR TH RECOR BAC INT FILE
2430 GOTO 2000                   ' RETURN FOR NEW NUMBER
2970 REM
2980 REM ***** PRINT MODULE
2990 REM
3000 LPRINT TAB(20);"PAYROLL LIST"
3010 LPRINT " "                  ' BLANK LINE
3020 LPRINT " SS. NUMBER  NAME";TAB(39);"PAY CODE        AMOUNT"
3030 LPRINT " "                  ' BLANK LINE
3040 FOR I=2 TO RECS             ' TO NUMBER IN FILE
3050        GET #1,I             ' GET RECORD BY NUMBER
3060        LPRINT MID$(SF$,1,3);"-";MID$(SF$,4,3);"-";MID$(SF$,7,4);
3070        LPRINT "  ";NF$;TAB(43);CF$;TAB(50);
3080        LPRINT USING "#,###.##";CVS(PF$)
3090        T=T+CVS(PF$)         ' ACCUMULATE TOTAL
3100 NEXT I
3110 LPRINT TAB(51);"---------"'UNDERLINE
3120 LPRINT "TOTAL";TAB(49);USING "##,###.##";T
3130 RETURN
3970 REM
3980 REM ***** EXIT MODULE
3990 REM
4000 CLOSE #1
4010 END
```

13. The changes for this program are as they were shown in the chapter. The new program is shown below:

```
10 REM ***** PROGRAM NAME: EX-13-13
20 REM
30 REM ***** EXERCISE 13-13 - 13 FIELD TREE FILE PROCESSING
40 REM
50 REM ***** WRITTEN BY EDWARD J. COBURN
60 REM
65 DIM P$(15),P(15),FD$(15)
70 OPEN "TREE13" AS #1 LEN=119
75 DATA SOC. SEC. #, 11, DEPT #, 5, NAME, 20, ADDR, 20
76 DATA CITY, 15, STATE, 2, ZIP CODE, 5, PHONE, 12
77 DATA # DEDUCT., 1, EMERG. PHONE, 12
78 DATA RATE OF PAY, 6, INS. DED., 6, MISC. DED., 6
80 FOR I=1 TO 13
82     READ P$(I),P(I)
83 NEXT I
88 FIELD #1, 2 AS RF$            ' DUMMY RECORD
90 GET 1,1                       ' GET THE FIRST RECORD
100 IF CVI(RF$)=0 THEN RECS=1 ELSE RECS=CVI(RF$)
```

(Program continues)

```
110 FIELD #1,11 AS FD$(1),5 AS FD$(2),20 AS FD$(3),20 AS FD$(4),
            15 AS FD$(5),  2 AS FD$(6),  5 AS FD$(7), 12 AS FD$(8),
             1 AS FD$(9), 12 AS FD$(10), 4 AS FD$(11), 4 AS FD$(12),
             4 AS FD$(13), 2 AS FD$(14), 2 AS FD$(15)
120 CLS                          ' CLEAR THE SCREEN
130 PRINT TAB(10);"PAYROLL MAINTENANCE"
140 PRINT                        ' BLANK LINE
150 PRINT "1.  ADD NEW RECORDS"
155 PRINT
160 PRINT "2.  CHANGE EXISTING RECORD"
165 PRINT
170 PRINT "3.  PRINT THE FILE"
175 PRINT
180 PRINT "4.  EXIT THE PROGRAM"
190 PRINT
200 P$= "WHAT OPTION (1-4)"
210 L=1                          ' LENGTH OF PROMPT
220 GOSUB 7000
230 IF B$>"0" AND B$<"5" THEN 270
240    M$="INPUT ERROR.  RETRY ENTRY"
250       GOSUB 6000             ' ERROR SUBROUTINE
260       GOTO 200               ' REPROMPT
270 ON VAL(B$) GOSUB 500, 2000, 3000, 4000
280 GOTO 120                     ' RETURN FOR ANOTHER INPUT
470 REM
480 REM ***** ADD MODULE
490 REM
500 CLS                          ' CLEAR THE SCREEN
510 PRINT TAB(20);"PAYROLL ENTRY"
520 PRINT                        ' BLANK LINE
530 FOR I=1 TO 7
540    LOCATE (I+1)*2,1
550    IF I<7 THEN PRINT STR$(I);". ";P$(I);TAB(40);
                        USING "##. &";I+7;P$(I+7)
            ELSE PRINT STR$(I);". ";P$(I)
560 NEXT I
570 FOR I=1 TO 13
580    IF I<8 THEN R=(I+1)*2 : C=17
            ELSE R=(I-6)*2 : C=60
590    L=P(I)                    ' PROMPT LENGTH
600    GOSUB 7070                ' PROMPT SUBROUTINE
610    IF I<>1 THEN 690          ' SKIP THE SEARCH
620       S$=B$                  ' ASSIGN THE SEARCH FIELD
630       IC=1                   ' ADD CODE FOR SEARCH
640       GOSUB 9000             ' SEARCH SUBROUTINE
650       IF SC=0 THEN 690       ' SKIP IF SEARCH OKAY
660          M$="DUPLICATE INDEX.  REENTER."
670          GOSUB 6000          ' ERROR SUBROUTINE
680          GOTO 580            ' REDO THE PROMPT
690    IF I<11 THEN LSET FD$(I)=B$ ELSE RSET FD$(I)=MKS$(VAL(B$))
700    IF I=1 THEN SVE$=B$       ' SAVE SS# FOR LATER USE
710 NEXT I
715 LSET FD$(14)=MKI$(0)         ' ASSIGN LOW NODE

(Program continues)
```

```
717 LSET FD$(15)=MKI$(0)              ' ASSIGN HIGH NODE
720 RECS=RECS+1                       ' INCREMENT RECORD NUMBER
730 PUT 1,RECS                        ' PUT THE RECORD
740 FIELD #1, 2 AS RF$                ' FIELD RECORD 1
750 LSET RF$=MKI$(RECS)               ' SET THE FIELD
760 PUT 1,1                           ' PUT RECORD 1
770 P$= "DO YOU WANT TO ADD ANY MORE (Y OR N)"
780 L=1                               ' LENGTH OF PROMPT
790 GOSUB 7000                        ' PROMPT SUBROUTINE
800 IF B$<>"Y" THEN RETURN
810 GOTO 500                          ' GET ANOTHER RECORD
1970 REM
1980 REM ***** CHANGE MODULE
1990 REM
2000 P$="SOCIAL SECURITY NUMBER (0 TO END)"
2010 L=11                             ' PROMPT LENGTH
2020 GOSUB 7000                       ' PROMPT SUBROUTINE
2030 IF B$="0" THEN RETURN            ' EXIT THE SUBROUTINE
2040 S$=B$                            ' ASSIGN SEARCH INDEX
2045 IC=0                             ' ADD CODE MUST BE ZERO
2050 GOSUB 9000                       ' SEARCH SUBROUTINE
2060 IF SC=1 THEN 2100                ' SKIP IF SEARCH FOUND
2070     M$="RECORD NOT FOUND.  REENTER."
2080       GOSUB 6000                 ' ERROR SUBROUTINE
2090       GOTO 2000                  ' GET INDEX AGAIN
2100 RN=TR                            ' SAVE RECORD NUMBER
2130 CLS                              ' CLEAR THE SCREEN
2140 PRINT TAB(20);"PAYROLL CHANGES"
2150 PRINT                            ' BLANK LINE
2160 FOR I=1 TO 7
2170    LOCATE (I+1)*2,1
2180    IF I<7 THEN PRINT STR$(I);". ";P$(I);TAB(40);
                        USING "##. &";I+7;P$(I+7)
            ELSE PRINT STR$(I);". ";P$(I)
2190    LOCATE (I+1)*2,17
2200    PRINT FD$(I);
2210    LOCATE (I+1)*2,60
2220    IF I<4 THEN PRINT FD$(I+7);
2230    IF I>3 AND I<7 THEN PRINT TAB(60);
                        USING "###.##";CVS(FD$(I+7));
2240 NEXT I
2250 P$="FIELD TO CHANGE (2-13, 0 TO END)"
2260 L=2                              ' PROMPT LENGTH
2270 GOSUB 7000                       ' PROMPT SUBROUTINE
2280 ITEM=VAL(B$)                     ' MAKE INTO NUMERIC
2290 IF ITEM>=0 AND ITEM<>1 AND ITEM<=13 THEN 2330
2300     M$="INVALID ENTRY.  TRY AGAIN"
2310       GOSUB 6000                 ' ERROR SUBROUTINE
2320       GOTO 2250                  ' REINPUT
2330 IF ITEM=0 THEN 2390              ' FIELD ENTRY
2340     IF ITEM<8 THEN R=(ITEM+1)*2 : C=17
                    ELSE R=(ITEM-6)*2 : C=60
2350       L=P(ITEM)                  ' PROMPT LENGTH
```

(Program continues)

PAGE 201

```
2360        GOSUB 7070              ' PROMPT SUBROUTINE
2370        IF ITEM<11 THEN LSET FD$(ITEM)=B$
                       ELSE RSET FD$(ITEM)=MKS$(VAL(B$))
2380        GOTO 2130               ' REPROMPT
2390 PUT #1,RN                      ' STORE THE RECORD BACK INTO FILE
2400 GOTO 2000                      ' RETURN FOR NEW NUMBER
2970 REM
2980 REM ***** PRINT MODULE
2990 REM
3000 LPRINT TAB(20);"PAYROLL LIST"
3010 LPRINT " "                     ' BLANK LINE
3020 LPRINT "SOC. SEC #   NAME";TAB(36);"PHONE       # DED      RATE";
         " INS.DED.   MISC.DED."
3030 LPRINT " "                     ' BLANK LINE
3040 FOR I=2 TO RECS                ' TO NUMBER IN FILE
3070     GET #1,I                   ' GET RECORD BY NUMBER
3080     LPRINT FD$(1);" ";FD$(3);" ";FD$(8);"      ";FD$(9);
3090     LPRINT USING "  #,###.##   #,###.##   #,###.##";
             CVS(FD$(11));CVS(FD$(12));CVS(FD$(13))
3100     TI=TI+CVS(FD$(12))         ' ACCUMULATE INSURANCE
3110     TM=TM+CVS(FD$(13))         ' ACCUMULATE MISCELLANEOUS
3120 NEXT I
3130 LPRINT TAB(61);"---------  ---------"
3140 LPRINT "TOTAL";TAB(61);USING "##,###.##   ##,###.##";TI,TM
3150 RETURN
3970 REM
3980 REM ***** EXIT MODULE
3990 REM
4000 CLOSE #1
4010 END
```

14. The only changes that are needed are to add routine lines 1315 and 1317; change routine line 2275 and in the tree access routine lines 9030, 9060, 9080, and 9120.

15. We use a stack to keep track of the previous nodes as we traverse the tree. The pseudocode follows:

```
Start
Open the file
Initialize the counter of the records printed to 1
Initialize the stack pointer to 0
Get the dummy record to determine the number of records
Initialize total field
Print the headings
Assign the current node to 2 (bypass the dummy)
DO-WHILE stack pointer > -1
   Get node record
   IF low node <> 0 THEN
      IF record has not been printed (check used array) THEN
         Push node on stack
```

(Pseudocode continues)

```
        Increment stack pointer
        Assign low node as new current node
      (ELSE)
      END-IF
   (ELSE)
   END-IF
   IF record has not been printed (check used array) THEN
      Print the record
      Accumulate total
      Assign node number to used array
      Increment the used counter
   (ELSE)
   END-IF
   IF high node <> 0 THEN
      Push node on stack
      Increment the stack pointer
      Assign low node as new current node
   ELSE
      Reduce the stack pointer
      Assign new node from stack
   END-IF
   Get node record from the file
END-DO
Print total
Close the file
End
```

The program should look like the following:

```
10 REM ***** PROGRAM NAME: EX-13-15
20 REM
30 REM ***** WRITTEN BY EDWARD J. COBURN
40 REM
50 REM EXERCISE 13-15 - TREE FILE SEQUENTIAL PRINT PROGRAM
60 REM
70 DIM STACK(25),USED(25)             ' SET UP STACK AND USED ARRAYS
80 U.CTR=1                            ' USED ARRAY COUNTER
90 PTR=0                              ' INITIALIZE STACK POINTER
100 OPEN "TREEDATA" AS #1 LEN=48
110 FIELD #1, 2 AS RF$
120 GET 1,1                           ' GET THE FIRST RECORD
130 IF CVI(RF$)=0 THEN RECS=1 ELSE RECS=CVI(RF$)
140 FIELD #1, 24 AS F$(1), 4 AS F$(2), 6 AS F$(3), 10 AS F$(4),
             2 AS F$(5), 2 AS F$(6)
150 T=0                              ' ZERO OUT TOTAL FIELD
160 PRINT TAB(25);"CONTRIBUTIONS LIST"
170 PRINT " "                        ' BLANK LINE
180 PRINT "NAME";TAB(28);"AMOUNT      DATE        PHONE NUMBER"
190 PRINT " "                        ' BLANK LINE
200 NODE=2                           ' CURRENT NODE NUMBER
210 GET 1,NODE
220 IF CVI(F$(5))=0 THEN 320         ' SKIP TO HIGH NODE
```

(Program continues)

```
230        FOR I=1 TO U.CTR
240            IF CVI(F$(5))=USED(I) THEN 320 ' ALREADY PRINTED
250        NEXT I
260        STACK(PTR)=NODE              ' PUSH ON STACK
270        PTR=PTR+1                    ' INCREMENT STACK POINTER
280        NODE=CVI(F$(5))              ' NEW NODE
290 GOTO 210
300                                     '
310                                     '
320 FOR I=1 TO U.CTR
330     IF NODE=USED(I) THEN 380       ' ALREADY PRINTED
340 NEXT I
350 GOSUB 560                          ' PRINT THE LINE
360 USED(U.CTR)=NODE                   ' KEEP TRACK OF LOW PRINTED
370 U.CTR=U.CTR+1                      ' INCREMENT COUNTER
380 IF CVI(F$(6))=0 THEN 480           ' SKIP TO GET NODE FROM STACK
390     FOR I=1 TO U.CTR
400         IF CVI(F$(6))=USED(I) THEN 480 ' ALREADY PRINTED
410     NEXT I
420     STACK(PTR)=NODE                ' PUSH ON STACK
430     PTR=PTR+1                      ' INCREMENT STACK POINTER
440     NODE=CVI(F$(6))                ' NEW NODE
450 GOTO 210
460                                     '
470                                     '
480 PTR=PTR-1                          ' REDUCE STACK POINTER
490 IF PTR=-1 THEN 620                 ' WE ARE DONE
500 NODE=STACK(PTR)                    ' GET NODE FROM STACK
510 GOTO 210
520 END
530 REM
540 REM ***** PRINT DETAIL LINE
550 REM
560 PRINT F$(1);TAB(25);
570 PRINT USING "##,###.##";CVS(F$(2));
580 PRINT "     ";MID$(F$(3),1,2);"/";MID$(F$(3),3,2);
        "/";MID$(F$(3),5,2);
590 PRINT "     ";MID$(F$(4),1,3);"-";MID$(F$(4),4,3);
        "-";MID$(F$(4),7,4)
600 T=T+CVS(F$(2))
610 RETURN
620 PRINT TAB(25);"---------"
630 PRINT "TOTAL";TAB(25); USING "######.##";T
640 END
```

16. The pseudocode for this program would be the same as before. The program follows:

```
10 REM ***** PROGRAM NAME: EX-13-16
20 REM
30 REM ***** EXERCISE 13-16 - XYZ CORPORATION EMPLOYEE FILE
40 REM
50 REM ***** WRITTEN BY EDWARD J. COBURN
60 REM
70 DIM A$(15),A(15),FD$(11)
80 OPEN "XYZPAYTR" AS #1 LEN=82      ' OPEN THE FILE
100 DATA NAME, 20, 3, ADDRESS, 20, 5, CITY, 15, 7, STATE, 2, 9
105 DATA ZIP, 5, 9, BIRTH DATE, 8, 11, PAY CODE, 1, 11
110 DATA EMP. DATE, 8, 13, # EXEMPT., 1, 13
120 FOR I=1 TO 9
130     READ A$(I),A(I),R(I)
140 NEXT I
150 FIELD #1, 2 AS RF$      ' DUMMY RECORD
160 GET 1,1                 ' GET THE FIRST RECORD
170 IF CVI(RF$)=0 THEN RECS=1 ELSE RECS=CVI(RF$)
180 FIELD #1,20 AS FD$(1), 20 AS FD$(2), 15 AS FD$(3), 2 AS FD$(4),
                5 AS FD$(5),  6 AS FD$(6),  1 AS FD$(7), 6 AS FD$(8),
                1 AS FD$(9), 2 AS FD$(10), 2 AS FD$(11)
200 CLS                      ' CLEAR THE SCREEN
210 PRINT TAB(10);"PAYROLL MAINTENANCE"
220 PRINT                    ' BLANK LINE
230 PRINT "1.  ADD NEW RECORDS"
240 PRINT
250 PRINT "2.  CHANGE EXISTING RECORD"
260 PRINT
270 PRINT "3.  PRINT THE FILE"
280 PRINT
290 PRINT "4.  EXIT THE PROGRAM"
300 PRINT
310 P$= "WHAT OPTION (1-4)"
320 L=1                      ' LENGTH OF PROMPT
330 GOSUB 7000
340 IF B$>"0" AND B$<"5" THEN 380
350    M$="INPUT ERROR.  RETRY ENTRY"
360    GOSUB 6000            ' ERROR SUBROUTINE
370    GOTO 310              ' REPROMPT
380 ON VAL(B$) GOSUB 500, 2000, 3000, 4000
390 GOTO 200                 ' RETURN FOR ANOTHER INPUT
470 REM
480 REM ***** ADD MODULE
490 REM
500 CLS                      ' CLEAR THE SCREEN
510 PRINT TAB(20);"PAYROLL ENTRY"
520 PRINT                    ' BLANK LINE
530 FOR I=1 TO 9                         ' DISPLAY LOOP
540     IF I<4 THEN PRINT STR$(I);". ";A$(I)
                ELSE PRINT STR$(I);". ";A$(I);TAB(35);
                        STR$(I+1);". ";A$(I+1) : I=I+1
```

(Program continues)

PAGE 205

```
550 PRINT
560 NEXT I
570 FOR J=1 TO 9                          ' ENTRY LOOP
580     L=A(J)
590     R=R(J)
600     IF J<5 OR J=6 OR J=8 THEN C=17 ELSE C=50
610     GOSUB 7070                         ' PROMPT SUBROUTINE
620     IF J<>1 THEN 690                   ' SKIP THE SEARCH
630         S$=B$                          ' ASSIGN THE SEARCH FIELD
635         IC=1                           ' ADD CODE FOR SEARCH
640         GOSUB 9000                     ' SEARCH SUBROUTINE
650         IF SC=0 THEN 690               ' SKIP IF SEARCH OKAY
660             M$="DUPLICATE INDEX.  REENTER."
670             GOSUB 6000                 ' ERROR SUBROUTINE
680             GOTO 580                   ' REDO THE PROMPT
690     IF J=7 AND B$<>"S" AND B$<>"H" THEN 610 ' ERROR
700     LSET FD$(J)=B$
710 NEXT J
720 P$="WHAT FIELD TO CHANGE (0 TO END)?"
730 L=1                                    ' LENGTH OF PROMPT
740 GOSUB 7000                             ' PROMPT SUBROUTINE
750 IF B$="0" THEN 950                     ' ZERO TO END
760 A=VAL(B$)                              ' SHOULD BE NUMBER
770 IF A>0 AND A<10 THEN 810               ' VALID ENTRY BRANCH
780     M$="INVALID ENTRY.  TRY AGAIN"
790     GOSUB 6000                         ' ERROR SUBROUTINE
800     GOTO 720                           ' RETURN FOR NEW INPUT
810 IF A<5 OR A=6 OR A=8 THEN C=17 ELSE C=50
820 R=R(A)
830 L=A(A)                                 ' LENGTH OF FIELD
840 GOSUB 7070                             ' PROMPT ENTRY
850     IF A<>1 THEN 930                   ' SKIP THE SEARCH
860         S$=B$                          ' ASSIGN THE SEARCH FIELD
870         GOSUB 9000                     ' SEARCH SUBROUTINE
880         IF SC=0 THEN 930               ' SKIP IF SEARCH OKAY
890             M$="DUPLICATE INDEX.  REENTER."
900             GOSUB 6000                 ' ERROR SUBROUTINE
910             GOTO 820                   ' REDO THE PROMPT
920     IF A=7 AND B$<>"S" AND B$<>"H" THEN 840 ' ERROR
930 LSET FD$(A)=B$                         ' SAVE CHANGED FIELD
940 GOTO 720                               ' RETURN TO FIELD PROMPT
950 RECS=RECS+1                            ' INCREMENT RECORD NUMBER
955 LSET FD$(10)=MKI$(0)                   ' SET LOW INDEX
957 LSET FD$(11)=MKI$(0)                   ' SET HIGH INDEX
960 PUT 1,RECS                             ' PUT THE RECORD
965 SV$=FD$(1)                             ' TEMPORARILY STORE INDEX
970 FIELD #1, 2 AS RF$                     ' FIELD RECORD 1
980 LSET RF$=MKI$(RECS)                    ' SET THE FIELD
990 PUT 1,1                                ' PUT RECORD 1
1000 FIELD #1,20 AS FD$(1), 20 AS FD$(2), 15 AS FD$(3), 2 AS FD$(4)
            5 AS FD$(5),  6 AS FD$(6),  1 AS FD$(7), 6 AS FD$(8)
            1 AS FD$(9), 2 AS FD$(10), 2 AS FD$(11)
1120 P$="DO YOU WANT TO ADD ANY MORE (Y or N)?"
```

(Program continues)

```
1130 L=1                              ' LENGTH OF PROMPT
1140 GOSUB 7000                       ' PROMPT SUBROUTINE
1150 IF B$<>"Y" THEN RETURN
1160 GOTO 500                         ' GET ANOTHER RECORD
1970 REM
1980 REM ***** CHANGE MODULE
1990 REM
2000 P$="ENTER NAME TO CHANGE (0 TO END)"
2010 L=20                             ' PROMPT LENGTH
2020 GOSUB 7000                       ' PROMPT SUBROUTINE
2030 IF B$="0" THEN RETURN            ' EXIT THE SUBROUTINE
2040 S$=B$                            ' ASSIGN SEARCH INDEX
2045 IC=0                             ' ADD CODE MUST BE 0
2050 GOSUB 9000
2060 IF SC=1 THEN 2100                ' SKIP IF SEARCH FOUND
2070      M$="RECORD NOT FOUND.  REENTER."
2080        GOSUB 6000                ' ERROR SUBROUTINE
2090        GOTO 2000                 ' GET INDEX AGAIN
2100 RN=TR                            ' RECORD TO ACCESS
2130 CLS                              ' CLEAR THE SCREEN
2140 PRINT TAB(20);"XYZ EMPLOYEE CHANGES"
2150 PRINT                            ' BLANK LINE
2160 FOR I=1 TO 9                     ' DISPLAY LOOP
2170    IF I<4 THEN PRINT STR$(I);". ";A$(I);TAB(17);FD$(I)
             ELSE IF I=4 THEN PRINT STR$(I);". ";A$(I);
             TAB(17);FD$(I);TAB(35);
             STR$(I+1);". ";A$(I+1);TAB(50);FD$(I+1) : I=I+1
2180    IF I=6 OR I=8 THEN PRINT STR$(I);". ";A$(I);TAB(17);
             LEFT$(FD$(I),2);"/";MID$(FD$(I),3,2);"/";
             RIGHT$(FD$(I),2);TAB(35);STR$(I+1);". ";
             A$(I+1);TAB(50);FD$(I+1) : I=I+1
2190 PRINT
2200 NEXT I
2205 PRINT
2207 PRINT "LOW =";CVI(FD$(10));"    HIGH =";CVI(FD$(11))
2210 P$="FIELD TO CHANGE (2-9, 0 TO END)"
2220 L=2                        ' PROMPT LENGTH
2230 GOSUB 7000                 ' PROMPT SUBROUTINE
2240 ITEM=VAL(B$)               ' MAKE INTO NUMERIC
2250 IF ITEM>=0 AND ITEM <>1 AND ITEM<=9 THEN 2290
2260      M$="INVALID ENTRY.  TRY AGAIN"
2270        GOSUB 6000          ' ERROR SUBROUTINE
2280        GOTO 2210           ' REINPUT
2290 IF ITEM=0 THEN 2380 ' FIELD ENTRY
2300 R=R(ITEM)
2310 IF ITEM<5 OR ITEM=6 OR ITEM=8 THEN C=17 ELSE C=50
2320      L=A(ITEM)                ' PROMPT LENGTH
2330        GOSUB 7070          ' PROMPT SUBROUTINE
2340        IF ITEM=7 AND B$<>"S" AND B$<>"H" THEN 2330' ERROR
2350      IF ITEM=6 OR ITEM=8 THEN
             B$=LEFT$(B$,2)+MID$(B$,4,2)+RIGHT$(B$,2)
2360        LSET FD$(ITEM)=B$
2370        GOTO 2130           ' REPROMPT

(Program continues)
```

```
2380 PUT #1,RN            ' STORE THE RECORD BACK INTO FILE
2390 GOTO 2000            ' RETURN FOR NEW NUMBER
2970 REM
2980 REM ***** PRINT MODULE
2990 REM
3000 LPRINT TAB(20);"XYZ CORPORATION"
3002 LPRINT TAB(21);"EMPLOYEE LIST"
3005 LPRINT " "           ' BLANK LINE
3020 LPRINT "NAME";TAB(22);"ADDRESS";TAB(43);"CITY";TAB(58);
        "STATE   ZIP"
3030 LPRINT " "           ' BLANK LINE
3040 FOR I=2 TO RECS      ' TO NUMBER IN FILE
3050     GET #1,I         ' GET RECORD BY NUMBER
3060     LPRINT FD$(1);" ";
3070     LPRINT FD$(2);" ";FD$(3);" ";FD$(4);"     ";FD$(5)
3090 NEXT I
3110 RETURN
3970 REM
3980 REM ***** EXIT MODULE
3990 REM
4000 CLOSE #1
4010 END
```

The new report should look like the following:

```
                    XYZ CORPORATION
                    EMPLOYEE LIST

NAME                ADDRESS              CITY            STATE   ZIP

ED COBURN           1400 SOUTH STREET    EL PASO         TX      76879
SARA SMITH          34567 WEST BLVD.     DENVER          CO      83789
TOM JONES           493 WESTERN          LOS ANGELES     CA      12837
HAROLD HARRIS       P.O. BOX 1O          BROOKINGS       SD      68594
EVERITT JOHNSON     3246 BOSQUE          DES MOINES      IA      39849
```

CHAPTER 14 . . . . . SORTING

14-1 Introduction

1. A **sort** is a program that orders a set of data.

2. This chapter covers four sorting methods:

   A. Selection

   B. Bubble

   C. Shell

   D. Quicksort (the fastest)

3. Three modules will be used with DATA:

   A. Input

   B. Sort

   C. Output

The Input Module

1. This module will READ the DATA and store it in an array.

2. The first number will be the number of items in the array.

3. The module is shown on page 384.

The Output Module

1. This module will print the sorted array on the screen.

2. The module is shown on page 385.

The DATA

1. The sort versions will be tested with 100 DATA items.

2. The data list is shown on page 385.

The Selection Sort

1. The Selection sort is a review from Chapter 6.

2. The sort scans through the array to find the smallest element.

3. This element is then switched with the element at the beginning of the array.

4. Each successive search begins at the next item in the list.

5. This continues until the item to begin with is the last item in the list.

6. A save variable is set up with the largest possible number so that any value in the list will be smaller.

7. The exchange requires a temporary storage variable.

8. The module is shown on page 387 (F-388).

9. This sort takes 50 seconds on the IBM.

14-3 The Bubble Sort

1. The **bubble sort** is probably one of the most widely used because it is easy to understand and write. It is also one of the slowest.

2. The sort starts at the bottom of the list and compares that item with the next.

3. If the next is less, the items are switched.

4. This will bubble the larger ones to the top.

5. As the list is bubbled, a count is made of the number of switches.

6. After a complete pass, if no switches were done, the list is sorted.

7. Each time the bubble process is done, the bubbling is done to one fewer than last time because each pass puts the larger number to the top of the list.

8. The module is shown on page 392 (F-391).

9. This sort requires 113 seconds on the IBM.

The Shell Sort

1. The **Shell sort** is named after its developer, D.L. Shell.

2. It is a modified bubble sort.

3. The switching takes place over larger distances.

4. This is more efficient than the bubble sort.

5. A gap pointer is set up to begin at one beyond the half-way point of the list.

6. The first item and the gap item are compared and switched if necessary.

7. Then the pointers move to the second item and the gap item plus 1.

8. The comparison and switching is done again as necessary.

9. After the pass, the gap is reduced in half and the entire process is repeated.

10. When the gap reaches 1, the pass becomes the same as the bubble sort.

11. A switch counter is kept. If any switches were made in a pass, the same gap is used again.

12. The module is on pages 394-396 (F-395).

13. This sort requires only 38 seconds on the IBM.

14-5 The Quicksort

1. The quicksort is the fastest sort known.

2. It was created by C.A.R. Hoare.

3. The sort divides the list into **partitions**.

4. It uses an item in the middle as a **key**.

5. All items less than the key are moved to the left and all larger are moved to the right.

6. This gives two partitions.

7. Each partition is then partitioned again until each partition is only one item long and the list is then sorted.

8. As the sort is run, the partitions are **pushed** onto a stack and **popped** off as they are needed (F-398 and 402).

9. The module is shown on page 403 (401).

10. The sort requires only 20 seconds.

14-6 Sorting Strings

1. Few changes are necessary in the program to sort strings.

2. The input module will have to be changed to READ strings and the array will have to be changed to a string.

3. The output will have to print the string array.

4. The DATA will have to be string items.

5. Finally, the sort module will need to handle strings instead of numbers.

6. The modules are on page 404.

14-7 Sorting Multiple Items

1. Generally a sort will arrange records, not fields.

2. The only changes to sort multiple items is that the sort routine will do several switches instead of just one.

3. The modules are on pages 405 and 406.

****

Answers to Questions to Aid Understanding

1. A sort is simply a method of arranging records into some type of sequence. Sorts are useful for mailing lists, customer lists, and employee files to name but a few.

* 2. As we used it in the chapter, it was used to indicate to the program how many elements were to be found in the DATA table.

3. The sorted list would be:

2, 3, 8, 9, 10, 22, 25, 35, 38, 44, 55, 56, 67, 87, 99

* 4. The Quicksort uses the key as a marker so that all the items less than the key can be moved to the left and all those larger than the key can be moved to the right. Then each segment is split around another key.

* 5. Only a few changes to the module are needed because the comparisons and switches are done on the array and the array will now be string. (Therefore, check the chapter for the flowchart and pseudocode.) The lines that need to be changed from numeric to string are; 370, 430, 470, 480, 490. Then we simply use the modules that have already been converted for strings to complete the program. The program follows:

```
10 REM ***** PROGRAM NAME: EX-14-5
20 REM
30 REM ***** WRITTEN BY EDWARD J. COBURN
40 REM
50 REM ***** QUICKSORT FOR STRING DATA
60 REM
70 READ NE                          ' NUMBER OF ELEMENTS
80 DIM A$(NE)                       ' ARRAY TO SORT
90 FOR I=1 TO NE
100     READ A$(I)                  ' READ IN ARRAY
110 NEXT I
270 REM
280 REM ***** QUICKSORT MODULE
290 REM
300 P=1                             ' PARTITION NUMBER
310 S(P,1)=1                        ' INITIAL LEFT MARGIN
320 S(P,2)=NE                       ' INITIAL RIGHT MARGIN
325 ' *********************** POP FROM STACK
330   LM=S(P,1)                     ' USE LEFT MARGIN
340   RM=S(P,2)                     ' USE RIGHT MARGIN
350   P=P-1                         ' REDUCE THE NUMBER OF PARTITIONS
355 ' *********************** ADJUST THE PARTITION
360   PM=INT((LM+RM)/2)             ' DETERMINE PARTITION MIDDLE
370   K$=A$(PM)                     ' GET KEY ELEMENT
380   LP=LM                         ' INITIALIZE LEFT POINTER
390   RP=RM                         ' INITIALIZE RIGHT POINTER
400   IF A$(LP)>=K$ THEN 430        ' IS LEFT GREATER
410     LP=LP+1                     ' MOVE LEFT POINTER
420     GOTO 400
430   IF A$(RP)<=K$ THEN 460        ' IS RIGHT LESS
440     RP=RP-1                     ' MOVE RIGHT POINTER
450     GOTO 430
460   IF LP>RP THEN 530             ' DO ITEMS NEED SWITCHING?
470     T$=A$(LP)                   ' SAVE LEFT ITEM
480     A$(LP)=A$(RP)               ' RIGHT TO LEFT
490     A$(RP)=T$                   ' REPLACE RIGHT
500     LP=LP+1                     ' MOVE LEFT POINTER
510     RP=RP-1                     ' MOVE RIGHT POINTER
520   IF LP<=RP THEN 400            ' IF MARGINS OKAY DO AGAIN
530   IF LP>=RM THEN 570            ' IS POINTER OKAY?
535 ' *********************** PUSH ONTO STACK
540     P=P+1                       ' UP PARTITION COUNTER
550     S(P,1)=LP                   ' LEFT MARGIN
560     S(P,2)=RM                   ' RIGHT MARGIN
570   RM=RP                         ' REDO MARGIN
580   IF LM<RM THEN 360             ' IS LEFT MARGIN REACHED?
590   IF P<>0 THEN 330              ' ANY MORE IN STACK?
870 REM
880 REM ***** OUTPUT MODULE
890 REM
895 CLS                            ' CLEAR THE SCREEN
910     FOR I=1 TO 10
```

(Program continues)

```
920        PRINT A$(I)
930     NEXT I
970 END
980 REM
985 REM ***** DATA TABLE
990 REM
1000 DATA 10
1010 DATA SAM SMITH, JOE BLOW, ED COBURN, AL SIMONS
1020 DATA FRED THOMPSON, JACK FRITZ, HARRY GARP
1030 DATA TOM JONES, PAM CONLEY, HARRISON FORD
RUN
AL SIMONS
ED COBURN
FRED THOMPSON
HARRISON FORD
HARRY GARP
JACK FRITZ
JOE BLOW
PAM CONLEY
SAM SMITH
TOM JONES
Ok
```

6. Check the chapter for the pseudocode. The program follows:

```
10 REM ***** PROGRAM NAME: EX-14-6
20 REM
30 REM ***** WRITTEN BY EDWARD J. COBURN
40 REM
50 REM ***** EXERCISE 14-6 - QUICKSORT WITH STRINGS
60 REM
70 READ NE                      ' NUMBER OF ELEMENTS
80 DIM A$(NE)                   ' ARRAY TO SORT
90 FOR I=1 TO NE
100     READ A$(I)              ' READ IN ARRAY
110 NEXT I
270 REM
280 REM ***** QUICKSORT MODULE
290 REM
300 P=1                         ' PARTITION NUMBER
310 S(P,1)=1                    ' INITIAL LEFT MARGIN
320 S(P,2)=NE                   ' INITIAL RIGHT PARTITION
325 ' ************************* POP FROM STACK
330     LM=S(P,1)               ' USE LEFT MARGIN
340     RM=S(P,2)               ' USE RIGHT MARGIN
350     P=P-1                   ' REDUCE NUMBER OF PARTITIONS
355 ' ************************* ADJUST THE PARTITION
360     PM=INT((LM+RM)/2)       ' DETERMINE PARTITION MIDDLE
370     K$=A$(PM)               ' GET KEY ELEMENT
380     LP=LM                   ' INITIALIZE LEFT POINTER
390     RP=RM                   ' INITIALIZE RIGHT POINTER
```

(Program continues)

PAGE 214

```
400        IF A$(LP)>=K$ THEN 430    ' IS LEFT GREATER
410              LP=LP+1             ' MOVE LEFT POINTER
420              GOTO 400
430        IF A$(RP)<=K$ THEN 460    ' IS RIGHT LESS
440              RP=RP-1             ' MOVE RIGHT POINTER
450              GOTO 430
460        IF LP>RP THEN 530         ' DO ITEMS NEED SWITCHING?
470              T$=A$(LP)           ' SAVE LEFT ITEM
480              A$(LP)=A$(RP)       ' RIGHT TO LEFT
490              A$(RP)=T$           ' REPLACE RIGHT
500              LP=LP+1             ' MOVE LEFT POINTER
510              RP=RP-1             ' MOVE RIGHT POINTER
520       IF LP<=RP THEN 400         ' IF MARGINS OKAY DO AGAIN
530       IF LP>=RM THEN 570         ' IS POINTER OKAY?
535 ' *************************** PUSH ONTO STACK
540              P=P+1               ' UP PARTITION COUNTER
550              S(P,1)=LP           ' LEFT MARGIN
560              S(P,2)=RM           ' RIGHT MARGIN
570       RM=RP                      ' REDO MARGIN
580       IF LM<RM THEN 360          ' IS LEFT MARGIN REACHED?
590       IF P<>0 THEN 330           ' ANY MORE IN STACK?
870 REM
880 REM ***** OUTPUT MODULE
890 REM
895 CLS                             ' CLEAR THE SCREEN
910       FOR I=1 TO NE
920              PRINT A$(I)
930       NEXT I
970 END
980 REM
985 REM ***** DATA TABLE
990 REM
1000 DATA 10
1010 DATA SAM SMITH, JOE BLOW, ED COBURN, AL SIMONS
1020 DATA FRED THOMPSON, JACK FRITZ, HARRY GARP
1030 DATA TOM JONES, PAM CONLEY, HARRISON FORD
RUN
AL SIMONS         4
ED COBURN         3
FRED THOMPSON     5
HARRISON FORD     10
HARRY GARP        7
JACK FRITZ        6
JOE BLOW          2
PAM CONLEY        9
SAM SMITH         1
TOM JONES         8
Ok
```

7. The only difference between this program and the previous
ones is the exchanging of four fields at the same time. The
program follows:

```
10 REM ***** PROGRAM NAME: EX-14-7
20 REM
30 REM ***** WRITTEN BY EDWARD J. COBURN
40 REM
50 REM ***** EXERCISE 14-7 - QUICKSORT WITH STRINGS
60 REM
70 DIM A$(25),B$(25),C$(25),D$(25)
80 OPEN "TREEDATA" AS #1 LEN=48
90 FIELD #1, 2 AS RF$
100 GET 1,1                              ' GET THE FIRST RECORD
110 IF CVI(RF$)=0 THEN RECS=1 ELSE RECS=CVI(RF$)
120 FIELD #1, 24 AS F$(1), 4 AS F$(2), 6 AS F$(3), 10 AS F$(4),
              2 AS F$(5), 2 AS F$(6)
130 FOR I=1 TO RECS-1
140     GET 1,I+1
150     A$(I)=F$(1)
160     B$(I)=F$(2)
170     C$(I)=F$(3)
180     D$(I)=F$(4)
190 NEXT I
200 REM
210 REM ***** QUICKSORT MODULE
220 REM
230 P=1                          ' PARTITION NUMBER
240 S(P,1)=1                      ' INITIAL LEFT MARGIN
250 S(P,2)=RECS-1                 ' INITIAL RIGHT PARTITION
260 ' ************************** POP FROM STACK
270     LM=S(P,1)                 ' USE LEFT MARGIN
280     RM=S(P,2)                 ' USE RIGHT MARGIN
290     P=P-1                     ' REDUCE NUMBER OF PARTITIONS
300 ' ************************** ADJUST THE PARTITION
310     PM=INT((LM+RM)/2)           ' DETERMINE PARTITION MIDDLE
320     K$=A$(PM)                 ' GET KEY ELEMENT
330     LP=LM                     ' INITIALIZE LEFT POINTER
340     RP=RM                     ' INITIALIZE RIGHT POINTER
350     IF A$(LP)>=K$ THEN 380    ' IS LEFT GREATER
360         LP=LP+1               ' MOVE LEFT POINTER
370         GOTO 350
380     IF A$(RP)<=K$ THEN 410    ' IS RIGHT LESS
390         RP=RP-1               ' MOVE RIGHT POINTER
400         GOTO 380
410     IF LP>RP THEN 570         ' DO ITEMS NEED SWITCHING?
420         T$=A$(LP)             ' SAVE LEFT ITEM
430         T1$=B$(LP)
440         T2$=C$(LP)
450         T3$=D$(LP)
460         A$(LP)=A$(RP)         ' RIGHT TO LEFT
470         B$(LP)=B$(RP)
```

(Program continues)

```
480              C$(LP)=C$(RP)
490              D$(LP)=D$(RP)
500              A$(RP)=T$          ' REPLACE RIGHT
510              B$(RP)=T1$
520              C$(RP)=T2$
530              D$(RP)=T3$
540              LP=LP+1            ' MOVE LEFT POINTER
550              RP=RP-1            ' MOVE RIGHT POINTER
560      IF LP<=RP THEN 350         ' IF MARGINS OKAY DO AGAIN
570      IF LP>=RM THEN 620         ' IS POINTER OKAY?
580 ' ************************* PUSH ONTO STACK
590              P=P+1              ' UP PARTITION COUNTER
600              S(P,1)=LP          ' LEFT MARGIN
610              S(P,2)=RM          ' RIGHT MARGIN
620      RM=RP                     ' REDO MARGIN
630      IF LM<RM THEN 310          ' IS LEFT MARGIN REACHED?
640      IF P<>0 THEN 270           ' ANY MORE IN STACK?
650 REM
660 REM ***** OUTPUT MODULE
670 REM
680 CLS                            ' CLEAR THE SCREEN
690 T=0                                ' ZERO OUT TOTAL FIELD
700 LPRINT TAB(25);"CONTRIBUTIONS LIST"
710 LPRINT " "                         ' BLANK LINE
720 LPRINT "NAME";TAB(28);"AMOUNT        DATE          PHONE NUMBER"
730 LPRINT " "                         ' BLANK LINE
740 FOR I=1 TO RECS-1
750     LPRINT A$(I);TAB(27);
760     LPRINT USING "####.##";CVS(B$(I));
770     LPRINT "      ";MID$(C$(I),1,2);"/";MID$(C$(I),3,2);
             "/";MID$(C$(I),5,2);
780     LPRINT "      ";MID$(D$(I),1,3);"-";MID$(D$(I),4,3);
             "-";MID$(D$(I),7,4)
790     T=T+CVS(B$(I))
800 NEXT I
810 LPRINT TAB(25);"--------"
820 LPRINT "TOTAL";TAB(25); USING "######.##";T
830 END
```

8. This sort and print are virtually the same design as in the past. The program follows:

```
10 REM ***** PROGRAM NAME: EX-14-8
20 REM
30 REM ***** WRITTEN BY EDWARD J. COBURN
40 REM
50 REM ***** EXERCISE 14-8 - QUICKSORT WITH RELATIVE REC. NO.
60 REM
70 DIM A$(25),RR(25)
80 OPEN "TREEDATA" AS #1 LEN=48
90 FIELD #1, 2 AS RF$
```

(Program continues)

```
100 GET 1,1                               ' GET THE FIRST RECORD
110 IF CVI(RF$)=0 THEN RECS=1 ELSE RECS=CVI(RF$)
120 FIELD #1, 24 AS F$(1), 4 AS F$(2), 6 AS F$(3), 10 AS F$(4),
              2 AS F$(5), 2 AS F$(6)
130 FOR I=1 TO RECS-1
140     GET 1,I+1
150     A$(I)=F$(1)
160     RR(I)=I+1
170 NEXT I
180 REM
190 REM ***** QUICKSORT MODULE
200 REM
210 P=1                           ' PARTITION NUMBER
220 S(P,1)=1                       ' INITIAL LEFT MARGIN
230 S(P,2)=RECS-1                  ' INITIAL RIGHT PARTITION
240 ' ************************* POP FROM STACK
250     LM=S(P,1)                 ' USE LEFT MARGIN
260     RM=S(P,2)                 ' USE RIGHT MARGIN
270     P=P-1                     ' REDUCE NUMBER OF PARTITIONS
280 ' ************************* ADJUST THE PARTITION
290     PM=INT((LM+RM)/2)         ' DETERMINE PARTITION MIDDLE
300     K$=A$(PM)                 ' GET KEY ELEMENT
310     LP=LM                     ' INITIALIZE LEFT POINTER
320     RP=RM                     ' INITIALIZE RIGHT POINTER
330     IF A$(LP)>=K$ THEN 360    ' IS LEFT GREATER
340             LP=LP+1           ' MOVE LEFT POINTER
350             GOTO 330
360     IF A$(RP)<=K$ THEN 390    ' IS RIGHT LESS
370             RP=RP-1           ' MOVE RIGHT POINTER
380             GOTO 360
390     IF LP>RP THEN 490         ' DO ITEMS NEED SWITCHING?
400             T$=A$(LP)         ' SAVE LEFT ITEM
410             T=RR(LP)
420             A$(LP)=A$(RP)     ' RIGHT TO LEFT
430             RR(LP)=RR(RP)
440             A$(RP)=T$         ' REPLACE RIGHT
450             RR(RP)=T
460             LP=LP+1           ' MOVE LEFT POINTER
470             RP=RP-1           ' MOVE RIGHT POINTER
480     IF LP<=RP THEN 330        ' IF MARGINS OKAY DO AGAIN
490     IF LP>=RM THEN 540        ' IS POINTER OKAY?
500 ' ************************* PUSH ONTO STACK
510             P=P+1             ' UP PARTITION COUNTER
520             S(P,1)=LP         ' LEFT MARGIN
530             S(P,2)=RM         ' RIGHT MARGIN
540     RM=RP                     ' REDO MARGIN
550     IF LM<RM THEN 290         ' IS LEFT MARGIN REACHED?
560     IF P<>0 THEN 250          ' ANY MORE IN STACK?
570 REM
580 REM ***** OUTPUT MODULE
590 REM
600 CLS                                   ' CLEAR THE SCREEN
610 T=0                                        ' ZERO OUT TOTAL FIELD
```

(Program continues)

```
620 LPRINT TAB(25);"CONTRIBUTIONS LIST"
630 LPRINT " "                              ' BLANK LINE
640 LPRINT "NAME";TAB(28);"AMOUNT        DATE        PHONE NUMBER"
650 LPRINT " "                              ' BLANK LINE
660 FOR I=1 TO RECS-1
670     GET 1,RR(I)
680     LPRINT F$(1);TAB(27);
690     LPRINT USING "####.##";CVS(F$(2));
700     LPRINT "     ";MID$(F$(3),1,2);"/";MID$(F$(3),3,2);
            "/";MID$(F$(3),5,2);
710     LPRINT "      ";MID$(F$(4),1,3);"-";MID$(F$(4),4,3);
            "-";MID$(F$(4),7,4)
720     T=T+CVS(F$(2))
730 NEXT I
740 LPRINT TAB(25);"---------"
750 LPRINT "TOTAL";TAB(25); USING "######.##";T
760 END
```

9. This program simply generates 1000 random numbers.

```
10 REM ***** PROGRAM NAME: EX-14-9
20 REM
30 REM ***** WRITTEN BY EDWARD J. COBURN
40 REM
50 REM ***** EXERCISE 14-9  - GENERATE A FILE WITH 1000 NUMBERS
60 REM
70 RANDOMIZE VAL(RIGHT$(TIME$,2))
80 OPEN "RNUMBERS" FOR OUTPUT AS #1
90 FOR I=1 TO 1000
100     R=INT(RND(1)*10000)+1
110     PRINT #1,R
120 NEXT I
130 CLOSE #1
140 END
```

Then we use the modules from the chapter to sort the numbers. The bubble sort is the slowest (as discussed in the chapter) and requires 2 hours, 10 minutes and 23 seconds. The selection sort requires 46 minutes and 50 seconds. The Shell sort takes 8 minutes and 49 seconds, while the quicksort is again the fastest, requiring only 3 minutes and 56 seconds. Quite a difference from the quicksort to the bubble sort.

10. The design of the sort and print program is the same as before and the program follows:

```
10 REM ***** PROGRAM NAME: EX-14-10
20 REM
30 REM ***** WRITTEN BY EDWARD J. COBURN
40 REM
50 REM EXERCISE 14-10 - SORT INDEXED FILE
60 REM
70 DIM A$(25),RR(25)
80 OPEN "INDXDATA" AS #1 LEN=44            ' OPEN DATA FILE
90 FIELD #1, 2 AS RF$
100 GET 1,1                                ' GET THE FIRST RECORD
110 IF CVI(RF$)=0 THEN RECS=1 ELSE RECS=CVI(RF$)
120 FIELD #1, 24 AS F$(1), 4 AS F$(2), 6 AS F$(3), 10 AS F$(4)
130 FOR I=2 TO RECS
140      GET 1,I
150      A$(I)=F$(3)
160      RR(I-1)=I
170 NEXT I
180 REM
190 REM ***** QUICKSORT MODULE
200 REM
210 P=1                                    ' PARTITION NUMBER
220 S(P,1)=1                               ' INITIAL LEFT MARGIN
230 S(P,2)=RECS-1                          ' INITIAL RIGHT PARTITION
240 ' ************************* POP FROM STACK
250    LM=S(P,1)                           ' USE LEFT MARGIN
260    RM=S(P,2)                           ' USE RIGHT MARGIN
270    P=P-1                               ' REDUCE NUMBER OF PARTITIONS
280 ' ************************* ADJUST THE PARTITION
290    PM=INT((LM+RM)/2)                   ' DETERMINE PARTITION MIDDLE
300    K$=A$(PM)                           ' GET KEY ELEMENT
310    LP=LM                               ' INITIALIZE LEFT POINTER
320    RP=RM                               ' INITIALIZE RIGHT POINTER
330    IF A$(LP)>=K$ THEN 360              ' IS LEFT GREATER
340         LP=LP+1                        ' MOVE LEFT POINTER
350         GOTO 330
360    IF A$(RP)<=K$ THEN 390              ' IS RIGHT LESS
370         RP=RP-1                        ' MOVE RIGHT POINTER
380         GOTO 360
390    IF LP>RP THEN 490                   ' DO ITEMS NEED SWITCHING?
400         T$=A$(LP)                      ' SAVE LEFT ITEM
410         T=RR(LP)
420         A$(LP)=A$(RP)                  ' RIGHT TO LEFT
430         RR(LP)=RR(RP)
440         A$(RP)=T$                      ' REPLACE RIGHT
450         RR(RP)=T
460         LP=LP+1                        ' MOVE LEFT POINTER
470         RP=RP-1                        ' MOVE RIGHT POINTER
480    IF LP<=RP THEN 330                  ' IF MARGINS OKAY DO AGAIN
490    IF LP>=RM THEN 540                  ' IS POINTER OKAY?
500 ' ************************* PUSH ONTO STACK
```

(Program continues)

```
510              P=P+1                    ' UP PARTITION COUNTER
520              S(P,1)=LP                ' LEFT MARGIN
530              S(P,2)=RM                ' RIGHT MARGIN
540     RM=RP                             ' REDO MARGIN
550     IF LM<RM THEN 290                 ' IS LEFT MARGIN REACHED?
560     IF P<>0 THEN 250                  ' ANY MORE IN STACK?
570 REM
580 REM ***** PRINT MODULE
590 REM
600 T=0                                              ' ZERO OUT TOTAL FIELD
610 LPRINT TAB(20);"DATE SORTED CONTRIBUTIONS LIST"
620 LPRINT " "                           ' BLANK LINE
630 LPRINT "NAME";TAB(28);"AMOUNT          DATE          PHONE NUMBER"
640 LPRINT " "                           ' BLANK LINE
650 FOR I=1 TO RECS-1
660    GET 1,RR(I)                        ' GET THE INDEX
670    LPRINT F$(1);TAB(27);
680    LPRINT USING "####.##";CVS(F$(2));
690    LPRINT "      ";MID$(F$(3),1,2);"/";MID$(F$(3),3,2);
           "/";MID$(F$(3),5,2);
700    LPRINT "       ";MID$(F$(4),1,3);"-";MID$(F$(4),4,3);
           "-";MID$(F$(4),7,4)
710    T=T+CVS(F$(2))
720 NEXT I
730 LPRINT TAB(25);"---------"
740 LPRINT "TOTAL";TAB(25); USING "######.##";T
750 END
```

11. The only substantial difference in this program is found
in lines 110 and 120 where the name field is turned around so
that it is last name first. The program follows:

```
10 REM ***** PROGRAM NAME: EX-14-11
20 REM
30 REM ***** WRITTEN BY EDWARD J. COBURN
40 REM
50 REM ***** EXERCISE 14-11 - QUICKSORT WITH LAST NAMES
60 REM
70 READ NE                       ' NUMBER OF ELEMENTS
80 DIM A$(NE)                     ' ARRAY TO SORT
90 FOR I=1 TO NE
100    READ A$(I)                 ' READ IN ARRAY
110    A=INSTR(A$(I)," ")
120    A$(I)=RIGHT$(A$(I),LEN(A$(I))-A)+", "+LEFT$(A$(I),A)
130 NEXT I
140 REM
150 REM ***** QUICKSORT MODULE
160 REM
170 P=1                          ' PARTITION NUMBER
180 S(P,1)=1                     ' INITIAL LEFT MARGIN
190 S(P,2)=NE                    ' INITIAL RIGHT PARTITION
200 ' ************************* POP FROM STACK
210    LM=S(P,1)                 ' USE LEFT MARGIN
```

(Program continues)

```
220     RM=S(P,2)                   ' USE RIGHT MARGIN
230     P=P-1                       ' REDUCE NUMBER OF PARTITIONS
240 ' ************************* ADJUST THE PARTITION
250     PM=INT((LM+RM)/2)           ' DETERMINE PARTITION MIDDLE
260     K$=A$(PM)                   ' GET KEY ELEMENT
270     LP=LM                       ' INITIALIZE LEFT POINTER
280     RP=RM                       ' INITIALIZE RIGHT POINTER
290     IF A$(LP)>=K$ THEN 320      ' IS LEFT GREATER
300             LP=LP+1             ' MOVE LEFT POINTER
310             GOTO 290
320     IF A$(RP)<=K$ THEN 350      ' IS RIGHT LESS
330             RP=RP-1             ' MOVE RIGHT POINTER
340             GOTO 320
350     IF LP>RP THEN 420           ' DO ITEMS NEED SWITCHING?
360             T$=A$(LP)            ' SAVE LEFT ITEM
370             A$(LP)=A$(RP)        ' RIGHT TO LEFT
380             A$(RP)=T$            ' REPLACE RIGHT
390             LP=LP+1             ' MOVE LEFT POINTER
400             RP=RP-1             ' MOVE RIGHT POINTER
410     IF LP<=RP THEN 290          ' IF MARGINS OKAY DO AGAIN
420     IF LP>=RM THEN 470          ' IS POINTER OKAY?
430 ' ************************* PUSH ONTO STACK
440             P=P+1               ' UP PARTITION COUNTER
450             S(P,1)=LP           ' LEFT MARGIN
460             S(P,2)=RM           ' RIGHT MARGIN
470     RM=RP                       ' REDO MARGIN
480     IF LM<RM THEN 250           ' IS LEFT MARGIN REACHED?
490     IF P<>0 THEN 210            ' ANY MORE IN STACK?
500 REM
510 REM ***** OUTPUT MODULE
520 REM
530 CLS                             ' CLEAR THE SCREEN
540     FOR I=1 TO NE
550         PRINT A$(I)
560     NEXT I
570 END
580 REM
590 REM ***** DATA TABLE
600 REM
610 DATA 10
620 DATA SAM SMITH, JOE BLOW, ED COBURN, AL SIMONS
630 DATA FRED THOMPSON, JACK FRITZ, HARRY GARP
640 DATA TOM JONES, PAM CONLEY, HARRISON FORD
RUN,
BLOW, JOE
COBURN, ED
CONLEY, PAM
FORD, HARRISON
FRITZ, JACK
GARP, HARRY
JONES,TOM
SIMONS, AL
SMITH, SAM
THOMPSON, FRED
Ok
```

12.   First we have to sort the file, which is no different than we have been doing. Then the tree must be balanced. The pseudocode to do this follows:

```
Start balance module
Initialize record counter to 2 (bypass dummy)
Open second file (first file opened before sort)
Read dummy from first file and put into second
Set partition number to 1
Set left margin to 1
Set right margin to the number of records
DO-WHILE number of partitions <> 0
   Assign margins from partition
   Reduce the partition counter
   IF the margins are the same THEN
      Get the record from the first file
      Assign the fields
      Put the record into the second file
      Increment the record counter (for the second file)
   ELSE
      Find partition middle
      Get that record from the first file
      Assign the fields
      Put the record into the second file
      Increment the record counter (second file)
      Increase the number of partitions
      Save the margins of the left partition
      Increase the number of partitions for the right
      Save the margins of the right partition
   END-IF
END-DO
Close the files
End
```

The program with all modules should look like the following:

```
10 REM ***** PROGRAM NAME: EX-14-12
20 REM
30 REM ***** WRITTEN BY EDWARD J. COBURN
40 REM
50 REM ***** EXERCISE 14-12 - QUICKSORT TREE BALANCING PROGRAM
60 REM
70 DIM A$(25),RR(25)
80 OPEN "TREEDATA" AS #1 LEN=48
90 FIELD #1, 2 AS RF$
100 GET 1,1                              ' GET THE FIRST RECORD
110 IF CVI(RF$)=0 THEN RECS=1 ELSE RECS=CVI(RF$)
120 FIELD #1, 24 AS F$(1), 4 AS F$(2), 6 AS F$(3), 10 AS F$(4),
                2 AS F$(5), 2 AS F$(6)
130 FOR I=1 TO RECS-1
140     GET 1,I+1
150     A$(I)=F$(1)
```

(Program continues)

```
160      RR(I)=I+1
170 NEXT I
180 REM
190 REM ***** QUICKSORT MODULE
200 REM
210 P=1                         ' PARTITION NUMBER
220 S(P,1)=1                     ' INITIAL LEFT MARGIN
230 S(P,2)=RECS-1                ' INITIAL RIGHT PARTITION
240 ' ************************* POP FROM STACK
250    LM=S(P,1)                 ' USE LEFT MARGIN
260    RM=S(P,2)                 ' USE RIGHT MARGIN
270    P=P-1                     ' REDUCE NUMBER OF PARTITIONS
280 ' ************************* ADJUST THE PARTITION
290    PM=INT((LM+RM)/2)         ' DETERMINE PARTITION MIDDLE
300    K$=A$(PM)                 ' GET KEY ELEMENT
310    LP=LM                     ' INITIALIZE LEFT POINTER
320    RP=RM                     ' INITIALIZE RIGHT POINTER
330    IF A$(LP)>=K$ THEN 360    ' IS LEFT GREATER
340            LP=LP+1           ' MOVE LEFT POINTER
350            GOTO 330
360    IF A$(RP)<=K$ THEN 390    ' IS RIGHT LESS
370            RP=RP-1           ' MOVE RIGHT POINTER
380            GOTO 360
390    IF LP>RP THEN 490         ' DO ITEMS NEED SWITCHING?
400            T$=A$(LP)         ' SAVE LEFT ITEM
410            T=RR(LP)
420            A$(LP)=A$(RP)     ' RIGHT TO LEFT
430            RR(LP)=RR(RP)
440            A$(RP)=T$         ' REPLACE RIGHT
450            RR(RP)=T
460            LP=LP+1           ' MOVE LEFT POINTER
470            RP=RP-1           ' MOVE RIGHT POINTER
480    IF LP<=RP THEN 330        ' IF MARGINS OKAY DO AGAIN
490    IF LP>=RM THEN 540        ' IS POINTER OKAY?
500 ' ************************* PUSH ONTO STACK
510            P=P+1             ' UP PARTITION COUNTER
520            S(P,1)=LP         ' LEFT MARGIN
530            S(P,2)=RM         ' RIGHT MARGIN
540    RM=RP                     ' REDO MARGIN
550    IF LM<RM THEN 290         ' IS LEFT MARGIN REACHED?
560    IF P<>0 THEN 250          ' ANY MORE IN STACK?
570 REM
580 REM ***** BALANCE ROUTINE
590 REM
600 I=2                         ' INITIALIZE RECORD COUNTER
610 OPEN "TREEOUT" AS #2 LEN=48
620 FIELD #2, 2 AS RF$
630 RSET RF$=MKI$(RECS)
640 PUT 2,1                              ' PUT THE FIRST RECORD
650 FIELD #2, 24 AS G$(1), 4 AS G$(2), 6 AS G$(3), 10 AS G$(4),
              2 AS G$(5), 2 AS G$(6)
660 P=1                         ' PARTITION NUMBER
670 S(P,1)=1                     ' INITIAL LEFT MARGIN

(Program continues)
```

PAGE 224

```
680 S(P,2)=RECS-1                   ' INITIAL RIGHT PARTITION
690 ' ************************** POP FROM STACK
700    LM=S(P,1)                    ' USE LEFT MARGIN
710    RM=S(P,2)                    ' USE RIGHT MARGIN
720    P=P-1                        ' REDUCE NUMBER OF PARTITIONS
730    IF LM<>RM THEN 810           ' DONE IF SAME
740             GET #1,RR(LM)        ' GET RECORD
750             FOR J=1 TO 6
760                LSET G$(J)=F$(J)
770             NEXT J
780             PUT #2,I             ' DUMP INTO SECOND FILE
790             I=I+1                ' INCREASE RECORD NUMBER
800             GOTO 940             ' CHECK FOR END OF PROGRAM
810      PM=INT((LM+RM)/2)           ' DETERMINE PARTITION MIDDLE
820      GET #1,RR(PM)               ' GET RECORD TO SAVE
830      FOR J=1 TO 6
840          LSET G$(J)=F$(J)
850      NEXT J
860      PUT #2,I                    ' DUMP INTO SECOND FILE
870      I=I+1                       ' INCREMENT RECORD NUMBER
880      P=P+1
890      S(P,1)=LM
900      S(P,2)=PM-1
910      P=P+1
920      S(P,1)=PM+1
930      S(P,2)=RM
940      IF P<>0 THEN 700
950 CLOSE #1, #2
960 END
```

13. The pseudocode for this program follows:

```
Start
Open the file
Get the dummy record to determine the number of records
Get the records assigning the fields to an array for sorting
Print the menu on the screen
Input a choice from the user
DO-WHILE choice not 0
   Use the choice as the subscript of the array for the sort
   Sort the records (for this pseudocode check the chapter)
   IF sort field is salary code or employment date THEN
      Print the records using address report form
   ELSE
      Print the records using birth date report form
   END-IF
   Input a choice from the user
END-DO
End
```

The program follows:


```
10 REM ***** PROGRAM NAME: EX-14-13
20 REM
30 REM ***** WRITTEN BY EDWARD J. COBURN
40 REM
50 REM ***** EXERCISE 14-13 - MULTIPLE CHOICE SORT FOR XYZ
60 REM
70 DIM A$(25,11),RR(25),FD$(11)
80 OPEN "XYZPAYTR" AS #1 LEN=82
90 FIELD #1, 2 AS RF$
100 GET 1,1                              ' GET THE FIRST RECORD
110 IF CVI(RF$)=0 THEN RECS=1 ELSE RECS=CVI(RF$)
120 FIELD #1,20 AS FD$(1), 20 AS FD$(2), 15 AS FD$(3), 2 AS FD$(4),
            5 AS FD$(5),  6 AS FD$(6),  1 AS FD$(7),  6 AS FD$(8),
            1 AS FD$(9), 2 AS FD$(10), 2 AS FD$(11)
130 FOR I=1 TO RECS-1
140     GET 1,I+1
150     FOR J=1 TO 11
160         IF J=8 THEN LSET FD$(J)=RIGHT$(FD$(J),2)+LEFT$(FD$(J),4)
170         A$(I,J)=FD$(J)
180         RR(I)=I+1
190     NEXT J
200 NEXT I
210 CLS
220 PRINT TAB(20);"XYZ CORPORATION EMPLOYEE LISTING"
230 PRINT
240 PRINT "WHAT SORT ORDER DO YOU WISH TO USE:"
250 PRINT
260 PRINT "1. NAME"
270 PRINT
280 PRINT "2. ADDRESS"
290 PRINT
300 PRINT "3. ZIP CODE"
310 PRINT
320 PRINT "4. SALARY CODE"
330 PRINT
340 PRINT "5. EMPLOYMENT DATE"
350 P$="CHOOSE A NUMBER FOR YOUR SORT (1-5, 0 TO END)"
360 L=1
370 GOSUB 7000
380 SORT=VAL(B$)
390 IF SORT<0 OR SORT>5 THEN 370
400 IF SORT=0 THEN 1200
410 IF SORT=3 THEN SORT=5
            ELSE IF SORT=4 THEN SORT=7
                            ELSE IF SORT=5 THEN SORT=8
420 PRINT SORT
430 STOP
440 REM
450 REM ***** QUICKSORT MODULE
460 REM
```

(Program continues)

PAGE 226

```
470 P=1                          ' PARTITION NUMBER
480 S(P,1)=1                     ' INITIAL LEFT MARGIN
490 S(P,2)=RECS-1                ' INITIAL RIGHT PARTITION
500 ' *********************** POP FROM STACK
510    LM=S(P,1)                 ' USE LEFT MARGIN
520    RM=S(P,2)                 ' USE RIGHT MARGIN
530    P=P-1                     ' REDUCE NUMBER OF PARTITIONS
540 ' *********************** ADJUST THE PARTITION
550    PM=INT((LM+RM)/2)         ' DETERMINE PARTITION MIDDLE
560    K$=A$(PM,SORT)            ' GET KEY ELEMENT
570    LP=LM                     ' INITIALIZE LEFT POINTER
580    RP=RM                     ' INITIALIZE RIGHT POINTER
590    IF A$(LP,SORT)>=K$ THEN 620 ' IS LEFT GREATER
600          LP=LP+1             ' MOVE LEFT POINTER
610          GOTO 590
620    IF A$(RP,SORT)<=K$ THEN 650  ' IS RIGHT LESS
630          RP=RP-1             ' MOVE RIGHT POINTER
640          GOTO 620
650    IF LP>RP THEN 750         ' DO ITEMS NEED SWITCHING?
660          T$=A$(LP,SORT)      ' SAVE LEFT ITEM
670          T=RR(LP)
680          A$(LP,SORT)=A$(RP,SORT)    ' RIGHT TO LEFT
690          RR(LP)=RR(RP)
700          A$(RP,SORT)=T$      ' REPLACE RIGHT
710          RR(RP)=T
720          LP=LP+1             ' MOVE LEFT POINTER
730          RP=RP-1             ' MOVE RIGHT POINTER
740    IF LP<=RP THEN 590        ' IF MARGINS OKAY DO AGAIN
750    IF LP>=RM THEN 800        ' IS POINTER OKAY?
760 ' *********************** PUSH ONTO STACK
770          P=P+1               ' UP PARTITION COUNTER
780          S(P,1)=LP           ' LEFT MARGIN
790          S(P,2)=RM           ' RIGHT MARGIN
800    RM=RP                     ' REDO MARGIN
810    IF LM<RM THEN 550         ' IS LEFT MARGIN REACHED?
820    IF P<>0 THEN 510          ' ANY MORE IN STACK?
830 REM
840 REM ***** DETERMINE PRINT ROUTINE
850 REM
860 IF SORT<7 THEN GOSUB 1090 ELSE GOSUB 920
870 GOTO 210                     ' RETURN TO MENU
880 END
890 REM
900 REM ***** PRINT MODULE FOR BIRTH DATE
910 REM
920 LPRINT TAB(20);"XYZ CORPORATION"
930 LPRINT TAB(21);"EMPLOYEE LIST"
940 LPRINT " "                   ' BLANK LINE
950 LPRINT "NAME";TAB(21);"BIRTH DATE    CODE    ";
         "EMP. DATE    # EXEMPT."
960 LPRINT " "                   ' BLANK LINE
970 FOR I=1 TO RECS-1            ' TO NUMBER IN FILE
980      GET #1,RR(I)            ' GET RECORD BY NUMBER

(Program continues)
```

```
990        LPRINT FD$(1);" ";
1000         LPRINT LEFT$(FD$(6),2);"/";MID$(FD$(6),3,2);
                    "/";RIGHT$(FD$(6),2);
1010         LPRINT TAB(36);FD$(7);"     ";
1020         LPRINT LEFT$(FD$(8),2);"/";MID$(FD$(8),3,2);
                    "/";RIGHT$(FD$(8),2);
1030         LPRINT "           ";FD$(9)
1040 NEXT I
1050 RETURN
1060 REM
1070 REM ***** PRINT MODULE FOR ADDRESSES
1080 REM
1090 LPRINT TAB(20);"XYZ CORPORATION"
1100 LPRINT TAB(21);"EMPLOYEE LIST"
1110 LPRINT " "                    ' BLANK LINE
1120 LPRINT "NAME";TAB(22);"ADDRESS";TAB(43);"CITY";TAB(58);
            "STATE    ZIP"
1130 LPRINT " "                    ' BLANK LINE
1140 FOR I=1 TO RECS-1             ' TO NUMBER IN FILE
1150       GET #1,RR(I)            ' GET RECORD BY NUMBER
1160       LPRINT FD$(1);" ";
1170       LPRINT FD$(2);" ";FD$(3);" ";FD$(4);"     ";FD$(5)
1180 NEXT I
1190 RETURN
1200 END
```

For a look at the report formats, please check the previous
chapter's programs.

CHAPTER 15 . . . . . GRAPHICS AND COLOR

15-1 Introduction

    1. This chapter explores graphics and color.

    2. The IBM and Apple can use color.

    3. Three types of **resolution**:

        A. Text

        B. Low

        C. High

    4. Resolution refers to the number of points or **pixels** on the screen that are accessible.

15-2 Text Resolution Graphics

    1. **Text resolution** refers to a group of pixels that are necessary to generate the textual letters on the screen.

    2. The machines have:

        A. IBM has 24 rows by 40 or 80 columns.

        B. Radio Shack Model III has 16 rows by 64 columns.

        C. Radio Shack Model 4 has 24 rows by 80 columns.

        D. Apple has 24 rows by 40 columns.

    3. Graphs in text resolution simply print a text character in the appropriate screen location.

    4. An example text graph is on page 413 as is the program.

    5. Improvement and improved program on pages 414-415.

    6. Vertical graph illustration is on page 415.

    7. The program is on page 416 (F-417).

15-3 Low Resolution Graphics

    1. **Low resolution graphics** allow access to a group of pixels smaller than text graphics.

    2. Each machine handles **low resolution graphics** differently.

Low Resolution Graphics - Radio Shack

1. The small pixel groups are called **blocks**.

2. The Model III has 128 blocks by 48 blocks.

3. The Model 4 has 160 blocks by 72 blocks.

4. Predefined graphics characters may be printed using the CHR$ function and codes 128-191 (see program 15-4, page 418).

5. The tic-tac-toe board program is on page 418.

6. Each block can be turned on with **SET(R,C)** (Model III only).

7. The block is turned off with **RESET(R,C)**.

8. The **POINT(R,C)** determines if a block is on or off.

9. Program 15-6 on page 419 uses SET command for tic-tac-toe.

10. The grade distribution program is on page 420.

Low Resolution Graphics - Apple

1. **Blocks** are half of a text character so the screen is 40 by 48.

2. The bottom four lines are reserved for text so graphics area is 40 by 40.

3. **GR** turns on low resolution mode.

4. Color is available with **COLOR** command.

5. Form of statement is:

   10 COLOR = color number

6. Color numbers are:

0 black	4 dark green	8 brown	12 green
1 magenta	5 gray 1	9 orange	13 yellow
2 dark blue	6 medium blue	10 gray 2	14 aqua
3 purple	7 light blue	11 pink	15 white

7. The blocks are addressable with **PLOT C,R** command.

8. Plotting is done on a coordinate system (thus C,R).

9. GRAPH1 program is on page 421.

10. Lines can be drawn with **HLIN** and **VLIN** as:

    100 HLIN column 1, column 2 AT row

    110 VLIN row 1, row 2 AT column

11. The GRDIST program is on pages 422-423 (F-423).

15-4 High Resolution Graphics

1. **High resolution graphics** allows access to each individual pixel.

2. Radio Shack computers do not have high resolution.

Low and High Resolution Graphics - IBM

1. Low resolution uses 320 by 200 and high resolution uses 640 by 200.

2. To use lines 192-199, you need to turn off line 25 with **KEY OFF**.

3. In low resolution four colors may be on the screen.

4. High resolution is strictly black and white.

5. Low resolution is turned on with **SCREEN 1** and **SCREEN 2** is for high resolution.

6. Text and graphics can be mixed on the screen.

7. The cursor is positioned with the LOCATE command.

8. Colors are set in text mode with:

    10 COLOR foreground, background, border

9. Eight colors are available in text mode:

    ```
    0 black    2 green   4 red      6 gold (brown)
    1 blue     3 cyan    5 magenta  7 white (gray)
    ```

10. In graphics mode (low) the color command is:

    10 COLOR background and border color, foreground palette

11. The colors are broken into two palettes:

Palette	Color 0	Color 1	Color 2	Color 3
0	background	green	red	gold
1	background	cyan	magenta	white

12. Blocks are turned on with PSET (C,R),color.

13. Graphics are done on coordinate system (thus C,R).

14. GRAPH1 is on page 425.

15. Lines can be drawn with LINE (C,R)-(C,R),color command.

16. GRAPH2 is on page 426.

17. Grade distribution program GRGRPH is on page 428 (F-427).

High Resolution Graphics - Apple

1. The Apple uses 280 by 160 points with the bottom four lines for text.

2. To turn on high resolution use HGR.

3. The COLOR command becomes HCOLOR.

4. The PLOT command becomes HPLOT.

5. The colors vary but are basically:

0 black 1   2 blue (depends) 4 black 2   6 (depends)
1 green (depends) 3 white 1   5 (depends) 7 white 2

6. High resolution program GRGRPH is on page 429 (F-430).

****

Answers to Questions to Aid Understanding

1. Resolution is simply the number of pixels that are accessible. Text resolution allows access only to whole characters (and predefined graphics characters). Low resolution allows access to smaller groups of pixels called blocks. High resolution allows access to each individual pixel.

* 2. A pixel is a single dot of resolution that can be turned on or off with a program command.

3. IBM:

High resolution is turned on with SCREEN 2.

Low resolution is turned on with SCREEN 1.

Graphics commands are LOCATE, COLOR, PSET, and LINE.

Radio Shack:

No high resolution.

Low resolution commands are SET, RESET, and POINT.

Apple:

Low resolution is turned on with GR and the commands are

COLOR, PLOT, HLIN, and VLIN.

High resolution is turned on with HGR and the commands

are HCOLOR and HPLOT.

4. The design for this program is basically PRINT
statements. The program follows:

```
10 REM ***** PROGRAM NAME: EX-15-4
20 REM
30 REM ***** EXERCISE 15-4 - OPINION GRAPH
40 REM
50 REM ***** PROGRAM WRITTEN BY EDWARD J. COBURN
60 REM
70 CLS                    ' CLEAR THE SCREEN
80 PRINT TAB(15);"OPINION DISPLAY"
90 PRINT
100 PRINT TAB(11);"5   10   15   20   25   30   35"
110 PRINT TAB(5);"+----+----+----+----+----+----+----+"
120 PRINT TAB(5);"!"
130 FOR I=1 TO 6
140     READ O$,N                     ' READ OPINION AND NUMBER
150     IF LEN(O$)<2 THEN PRINT " ";   ' EXTRA BLANK
160     PRINT O$;"  ";
170     PRINT"! ";
180     FOR J=1 TO N
190         PRINT "X";
200     NEXT J
210     PRINT                          ' FOR CARRIAGE RETURN
220 PRINT TAB(5);"!"
230 NEXT I
240 PRINT TAB(5);"+----+----+----+----+----+----+----+"
250 END
260 DATA TD,10,D,25,MS,30,S,20,TS,5,NO,10
```

```
RUN
                OPINION DISPLAY

              5   10   15   20   25   30   35
         +-----+----+----+----+----+----+----+
         !
   TD    ! XXXXXXXXXX
         !
    D    ! XXXXXXXXXXXXXXXXXXXXXXXXX
         !
   MS    ! XXXXXXXXXXXXXXXXXXXXXXXXXXXXXX
         !
    S    ! XXXXXXXXXXXXXXXXXXXX
         !
   TS    ! XXXXX
         !
   NO    ! XXXXXXXXXX
         !
         +-----+----+----+----+----+----+----+
   Ok
```

   * 5. The flowchart for this program can be seen in Figure F-
14 (in the book), the screen design is shown in Figure F-15 (in
the book) and the pseudocode follows:

```
Start
Read data items and store them in array
Print heading
Initialize counter to 50 (I)
DO-WHILE counter (I) is not less than 1
    Print counter (I) for scale and wall
    Initialize counter to 1 (J)
    DO-WHILE counter (J) is not greater than 6
        Print marker or blanks
        Increase counter (J) by 1
    END-DO
    Print blank line
    Decrease counter (I) by 5
END-DO
Print graph bottom and labels
End
```

The program follows:

```
10 REM ***** PROGRAM NAME: EX-15-5
20 REM
30 REM ***** TEXT RESOLUTION GRAPH - EXERCISE 15-5
40 REM
50 FOR I = 1 TO 5
60     READ A(I)
70 NEXT I
80 PRINT TAB(7);"GOVERNMENT SATISFICATION"
90 PRINT "50% +";                    ' PRINT REFERENCE NUMBER
100 FOR J = 50 TO 1 STEP -5          ' SCALE LOOP
110     IF J<>50 THEN PRINT "    !";
120     FOR I = 1 TO 5
130         IF A(I)>=J THEN PRINT " ***"; ELSE PRINT "    ";
140     NEXT I
150     PRINT                        ' CARRIAGE RETURN
160 NEXT J
170 PRINT " 0% +--------------------------"
180 PRINT TAB(8);"TD    D   MS    S    TS   NO"
190 END
RUN
      GOVERNMENT SATISFACTION
50% +
     !
     !
     !
     !               ***
     !         ***   ***
     !         ***   ***   ***
     !         ***   ***   ***
     !   ***   ***   ***   ***         ***
     !   ***   ***   ***   ***   ***   ***
  0% +--------------------------------
         TD    D    MS    S    TS   NO
```

6. The design for this program closely follows the one in the chapter. The program follows:

```
10 REM ***** PROGRAM NAME: EX-15-6
20 REM
30 REM ***** EXERCISE 15-6 - RANDOM NUMBER GRAPH
40 REM
50 REM ***** PROGRAM WRITTEN BY EDWARD J. COBURN
60 REM
70 CLS                       ' CLEAR THE SCREEN
80 SCREEN 1                  ' TURN ON GRAPHICS
90 COLOR 0,0                 ' BACKGROUND BLACK, PALETTE 0
100 PRINT "10"               ' SCALE MARKER
110 LOCATE 14,1              ' MOVE THE CURSOR
```

(Program continues)

```
120 PRINT "  1"                     ' SCALE MARKER
130 LINE (26,1)-(26,110),2          ' GRAPH WALL
140 LINE (26,55)-(310,55),2         ' GRAPH BOTTOM
150 OPEN "RANDOM1" FOR INPUT AS #1
160 OPEN "RANDOM2" FOR INPUT AS #2
165 B=50
170 FOR I=36 TO 326 STEP 10
180     INPUT #1,R1
190     INPUT #2,R2
200     A=(R1-R2)*10
210     A=100-A                     ' REVERSE FOR SCALE
220     A=A-50
230     LINE (I-10,B)-(I,A),3       ' PLOT LINE
240     B=A                         ' SAVE LAST POINT
250 NEXT
260 LOCATE 16,10                    ' POSITION FOR MESSAGE
270 PRINT "GRADE DISTRIBUTION"
280 END
```

7. This program is accomplished the same way the vertical
graph in the chapter is. The program should look like the
following:

```
10 REM ***** PROGRAM NAME: EX-15-7
20 REM
30 REM ***** TEXT RESOLUTION GRADE DISPLAY
40 REM
50 REM ***** PROGRAM WRITTEN BY EDWARD J. COBURN
60 REM
70 CLS                                 ' CLEAR THE SCREEN
80 OPEN "STUDENTS" FOR INPUT AS #1
90 FOR I=1 TO 4
100      INPUT #1,SS$,NL$(I),NF$(I),C$
110      FOR J=1 TO 5
120          INPUT #1,G(I,J)
130          G(I,J)=G(I,J)/5              ' REVERSE SCALE OF NUMBER
150      NEXT J
170 NEXT I
180 FOR I=100 TO 0 STEP -5
190      IF I/25=INT(I/25) THEN PRINT USING "### +";I
                          ELSE PRINT "    !"
200 NEXT I
210 LOCATE 21,6
220 PRINT STRING$(68,"-")
230 FOR I=1 TO 20
240      LOCATE I,6
250      FOR J=1 TO 4
260          FOR K=1 TO 5
270              IF G(J,K)>=21-I THEN PRINT " * ";
                          ELSE PRINT "   ";
280          NEXT K
290      PRINT "   ";
300      NEXT J
310 NEXT I
320 FOR I=1 TO 5                ' NAME PRINT LOOP
330      LOCATE 22,(I-1)*18+7
340      PRINT NL$(I)
350 NEXT I
360 PRINT
370 PRINT TAB(30);"GRADE LIST";
380 GOTO 380                    ' DEAD LOOP TO PRESERVE DISPLAY
390 END
```

(Output on next page)

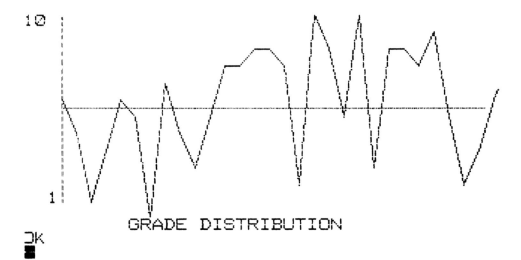

```
1 0
```

```
1
```

GRADE DISTRIBUTION

8. The program should look like the following:

```
10 REM ***** PROGRAM NAME: EX-15-8
20 REM
30 REM ***** TEXT RESOLUTION TOTAL LETTER GRADE DISPLAY
40 REM
50 REM ***** PROGRAM WRITTEN BY EDWARD J. COBURN
60 REM
70 CLS                                   ' CLEAR THE SCREEN
80 OPEN "STUDENTS" FOR INPUT AS #1
90 FOR I=1 TO 4
100      INPUT #1,SS$,NL$,NF$,C$
110      FOR J=1 TO 5
120           INPUT #1,G
130           IF G>=90 THEN G(1)=G(1)+1  ' TOTAL GRADES
140           IF G>=80 AND G<90 THEN G(2)=G(2)+1
150           IF G>=70 AND G<80 THEN G(3)=G(3)+1
160           IF G>=60 AND G<70 THEN G(4)=G(4)+1
170           IF G<60 THEN G(5)=G(5)+1
180      NEXT J
190 NEXT I
200 FOR I=15 TO 0 STEP -1
210      IF I/5=INT(I/5) THEN PRINT USING "### +";I
                         ELSE PRINT "    !"
220 NEXT I
230 LOCATE 16,6
240 PRINT STRING$(68,"-")
250 FOR I=1 TO 15
260      LOCATE I,6
270      FOR J=1 TO 5
280           IF G(J)>=16-I THEN PRINT " *****   ";
                         ELSE PRINT "         ";
```

(Program continues)

```
290         PRINT "        ";
300     NEXT J
310 NEXT I
320 FOR I=1 TO 5              ' NAME PRINT LOOP
330     LOCATE 17,(I-1)*13+9
340     IF I<5 THEN PRINT CHR$(64+I) ELSE PRINT "F"
350 NEXT I
360 PRINT
370 PRINT TAB(30);"GRADE LIST";
380 GOTO 380                  ' DEAD LOOP TO PRESERVE DISPLAY
390 END
```

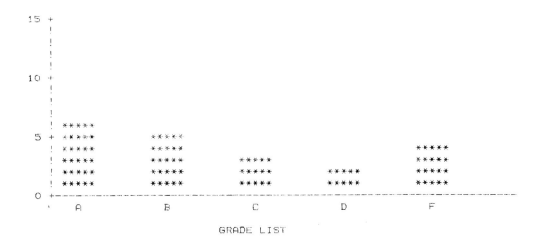

CHAPTER 1 . . . . . MICROCOMPUTERS AND BASIC

Circle the correct response for the following true-false questions.

T   F   1. The keyboard would be considered a piece of software.

T   F   2. Software is another name for programs.

T   F   3. BASIC was developed in about 1975.

T   F   4. BASIC is one of the more difficult languages to learn how to program.

T   F   5. Information is stored in the memory of the computer.

T   F   6. The BREAK key is pressed to stop the execution of a program.

T   F   7. The CLEAR key will erase the program from memory.

T   F   8. A diskette is also known as a floppy disk.

Put the correct choice in the blank to answer the following multiple choice questions.

-----   1. A single memory switch is called
        a. character   c. byte
        b. bit   d. cursor

-----   2. Which of the following is not one of the three major functions of a computer?
        a. input   c. output
        b. memory   d. process

-----   3. A disk surface is set up in a series of concentric circles known as
        a. tracks   c. sectors
        b. files   d. directories

-----   4. The protective plastic covering on the disk is known as the
        a. file   c. jacket
        b. envelope   d. cover

Write the correct response in the blank.

1. The storage code for microcomputers is called ....

2. The upper left-hand corner is known as the ....

3. The display indicator on the screen is called the ....

4. To signal the computer that we have tried to communicate with it we generally use the .... key.

5. Information about what is stored on a disk is stored on the disk in the ....

6. The command to store a program on disk is ....

7. The command to retrieve a program from disk is ....

Answer key for Chapter 1

True-false	Multiple choice	Short answer
1. F	1. b	1. ASCII
2. T	2. b	2. home position
3. F	3. a	3. cursor
4. F	4. c	4. RETURN
5. T		5. directory
6. T		6. SAVE
7. F		7. LOAD
8. T		

CHAPTER 2 . . . . . FLOWCHARTS, PSEUDOCODE, AND STRUCTURES

Circle the correct response for the following true-false questions.

T   F   1. Communication problems are mainly related to businesses.

T   F   2. Pseudocode is an informal language used to show
              solutions to programming problems.

T   F   3. All programmers design programs.

T   F   4. Structured programming was first proposed by Dijkstra
              in the early 1980s.

T   F   5. Structured programming can help save programming time
              by making debugging easier.

T   F   6. We would show an input using an I/O symbol.

T   F   7. A loop and iteration are the same thing.

T   F   8. The small circular symbol is called either a collector
              on connector depending upon its use.

T   F   9. The small circular symbol used on the IF-THEN-ELSE
              structure signifies the entry point into the structure.

T   F   10. The IF-THEN-ELSE structure has two flow lines exiting
               from the structure.

Put the correct choice in the blank to answer the following
multiple choice questions.

-----   1. The committee that has standardized the symbols used
            in the book is called
            a. ASCII   c. ANSI
            b. EBCDIC   d. NASA

-----   2. A calculation would be shown using which symbol?
            a. process   c. decision
            b. I/O   d. none of these

-----   3. Which of the following structures does not DIRECTLY
            contain the decision test?
            a. IF-THEN-ELSE   c. simple sequence
            b. DO-WHILE   d. all of them do

-----   4. The symbol used to depict initialization is
            a. preparation   c. counter
            b. predefined process   d. annotation

PAGE 242

----- 5. The shape of the symbol used to show output from the
program is the
a. rectangle   c. circle
b. diamond   d. none of them

Write the correct response in the blank.

1. A pictorial diagram of a problem solution is called a

....

2. A group of programs that together perform a function is known

as a ....

3. List the three programming structures proposed by Dijkstra.

....

....

....

4. Each flowchart must begin with a .... symbol.

5. An IF-THEN-ELSE is an example of the use of the

.... structure as proposed by Dijkstra.

6. The IF-THEN-ELSE structure with only one option to be

performed is know as a(n) ....

7. The first thing in the DO-WHILE structure is the

....

8. When one structure is wholly inside another, it is said to be

....

Answer key for Chapter 2

True-false	Multiple choice	Short answer
1. F	1. c	1. flowchart
2. T	2. a	2. system
3. T	3. c	3. simple sequence
4. F	4. a	selection
5. T	5. d	repetitive block
6. T		4. terminal
7. T		5. selection
8. T		6. null ELSE
9. F		7. test
10. F		8. nested

CHAPTER 3 . . . . . BEGINNING BASIC

Circle the correct response for the following true-false questions.

T   F   1. If you use the command PRINT 5,16 the digit 6 will appear in column 16 on the screen.

T   F   2. The blank printed in front of a number printed on the screen is for the plus sign that is understood.

T   F   3. Blanks generally do not make any difference in BASIC.

T   F   4. To remove line 10 from our program we would simply key the number 10 and press RETURN.

T   F   5. The number 0 is a valid line number.

T   F   6. The DELETE command will erase the whole program from memory.

T   F   7. A$RT is a valid variable name.

T   F   8. Using A and A$ in the same program might cause a conflict in the memory of the machine.

T   F   9. A$="T@is" is a valid assignment.

T   F   10. BASIC does not require the END statement.

Put the correct choice in the blank to answer the following multiple choice questions.

-----   1. If you typed PRINT "4+5" in the machine you would see displayed
    a. 9   c. "4+5"
    b. 4 + 5   d. none of them

-----   2. The value of   5*4+6 is
    a. 50   c. 26
    b. 24   d. none of them

-----   3. The value of 3+4*5-2+8/2 is
    a. 25   c. 20.5
    b. 37   d. none of them

-----   4. Which of the following assignment statements is invalid?
    a. 10 A$ = 25   c. 05 A$ = "BYE"
    b. 01 B$ = A$ d. 100 C$ = ""

-----   5. The statement X = B ^ 3 is the same as
    a. X = B * 3 * 3   c. X = 3 * 3 * 3
    b. X = B * B * B   d. none of them

----- 6. In the order of operations, addition is
   a. highest in the order   c. lowest in the order
   b. same level as subtraction d. same level as division

----- 7. If A = 4 and B = 3 what is the value of C?
   C = A * B ^ (A / 2)
   a. 24   c. 36
   b. 144   d. none of them

----- 8. When you PRINT a variable, the value stored for the
   variable will
   a. not change   c. be erased
   b. change   d. none of them

----- 9. An END statement
   a. is not required
   b. indicates the end of the program
   c. can actually be used anywhere in a program
   d. all of the above

Write the correct response in the blank.

1. If you enter a command incorrectly, you will usually get a

   .... error.

2. A PRINT statement with nothing else after it will

   ....

3. "HI THERE" is called a ....

4. A comma and semicolon are called ....

5. The SPC statement will ....

   ....

6. The TAB statement will ....

   ....

7. The BASIC execution command is ....

8. We number our programs by 10s so ....

   ....

9. To display the program on the screen we would type

   ....

10. The clear screen command on my machine is ....

11. All numeric variables start out automatically assigned as

....

12. All string variables start out automatically assigned as

....

Answer key for Chapter 3

True-false	Multiple choice	Short answer
1. F	1. d	1. syntax
2. T	2. c	2. print a blank line
3. T	3. a	3. literal
4. T	4. a	4. delimiters
5. T	5. b	5. move the cursor over the specified number of spaces
6. F	6. b	6. Move the cursor over to the specified column
7. F	7. c	7. RUN
8. F	8. a	8. 10s
9. T	9. d	9. LIST
10. T		10. CLS or HOME
		11. zero
		12. null

CHAPTER 4 . . . . . DOCUMENTATION AND INPUT

Circle the correct response for the following true-false questions.

T   F   1. The ? (question mark) can substitute for the REM statement in the IBM and Radio Shack versions of BASIC.

T   F   2. An INPUT statement is basically an assignment.

T   F   3. If you are using a program to INPUT data and two question marks appear, you have made an error.

T   F   4. If we wish to have structured BASIC programs, we cannot use the GOTO statement.

T   F   5. It is not a good idea to use a STOP statement as a permanent substitute for an END statement in a program.

Put the correct choice in the blank to answer the following multiple choice questions.

-----   1. REM statements
         a. give information to the computer
         b. are executed by the computer
         c. contain information for the programmer
         d. must be the first statement in the program

-----   2. If you enter the wrong type of data in response to an INPUT statement you will see
         a. a Syntax error   c. a Redo from start error
         b. an INPUT error   d. none of them

-----   3. Which of the following is an incorrect statement?
         a. 10 INPUT "WHAT IS YOUR NAME";N$
         b. 20 INPUT "ADD, CHANGE, OR DELETE";A$
         c. 30 PRINT "INPUT A NUMBER";N$
         d. 40 INPUT "PLEASE ENTER A NUMBER"N$

-----   4. The command T = A + T is called
         a. accumulator   c. counter
         b. running total   d. both a and b

-----   5. The command that can cause an infinite loop is the
         a. INPUT   c. PRINT
         b. GOTO   d. none of them

Write the correct response in the blank.

1. Name the three different types of documentation

   ....

   ....

   ....

2. A REM statement would be considered what type of documentation?

   ....

3. The literal on the INPUT statement is called a

   ....

4. Any character may be used between the quotation marks of a

   literal except ....

5. The unconditional branch statement is the ....

6. To get out of a infinite loop we use ....

7. In the use of the statement, there is only one difference
   between the STOP and END statements which is

   ....

8. To restart a program after it has been stopped we would use

   ....

Answer key for Chapter 4

True-false	Multiple choice	Short answer
1. F	1. c	1. user
2. T	2. c	program
3. F	3. d	programmer
4. F	4. d	2. program
5. T	5. b	3. prompt
		4. quotation mark
		5. GOTO
		6. BREAK key
		7. STOP prints line number
		8. CONT or continue

CHAPTER 5 . . . . . DECISIONS AND LOOPS

Circle the correct response for the following true-false questions.

T   F   1. An IF-THEN test is necessary to create a DO-WHILE loop.

T   F   2. If A$="HIGH" and B$="HI" then A$<B$.

T   F   3. Any valid BASIC statement can be used as the action part of an IF-THEN test.

T   F   4. In certain cases the IF-THEN statement becomes an unconditional branch.

T   F   5. If we used a STOP statement on an IF-THEN, we could easily use the CONT statement to continue the program.

T   F   6. You cannot reuse a variable within a loop that was used as the start value of the loop as this will cause the program to have problems.

T   F   7. You can use negative numbers on the start, end, or STEP values on the FOR statement.

T   F   8. It is okay to assign to the counter within the body of the loop as long as care is exercised.

T   F   9. The following FOR statement would cause the loop to execute seven times.
10 FOR I = 4 TO 25 STEP 3

T   F   10. A FOR-NEXT loop will automatically increment the counter by one each time through the loop.

T   F   11. It is sometimes useful to use the colon to continue an IF-THEN action.

Put the correct choice in the blank to answer the following multiple choice questions.

_____   1. Which of the following is the symbol for not equal to?
a. ≠   c. <>
b. <=   d. none of them

_____   2. Which of the following statements will NEVER branch to line 50?
a. 10 GOTO 50   c. IF A=B THEN 50
b. IF A$=B THEN 50   d. all of them can

----- 3. After the following statements are executed, A will have the value of

    10 A=5
    20 IF A>0 THEN A=A+A

    a. 10   c. 15
    b. 0   d. 5

----- 4. Which of the following statements is invalid?
    a. IF A=B THEN PRINT "ERROR"
    b. IF A$=B$ THEN R=5
    c. IF R9$=PROMPT$ THEN PROMPT$="THIS IS CRAZY"
    d. all of them are correct statements

----- 5. Which of the following numbers would we use if we wished the loop to process 15 times?
    10 FOR I = 1 TO 150
    a. 15   c. 9
    b. 10   d. 11

----- 6. A boolean operator is also known as
    a. test operator   c. logical operator
    b. repeat operator   d. none of them

----- 7. How may times will the following loop?

    10 E = 10
    20 S = 5
    30 FOR I = 1 TO E
    40   E = 12
    50 NEXT I
    60 END

    a. 10   c. 5
    b. 12   d. none of them

Write the correct response in the blank.

1. The < symbol is called a .... operator.

2. There are three commonly used boolean operators which are

    ...., ..., and ....

3. If the condition check of an IF-THEN test is false, control

    ....

4. Give three examples of a FOR statement that would loop 6 times using three different STEP values.

   FOR I = 1.......................................

   FOR I = 2.......................................

   FOR I = 5.......................................

5. Given A$="10/15/86" show a literal that is less than A$ and another that is greater than A$.

   Greater ....

   Less ....

6. The REPEAT-UNTIL differs from the DO-WHILE in only one

   significant respect which is ....

   ....

In the following, if the statement is incorrect, explain what is wrong on the blank provided. If it is correct, enter CORRECT in the blank.

   1. 10 IF A$="5" THEN 20

   ....

   2. 10 FOR I = I TO 10

   ....

   3. 10 IF B$=A$ THEN B

   ....

   4. 10 FOR I = -1 TO 10 STEP -1

   ....

   5. 10 FOR J = 2 TO 5 STEP J

   ....

   6. 10 FOR 2 TO 8

   ....

   7. 10 IF A>=< THEN 100

   ....

8.   10 IF A<B THEN A<5+B

....

9.   10 IF A=5 THEN B+A=6

....

10.   10 FOR I=1 TO 10 : PRINT I : NEXT

....

As the computer executes the following program, it will print values on the screen. Show the values that would be printed by finishing the given table (there are probably more blanks than necessary).

```
10 REM ***** EXAMPLE PROGRAM
20 REM
30 CLS
35 K=1
40 FOR I=1 TO 15 STEP 3
50     PRINT I,J,K
60     IF I<10 THEN J=J+1
70     K=I*J/K
80     IF I<6 THEN I=I+1
90     IF K>5 THEN K=2
100 NEXT I
110 END
```

I = ..., ..., ..., ..., ..., ..., ..., ..., ..., ..., ...

J = ..., ..., ..., ..., ..., ..., ..., ..., ..., ..., ...

K = ..., ..., ..., ..., ..., ..., ..., ..., ..., ..., ...

Answer key for Chapter 5

True-false	Multiple choice	Short answer
1. F	1. c	1. relational
2. F	2. b	2. AND, OR, NOT
3. T	3. a	3. falls through to next stmt.
4. F	4. d	4. many possible answers
5. T	5. b	5. many possible answers
6. F	6. c	6. position of test
7. T	7. a	
8. T		
9. F		
10. F		
11. T		

Program statements

1. correct   6. incorrect
2. correct   7. incorrect
3. incorrect   8. incorrect
4. correct   9. incorrect
5. correct   10. correct

Program variables

I = 1, 5, 9, 12, 15

J = 0, 1, 2, 3, 3

K = 1, 1, 2, 2, 2

Circle the correct response for the following true-false questions.

T   F   1. An array dimensioned as A$(11) actually has 12 elements.

T   F   2. We need to be careful to dimension our array to precisely the number of elements that we are going to need, otherwise the program might run into trouble with the unused elements.

T   F   3. There are no limits to the number of data items on each DATA statement.

T   F   4. The DATA statement must be placed at the end of the program.

T   F   5. We need to be sure that our DATA statements don't contain more items than the program is going to access.

T   F   6. On the IBM we can use the RESTORE statement to restore the DATA pointer to a particular DATA item.

T   F   7. When using two dimensional arrays it is conventional to use the first dimension as the row number.

T   F   8. You will get an error in your program if you have READ statements without DATA statements.

T   F   9. You will get an error in your program if you have DATA statements without READ statements.

T   F   10. The variables A1 and A(1) bear no relationship to each other.

T   F   11. A READ statement is basically an assignment.

T   F   12. Subroutines are only important if you are using a group of code a number of times in the program.

Put the correct choice in the blank to answer the following multiple choice questions.

-----   1. Which pair of statements is unrelated?
        a. READ and DATA   c. LET and INPUT
        b. GOSUB and RETURN   d. all are related pairs

-----   2. Which of the following statements would not give you an error if executed as a program by itself.
        a. 10 GOTO 100   c. 10 PRINT B(15)
        b. 10 GOSUB 100   d. all cause an error

----- 3. Given the following program, which of the choices is
         correct?

```
10 REM ***** SAMPLE PROGRAM
20 REM
30 FOR I = 1 TO 4 STEP 2
40     READ B(I)
50 NEXT I
60 READ B(3)
70 DATA 1,2,3,4
80 END
```

    a. B(2)=2
    b. an error will occur because there is not enough data
    c. B(3)=4
    d. none of them are correct

Write the correct response in the blank.

1. An index may also be called ....

2. An array is automatically dimensioned with

   .... elements.

3. If we try to READ more DATA items than are available we will

   get an .... error.

4. If we are going to use an end-of-data marker with a READ-DATA
   combination, we will also have to include a

   .... statement.

5. What type of error would occur if you used a GOTO statement to
   jump into the middle of a subroutine?

   ....

6. A series of conditional branch statements can be converted

   into the BASIC .... statement which is

   known as the .... structure.

7. We used the bubble sort for our example sort because

   ....

8. In order to use a comma in a DATA item the entire DATA item

   must ....

Examine the following program and then answer the questions.

```
10 REM ***** SAMPLE PROGRAM
20 REM
30 DIM B(15)
40 FOR I = 1 TO 20 STEP 3
50     READ B(I)
60 NEXT I
70 DATA 5,7,9,1,2,4,6,7,5,4,7,8,4,5,3,2
80 END
```

1. After the program executes, what will be the value of:

   B(1) ....

   B(3) ....

   B(4) ....

   B(8) ....

   B(13) ....

   B(19) ....

2. This program will cause an error. What type of error will

   occur? ....

3. How many loops will the program go through before the error

   causes the program's termination?.......................

In the following, if the statement is incorrect, explain what is
wrong on the blank provided. If it is correct, enter CORRECT in
the blank.

   1. 10 RETURN A

   ....

   2. 10 DIM A,B,C

   ....

   3. 10 GOSUB 10000

   ....

   4. 10 READ A;B,C,D

   ....

```
5. 10 FOR 2 = I TO 10

........................................................

6. 10 A(I)=B(J)+C$(R)

........................................................

7. 10 READ A,A$,B,B$,D,C$,R,G$,H,H,J

........................................................

8. 10 READ "WHAT IS YOUR NAME";N$

........................................................

9. 10 DATA "WACO, NEW YORK, DENVER",2,12/15/57

........................................................

10. 10 ON A$ GOSUB 50,100,500,60,80,90

........................................................
```

Which of the following pairs of READ and DATA statements are incorrect and why? Assume that the DATA statement is to be processed by the READ statement.

```
1. 10 READ A,B,C
   90 DATA 5,7,8

........................................................

2. 10 READ A,A$,B,B$
   90 DATA 5,BYE,6

........................................................

3. 10 READ A$,B$,C$
   90 DATA "THIS IS A FUN GAME",7,8,9,THIS

........................................................

4. 10 READ A,B,C
   90 9,8,7

........................................................

5. 10 READ A,B
   90 DATA 5,      6,      2,      334,      6,      7

........................................................
```

```
6. 10 READ A,B,C
   90 DATA 90,MARY,2
```

....

Answer key for Chapter 6

True-false	Multiple choice	Short answer
1. T	1. c	1. subscript
2. F	2. d	2. 11
3. T	3. d	3. Out of data
4. F		4. IF-THEN
5. F		5. Return without GOSUB
6. F		6. ON ... GOTO
7. T		CASE
8. T		7. easy to understand
9. F		8. be enclosed with quotes
10. T		
11. T		
12. F		

Array program	Program statements	READ-DATA pairs
1. B(1) = 5	1. incorrect	1. correct
B(3) = 0	2. incorrect	2. incorrect
B(4) = 7	3. correct	3. correct
B(8) = 0	4. incorrect	4. incorrect
B(13)= 2	5. incorrect	5. correct
B(19)= 0	6. incorrect	6. incorrect
2. Subscript out	7. correct	
of range	8. incorrect	
3. 5	9. correct	
	10. incorrect	

CHAPTER 7 . . . . . STRING HANDLING AND FUNCTIONS

Circle the correct response for the following true-false questions.

T F 1. The INKEY$ (or GET) command doesn't allow prompting.

T F 2. If we need to print a quotation mark, we can do it
         with the STR$ function.

T F 3. 10 IF LEFT$(B$,3)=115 THEN 100 is a correct statement.

T F 4. If B$="ABCCBA" then it is true that
         LEFT$(B$,3)=RIGHT$(B$,3).

Put the correct choice in the blank to answer the following
multiple choice questions.

----- 1. To convert the number 13 into one printable character,
          we would use which command?
          a. CHR$ c. VAL
          b. ASC   d. none of them

----- 2. If we used the command M$=ASC(65) M$ would be
          a. A   c. I
          b. 65   d. none of them

----- 3. Which function will allow you to search a string for a
          particular character?
          a. INSTR   c. INSTRING$
          b. INS   d. STRING$

----- 4. Which of the following will round A to the nearest
          hundredth?
          a. A=INT(A * .01)   c. A=INT((A+.005)*100/100
          b. A=RND(A TO .01)   d. none of them

----- 5. Which of the following will return the number 5 when
          A=5.05?
          a. A=INT(A)   c. A=INT(A+.05)
          b. A=VAL(A+.5)   d. none of them

Write the correct response in the blank.

1. Combining two or more strings is called ....

2. A partial string extracted from a larger string is called a

   ....

3. Write the second statement that should go along with 10 A$=INKEY$

   ....

4. What will the following statement do? 10 A=INT(A+.5)

    ....

5. The statement 10 A=INT(B/5) is doing what?

    ....

6. Write the statement that would give us a random number
   from 5 and 10 inclusive.

    ....

Use the assignment B$="ABCDEFGHIJKLMNOPQRSTUVWXYZ" to answer the
following questions.

1. The command C$=LEFT$(B$,3) would put what into C$?

    ....

2. The command D$=RIGHT$(B$,5) would put what into D$?

    ....

3. The command E$=MID$(B$,6,8) would put what into E$?

    ....

4. The command A=INSTR(B$," ") would put what into A?

   ....

5. The command F$=MID$(B$,3,4)+RIGHT$(B$,2) would put what into F$?

    ....

6. The command G$=ASC(MID$(B$,1,5)) would put what into G$?

    ....

7. The command H$=VAL(LEFT$(B$,2)) would put what into H$?

    ....

8. The command I$=CHR$(ASC(LEFT$(B$,1)) would put what into I$?

    ....

9. How many times would this FOR statement cause a loop to
   function?   10 FOR I=1 TO LEN(B$)

    ....

Use the assignment B$="0123456789" to answer the following questions.

1. The command A=INSTR(B$,"4") would put what into A?

   ....

2. The command G=VAL(MID$(B$,1,5)) would put what into G?

   ....

3. The command I$=CHR$(ASC(LEFT$(B$,1)) would put what into I$?

   ....

4. The command B=VAL(LEFT$(B$,2)+RIGHT$(B$,2))/3 would put what into B?

   ....

5. The command C=LEN(MID$(B$,8,5)) would put what into C

   ....

Answer key for Chapter 7

True-false	Multiple choice	Short answer
1. F	1. d	1. concatenation
2. F	2. d	2. substring
3. F	3. a	3. 20 IF A$="" THEN 10
4. F	4. c	4. round off A
	5. a	5. test the mod
		6. A=INT(RND(0)*5)+6

B$="ABC, etc.

1. ABC
2. VWXYZ
3. FGHIJKLM
4. 0
5. CDEFYZ
6. 65
7. 0
8. A
9. 26

B$="0123456789"

1. 5
2. 01234
3. 49
4. 63
5. 3

CHAPTER 8 . . . . . SEQUENTIAL FILE HANDLING

Circle the correct response for the following true-false questions.

T   F   1. The smallest storage location used in the computer is called a bit.

T   F   2. A bit is enough storage space for one character.

T   F   3. It is okay to let the computer close your file for you to save having to create the appropriate command in your program.

T   F   4. We are limited in the number of files we may open at one time unless we use special coding to exceed this number.

T   F   5. Sequential processing is generally the best type for most needs.

T   F   6. The close statement can be used to close particular files or all of them that are open.

T   F   7. File names are limited to a certain number of characters.

T   F   8. Before you store any files, you need to decide how many you are going to need because the file must be set up as a certain size.

Put the correct choice in the blank to answer the following multiple choice questions.

-----   1. The names for the various methods of accessing files include
      a. direct   c. sequential
      b. random   d. all of them

-----   2. If we need to put data at the end of a previously created file, we would
      a. append the records   c. add the records
      b. output the records   d. none of these

-----   3. Before we can read information from a file, it must be
      a. closed   c. opened
      b. dimensioned   d. none of them

-----   4. The usual order when working with a sequential file is
      a. open, close, read   c. write, close, open, read
      b. open, write, close, read d. none of them

Write the correct response in the blank.

1. A variable is also called a ....

2. A group of data stored on a disk is called a ....

3. Why would we probably not store a date as 10/15/86

   ....

4. In the file name RATES.CMD the CMD is known as the

   ....

5. Why is random access preferable in some cases?

   ....

6. Give the open statement for your machine to open a file called
   MASTFILE to input the information.

   ....

7. Give the command for your machine to read records from the
   opened MASTFILE.

   ....

8. Why do we need to put commas between the fields to be stored?

   ....

9. When we are inputting data from a file, we can know we are
   out of data with an

   ....

Answer key for Chapter 8

True-false	Multiple choice	Short answer
1. T	1. d	1. field
2. F	2. a	2. file
3. F	3. c	3. slashes take space
4. T	4. d	4. extension
5. F		5. access a particular record
6. T		6. various answers
7. T		7. various answers
8. F		8. otherwise the fields are pushed together into one
		9. end-of-file check

CHAPTER 9 . . . . . MENUS AND REPORTS

Circle the correct response for the following true-false questions.

T   F   1. We should always print a heading at the top of a
            screen display.

T   F   2. We should always make sure our prompts contain enough
            information without being too lengthy.

T   F   3. When designing a report layout, a line spacing chart
            can be a valuable tool.

T   F   4. We can use the variables A and A% in the program at
            the same time.

T   F   5. We can store the number 999,999.99 as a single
            precision number.

Put the correct choice in the blank to answer the following
multiple choice questions.

-----   1. To make a screen display visually pleasing you can
            a. print blank lines between items
            b. balance entries across the screen
            c. put as much information on the screen as you can
               and avoid using two screens for one function
            d. all of them
            e. a and b only

-----   2. We discussed putting something at the bottom of the
            screen, that was
            a. prompts   c. headings
            b. footings   d. none of them

-----   3. The number 9.99 should be (most economically) stored as
            a. double precision   c. single precision
            b. integer   d. none of them

-----   4. The number A# is notation for
            a. double precision   c. single precision
            b. integer   d. none of them

-----   5. The largest number that may be represented in the
            computer using scientific notation is
            a. 9.0E15   c. 9.0E25
            b. unlimited   d. none of them

-----   6. The smallest number that may be stored using an
            integer is
            a. unlimited   c. 0
            b. -3000   d. none of them

----- 7. Which of the following is least directly related to
        the others
        a. subtotal   c. control break
        b. test field   d. heading

----- 8. A subtotal is also known as
        a. control total   c. final total
        b. break total   d. summary total

Write the correct response in the blank.

1. A menu-driven program is an effort to produce programs that are

   ....

2. If we input a number as a string variable we can change it to

   a number so we can test it with the .... function.

3. Give an example of a statement (or statements) that would
   allow your machine to position the cursor to row 5, column 6.

   ....

   ....

4. Positioning the cursor at a particular location on the screen

   is known as ....

5. We caused our error message to flash by

   ....

6. When printing a report, there are two different types of
   headings; list them.

   ....

   ....

7. When printing a report, there are two different types of
   totals; list them.

   ....

   ....

8. Lines of information in the printing of a report are called

   ....

9. The only purpose of the PRINT USING statement is

. . . .

10. Using two dollar signs in the PRINT USING will cause

. . . .

11. To do a control break report what must be true of the file?

. . . .

12. If we remove the lines of information in a control break
    report, we are left with what type of report?

. . . .

Answer key for Chapter 9

True-false	Multiple choice	Short answer
1. T	1. e	1. user-oriented
2. T	2. a	2. VAL
3. T	3. c	3. various answers
4. T	4. a	4. direct cursor addressing
5. F	5. b	5. printing and erasing line
	6. d	6. page
	7. d	column
	8. a	7. subtotals
		final totals
		8. detail lines
		9. printing edited data
		10. floating dollar sign
		11. must be in sorted order
		12. summary report

CHAPTER 10 . . . . . PROMPTS AND ERRORS

Circle the correct response for the following true-false questions.

T   F   1. With the prompting input routine we set up, virtually
            any length of field can be input just by adjusting the
            end point of the input loop.

T   F   2. It is necessary to check for a blank after a character
            input to be sure a key was pressed.

T   F   3. Printing the character input with the INKEY$ or GET is
            called echoing the character.

Put the correct choice in the blank to answer the following
multiple choice questions.

-----   1. Which of the following keystrokes can the INKEY$
            routine not capture?
            a. the letter A   c. the escape key
            b. the backspace   d. it can get them all

-----   2. A string that has a length of zero would be called
            a. empty   c. null
            b. blank   d. none of them

-----   3. One method of testing for a carriage return would be
            a. IF A$=CHR$(13)   c. IF A$=ASC(13)
            b. IF A$=STR$(13)   d. none will work

-----   4. Another method of testing for a carriage return would be
            a. IF A=VAL(13)   c. IF A=ASC(13)
            B. IF 13=ASC(A$)   d. none will work

-----   5. The ERL statement will
            a. print the error number
            b. print the machine's error message
            c. print the line number that the error occurred on
            d. none of them

-----   6. After the error routine is used, which statement will
            cause the program to retry the statement that caused
            the error?
            a. RESUME   c. RESUME NEXT
            b. RESUME AGAIN   d. REPEAT RESUME

-----   7. When would you not want to print the character on the
            screen that was input with the INKEY$ or GET?
            a. when you are entering a password
            b. when the character is incorrect
            c. when the character is not printable
            d. all of the above

Write the correct response in the blank.

1. When we use 10 A$=INKEY$ (or GET) statement we also need to use
   another statement to capture the keystroke, show that statement.

   ....

2. List two of the three differences between use of the INPUT
   statement versus the INKEY$ or GET.

   ....

   ....

3. Why did we construct the prompting routine as a subroutine?

   ....

   ....

4. In our prompting routine we captured the character in A$ and
   then used B$=B$+A$. What is the purpose of B$=B$+A$?

   ....

   ....

5. What will the statement PRINT STRING$(39," ") accomplish?

   ....

   ....

6. When we press the backspace using the prompt subroutine, we
   need to remove a character from the accumulated data; show a
   statement that will accomplish this.

   ....

7. Write the form of the error trap for your machine.

   ....

8. Write the statement that allows you to check the error number
   on your machine.

   ....

9. What will occur on the IBM and Radio Shack if you do not
   RESUME your program processing after an error?

   ....

10. Write the command that will disable error trapping on your machine.

    ●

11. What is the purpose of printing asterisks on the screen in the prompting routine?

    ●

Answer key for Chapter 10

True-false	Multiple choice	Short answer
1. T	1. d	1. 20 IF A$="" THEN 10
2. F	2. c	2. no return needed
3. T	3. a	only character input
	4. b	no echo of input
	5. c	3. multiple accesses
	6. a	4. accumulate input data
	7. d	5. blank out display line
		6. B$=MID$(B$,1,LEN(B$)-1)
		7. various answers
		8. various answers
		9. next error not trapped
		10. various answers
		11. show length of entry

CHAPTER 11 . . . . . RANDOM ACCESS FILE PROCESSING

Circle the correct response for the following true-false questions.

T   F   1. We cannot sequentially process a random access file.

T   F   2. We cannot randomly access a sequential file.

T   F   3. Random file processing is also known as direct access.

T   F   4. Unlike sequential processing, when using random
           processing, the length of the records needs to be
           established.

T   F   5. If we store the same number of records in a sequential
           file and in a random file, the file lengths will be
           the same.

T   F   6. The statement to close a random file is the same
           statement used to close a sequential file.

T   F   7. If the FIELD statement does not fill the available
           area, the rest is automatically filled with blanks.

T   F   8. When storing and retrieving random records, it is
           important to know the relative record position in the
           file so we can access the proper record.

T   F   9. We used the dummy record so that we could keep track
           of the number of records in the file.

T   F   10. When we print the random file, it will be in sorted
           order.

T   F   11. All random file records are the same length.

T   F   12. We need to specify the record length of a random file
           when we close it.

Put the correct choice in the blank to answer the following
multiple choice questions.

-----   1. Which of the following is not a valid technique for
              updating a sequential file?
              a. read all the records into an array
              b. use two separate data files
              c. change the records directly
              d. all are proper techniques

-----   2. Which of the following terms is not related to the
              others?
              a. FIELD   c. buffer
              b. random file   d. all terms are related

----- 3. Which of the following terms is not related to the others?
   a. MKD$ c. LSET
   b. CVD   d. all terms are related

----- 4. Which of the following commands does not relate to use of integers?
   a. MKI$ c. CVI$
   b. CVS   d. both b and c

----- 5. When we are processing a random file, if we access a record beyond the last record in the file
   a. we will get an error
   b. we will simply access an empty record
   c. we will retrieve whatever junk happened to be on the disk in that area
   d. none of the above is correct

----- 6. When changing random records, which of the following is the least important part of the process?
   a. updating the dummy record
   b. opening the file
   c. displaying the record on the screen for changes
   d. getting the record from the file

Write the correct response in the blank.

1. Write the open statement that would be used on your machine to open the MASTFILE with a length of 35.

   ....

2. When using the IBM and Radio Shack what is the purpose of the LSET and RSET statements?

   ....

   ....

3. What does left justification mean?

   ....

   ....

4. When accessing records in the random file, we used the record number plus one. Why?

   ....

5. In our random file processing example programs, the last thing we need to do after adding a record to the file is

....

6. When changing records, how can we verify that the record asked for by the user is an actual record we have on file?

....

Answer key for Chapter 11

True-false	Multiple choice	Short answer
1. F	1. c	1. various answers
2. F	2. d	2. to store data in buffer
3. T	3. d	3. characters aligned to left
4. T	4. d	4. by-pass dummy record
5. F	5. c	5. update dummy record
6. T	6. a	6. by checking against dummy
7. T		
8. T		
9. T		
10. F		
11. T		
12. F		

CHAPTER 12 . . . . . INDEXED FILE PROCESSING

Circle the correct response for the following true-false questions.

T   F   1. The major problem with using random files is that the user has to know the record number which usually has nothing to do with the record itself.

T   F   2. It is necessary to have an index file without duplicates.

T   F   3. The field with which we access the indexed file is called the index.

T   F   4. In order to access the index file, it must be in sorted sequence.

T   F   5. When doing the binary search, we know when the record is not in the file when the record we access is blank.

T   F   6. When creating an indexed file, it is generally a good idea to construct the main file without the index to conserve disk space.

T   F   7. There is no limit (other than allowable disk space) to the number of records that may be used in an indexed file.

T   F   8. Because of the way we used the dummy record, it was necessary to put one in the index file as well as one in the main file.

T   F   9. We can print the list from an indexed file by accessing the index file first.

T   F   10. The problem with changing the name of the index in the program we used in the book is that although the index in the main file is changed, the one in the index file is not.

T   F   11. The strings "1", "3", "5", "10", "20" are in sorted sequence.

Put the correct choice in the blank to answer the following multiple choice questions.

-----   1. The real purpose of the bubble insert procedure is to
         a. keep the index file in sequence
         b. search for the item needed
         c. put a newly added index in the file
         d. both a and c

----- 2. We can assure that there are no duplicates in our
       index file by
       a. checking the file before allowing additions
       b. checking the file for duplicates before allowing
          changes to the index
       c. delete the old record before the duplicate is added
       d. only a and b

----- 3. Which of the following fields would be sorted before "4"?
       a. "yes"   c. "YES"
       b. "10"   d. none of them

Write the correct response in the blank.

1. Demonstrate the technique used to turn two items around.

       ....
       ....
       ....

2. Name one technique that can be helpful when the insertion
   technique for the index file becomes too slow.

       ....
       ....

Answer key for Chapter 12

True-false	Multiple choice	Short answer
1. T	1. d	1. 10 T = A
2. T	2. d	20 A = B
3. T	3. b	30 B = T
4. T		2. bring index into memory
5. F		
6. F		
7. F		
8. F		
9. T		
10. T		
11. F		

CHAPTER 13 . . . . . TREE STRUCTURES

Circle the correct response for the following true-false questions.

T   F   1. The first entry into the tree structure is called the branch entry.

T   F   2. Each entry in a tree is called a node.

T   F   3. All entries less than the beginning entry in the tree branch to the left.

T   F   4. When creating our tree file, all the pointers to the higher and lower entries begin as zero.

T   F   5. In order to use the tree structure with a file with the same fields as before, we need to change our OPEN statement.

T   F   6. It would be only a minor inconvenience to let our program change the index field when using a tree structure file.

T   F   7. If you access the various nodes in the tree you are said to be traversing the tree.

T   F   8. When using a tree, the records are stored in the file in the order that they are entered.

T   F   9. With very little effort we could change our tree access programs to create a self-balancing tree.

Write the correct response in the blank.

1. List two advantages tree structures have over indexed files.

   . . . .

   . . . .

2. Name one advantage indexed files have over tree structure files.

   . . . .

3. We know the item we are looking for is not in the tree when

   . . . .

   . . . .

4. Why can't we delete a record from the tree file without rearranging the file?

....

....

5. Show the routine to convert a number from 1 to 65,000 into a two byte representation.

....

....

Answer key for Chapter 13

True-false	Multiple choice	Short answer
1. F	none	1. faster additions
2. T		no index file needed
3. T		2. can easily print sorted list
4. T		3. there are no nodes
5. T		remaining on that branch
6. F		4. it disturbs the node pointers
7. T		5. A=INT(N/256) ' HIGH BYTE
8. T		B=N-A*256 ' LOW BYTE
9. F		

Circle the correct response for the following true-false questions.

T   F   1. In the sort that uses partitions, they are divided in half by the element in the middle which is known as the key.

T   F   2. The stack we used for the partitioned sort would be called a first-in-first-out stack.

T   F   3. Removing an entry from a stack is called popping.

T   F   4. Putting an element into a stack is called stacking.

T   F   5. Sorting strings is much more difficult than sorting numbers from a programming point of view.

T   F   6. The quicksort is basically a selection sort.

T   F   7. When a partition is divided into two, the two new partitions are usually the same size.

Put the correct choice in the blank to answer the following multiple choice questions.

-----   1. Of the sorts discussed, the fastest was
     a. bubble   c. selection
     b. Shell   d. quicksort

-----   2. Of the sorts discussed, the slowest was
     a. bubble   c. selection
     b. Shell   d. quicksort

-----   3. Which of the sorts requires a counter to keep track of the number of passes?
     a. bubble   c. quicksort
     b. selection   d. a and b

-----   4. Which sort uses partitions?
     a. bubble   c. selection
     b. Shell   d. quicksort

-----   5. Which sort looks through the whole list searching for the smallest item?
     a. bubble   c. selection
     b. Shell   d. quicksort

-----   6. Which sort was listed as the one most widely used by beginning programmers?
     a. bubble   c. selection
     b. Shell   d. quicksort

----- 7. Which sort uses a gap pointer?
      a. bubble   c. selection
      b. Shell   d. quicksort

----- 8. The easiest way to sort file entries is to sort what with the index
      a. the record number   c. the rest of the fields
      b. the partition   d. none of them

Write the correct response in the blank.

1. Define a sort.

   . . . .

   . . . .

   . . . .

2. Why did we remove the counter variable from the NEXT statements in the sort programs?

   . . . .

   . . . .

3. With the quicksort, when do we know that the list is sorted?

   . . . .

   . . . .

4. There is only one significant difference between sorting a single item and sorting multiple items. What is it?

   . . . .

Answer key for Chapter 14

True-false	Multiple choice	Short answer
1. T	1. d	1. puts list in sequence
2. F	2. a	2. speed
3. T	3. a	3. all partitions have one
4. F	4. d	element
5. F	5. c	4. switching multiple items
6. F	6. a	
7. F	7. b	
	8. a	

CHAPTER 15 . . . . . GRAPHICS AND COLOR

Circle the correct response for the following true-false questions.

T F 1. Each point that can be accessed on the screen is
         called a pixel.

T F 2. A vertical graph is easier to program than a
         horizontal graph.

T F 3. Low resolution graphics allow access to smaller groups
         of points than does high resolution.

T F 4. In low resolution, all three of the computers discussed
         in the text have special predefined graphics characters.

T F 5. Plotting functions use (column,row).

T F 6. High resolution graphics allows only black and white
         displays on the IBM.

Put the correct choice in the blank to answer the following
multiple choice questions.

-----   1. The command used on the Radio Shack to turn on a low
            resolution block is
            a. RSET   c. POINT
            b. RESET   d. none of them

-----   2. The command used on the Radio Shack to test for a
            turned on low resolution block is
            a. RSET   c. POINT
            b. RESET   d. none of them

-----   3. Apple low resolution graphics are turned on with
            a. GR   c. HGR
            b. GRPH   d. none of them

-----   4. Which of the following is not a high resolution
            graphics Apple command?
            a. HGR   c. HCOLOR
            b. HDRAW   d. all of them are

-----   5. Which of the following is not a low resolution
            graphics command on the Apple?
            a. PLOT   c. COLOR
            b. GR   d. all of them are

-----   6. The IBM uses which command for cursor positioning in
            high resolution graphics?
            a. LOCATE   c. PLOT
            b. SCREEN   d. none of them

----- 7. Which command is used to turn on high resolution
graphics on the IBM?
a. HGR   c. COLOR 2
b. KEY ON   d. none of them

----- 8. Which computer has access to the most graphics points.
a. Radio Shack   c. IBM
b. Apple   d. b and c are the same

Answer key for Chapter 15

True-false	Multiple choice	Short answer
1. T	1. d	1. various answers
2. F	2. c	
3. F	3. a	
4. T	4. b	
5. T	5. d	
6. T	6. a	
	7. d	
	8. c	

TRANSPARENCY MASTERS

The illustrations on pages 283-330 are included for your
use in overhead projection. The figure numbers given are those
used in MICROCOMPUTER BASIC: Structures, Concepts, and Techniqu
the captions have been included to help identify the figures
in AN INTRODUCTION TO BASIC and ADVANCED BASIC.

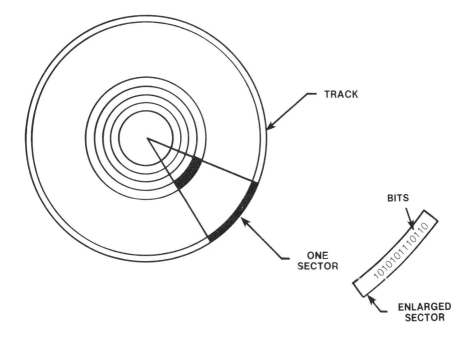

FIGURE 1-4
Diagram of a sector.

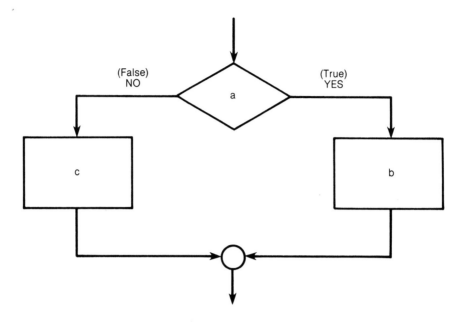

FIGURE 2-8
Basic IF-THEN-ELSE structure.

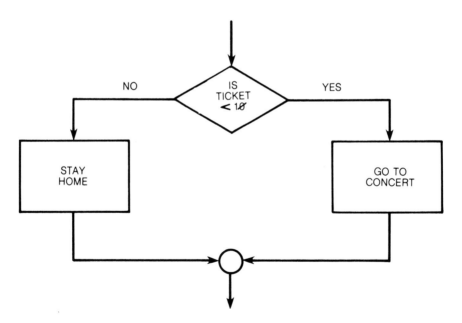

FIGURE 2-9
IF-THEN-ELSE example.

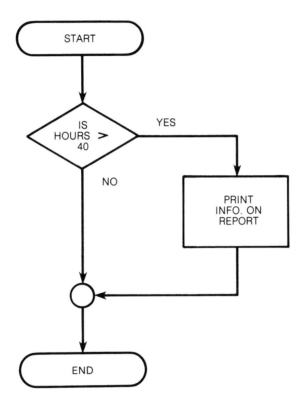

FIGURE 2-11
Null ELSE example.

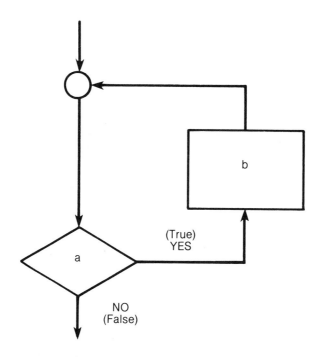

FIGURE 2-12
Basic DO-WHILE structure.

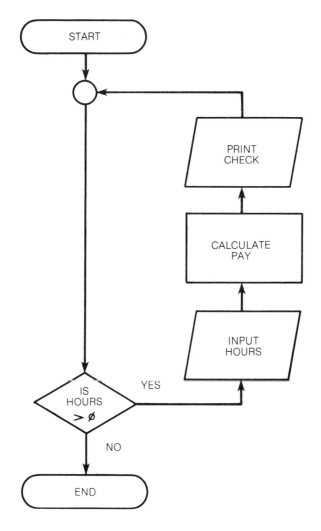

FIGURE 2-15
End-of-data marker example with one input.

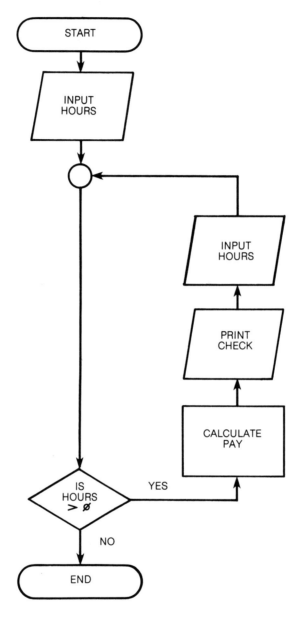

FIGURE 2-16
End-of-data marker example with two inputs.

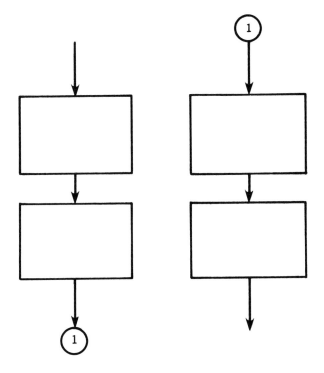

FIGURE 2-17
Example of second use of connectors.

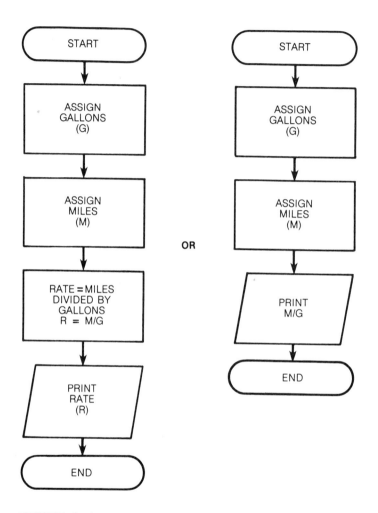

FIGURE 3-4
Two different methods of flowcharting the
miles-per-gallon problem.

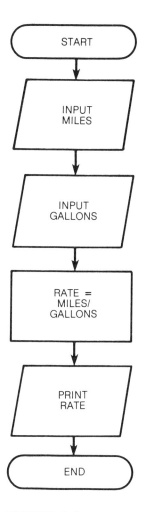

FIGURE 4-1
Flowchart of mileage problem.

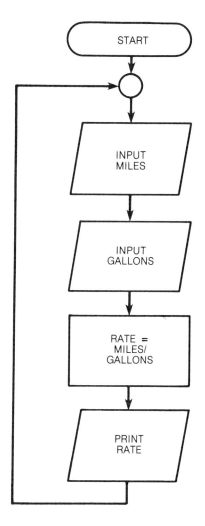

FIGURE 4-2
Flowchart with nonending loop.

TABLE 5–1 Relational Operators

OPERATOR	MEANING	SAMPLE
=	equal to	A = B
<	less than	A < B
>	greater than	A > B
<>	not equal to	A <> B
<=	less than or equal to	A <= B
>=	greater than or equal to	A >= B

From Coburn, *Microcomputer BASIC: Structures, Concepts, and Techniques,*
copyright © 1986 by Delmar Publishers Inc.

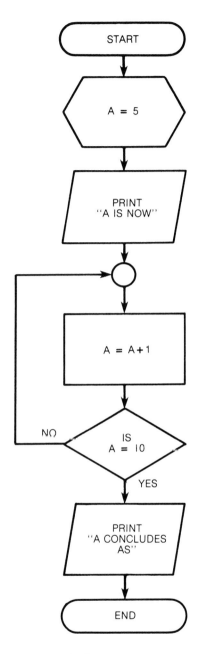

FIGURE 5-4
REPEAT-UNTIL structure.

From Coburn, *Microcomputer BASIC: Structures, Concepts, and Techniques,*
copyright © 1986 by Delmar Publishers Inc.

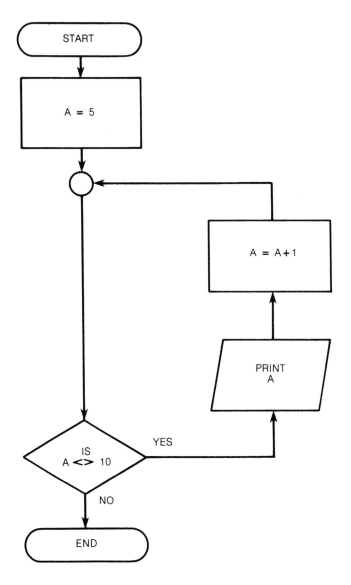

FIGURE 5-5
DO-WHILE structure.

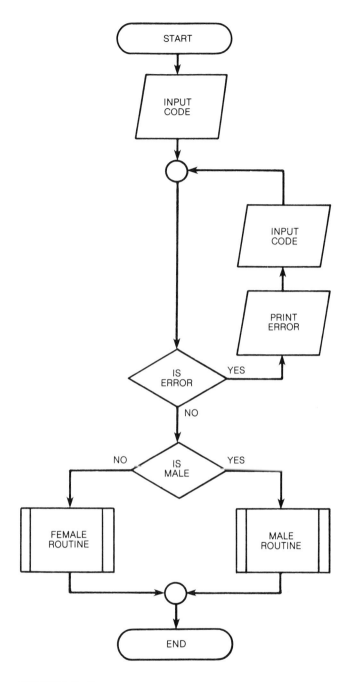

FIGURE 5-8
Flowchart using error trap.

From Coburn, *Microcomputer BASIC: Structures, Concepts, and Techniques,*
copyright © 1986 by Delmar Publishers Inc.

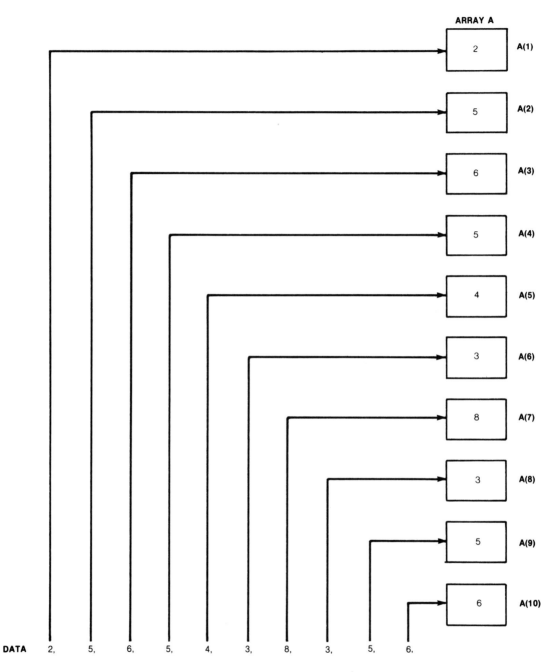

FIGURE 6-2
Assigning data into an array.

From Coburn, *Microcomputer BASIC: Structures, Concepts, and Techniques,*
copyright ©1986 by Delmar Publishers Inc.

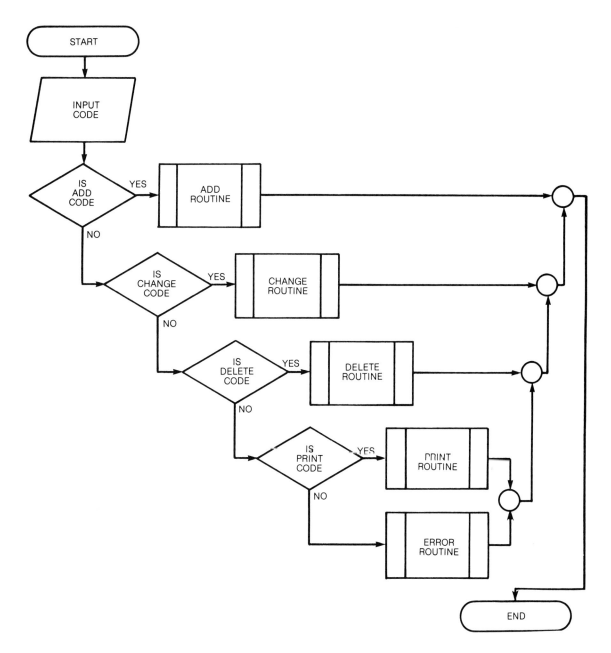

FIGURE 6-5
Flowchart with nested IF-THEN-ELSE.

From Coburn, *Microcomputer BASIC: Structures, Concepts, and Techniques,*
copyright © 1986 by Delmar Publishers Inc.

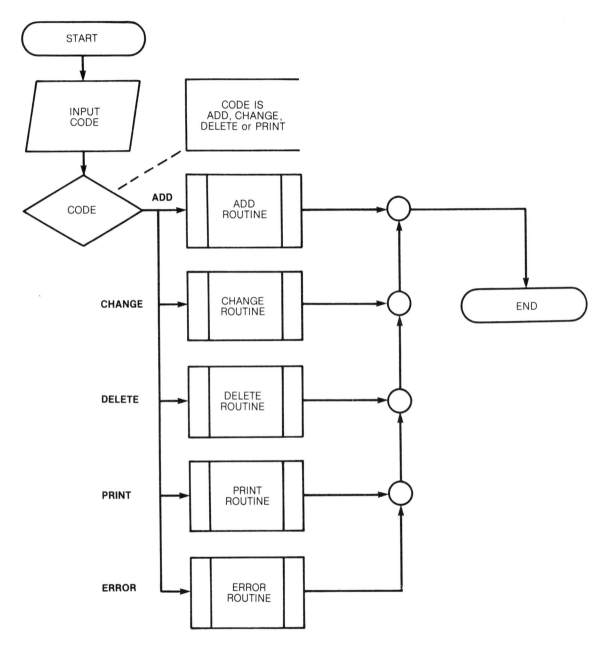

FIGURE 6-6
Flowchart of CASE structure.

From Coburn, *Microcomputer BASIC: Structures, Concepts, and Techniques*,
copyright ©1986 by Delmar Publishers Inc.

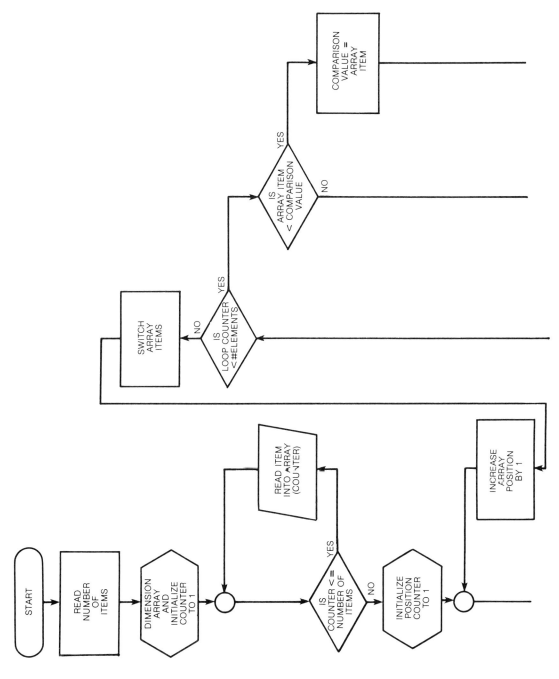

FIGURE 6-7
Flowchart of selection sort, part 1.

From Coburn, *Microcomputer BASIC: Structures, Concepts, and Techniques,*
copyright © 1986 by Delmar Publishers Inc.

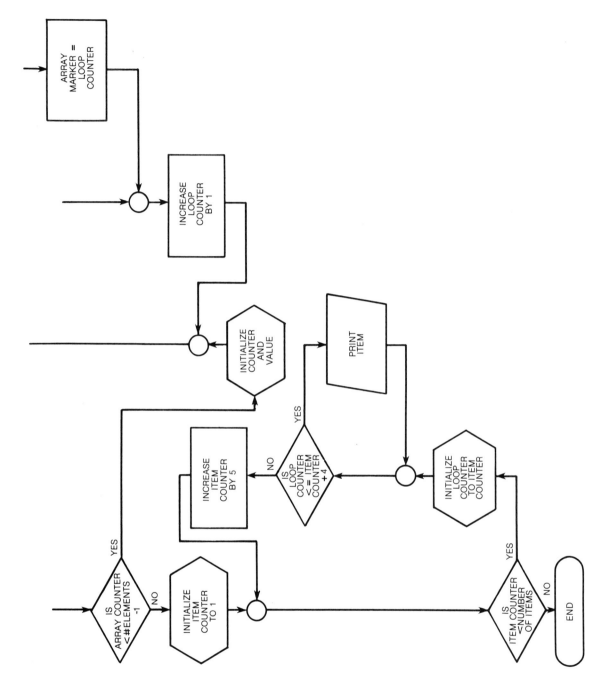

FIGURE 6-7
Flowchart of selection sort, part 2.

From Coburn, *Microcomputer BASIC: Structures, Concepts, and Techniques,*
copyright ©1986 by Delmar Publishers Inc.

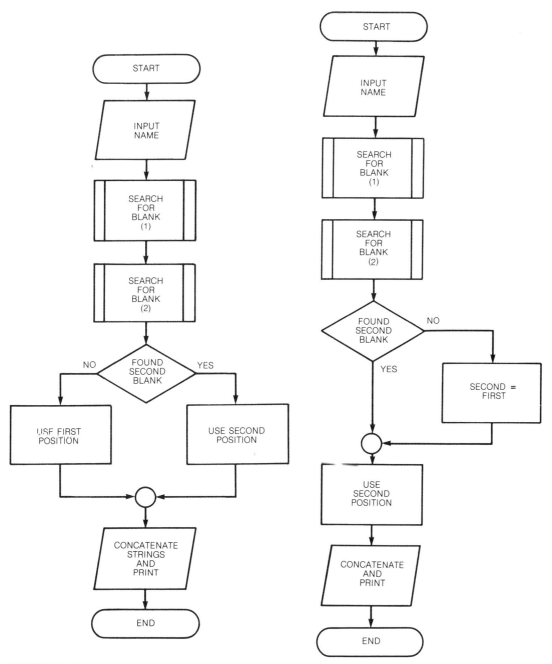

FIGURE 7-1
Flowchart of search for blank.

FIGURE 7-2
Better solution for search problem.

From Coburn, *Microcomputer BASIC: Structures, Concepts, and Techniques,*
copyright © 1986 by Delmar Publishers Inc.

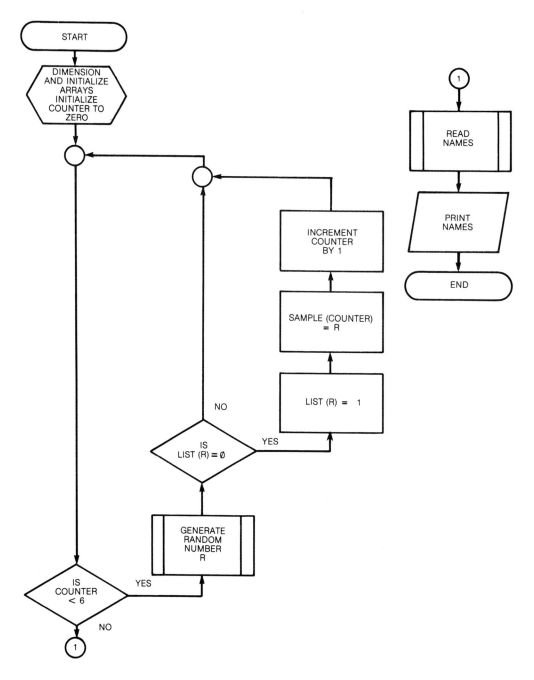

FIGURE 7-3
Flowchart of random names list.

From Coburn, *Microcomputer BASIC: Structures, Concepts, and Techniques,*
copyright © 1986 by Delmar Publishers Inc.

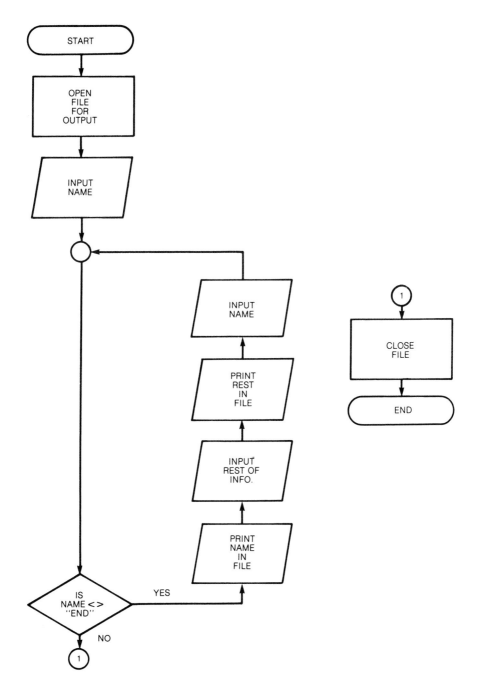

FIGURE 8-1
Flowchart of program to store mailing labels.

From Coburn, *Microcomputer BASIC: Structures, Concepts, and Techniques,*
copyright © 1986 by Delmar Publishers Inc.

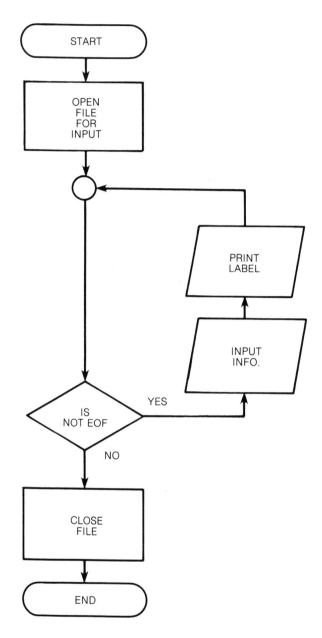

FIGURE 8-2
Flowchart of program to print mailing labels.

LINE SPACING CHART
COLUMNS

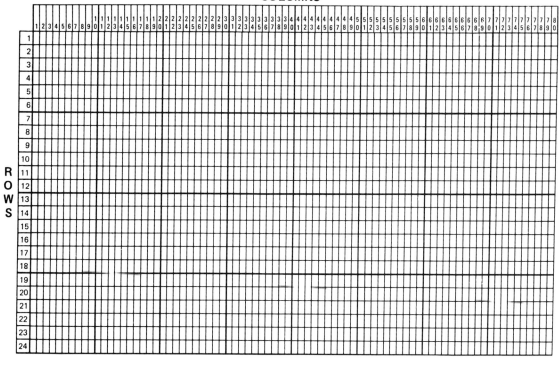

FIGURE 9-1
Typical line spacing chart.

LINE SPACING CHART

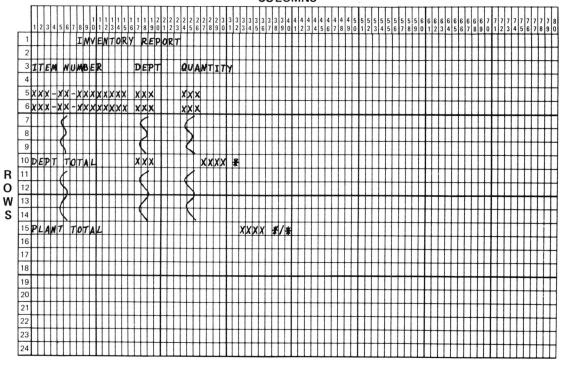

FIGURE 9-2
Design of report using line spacing chart.

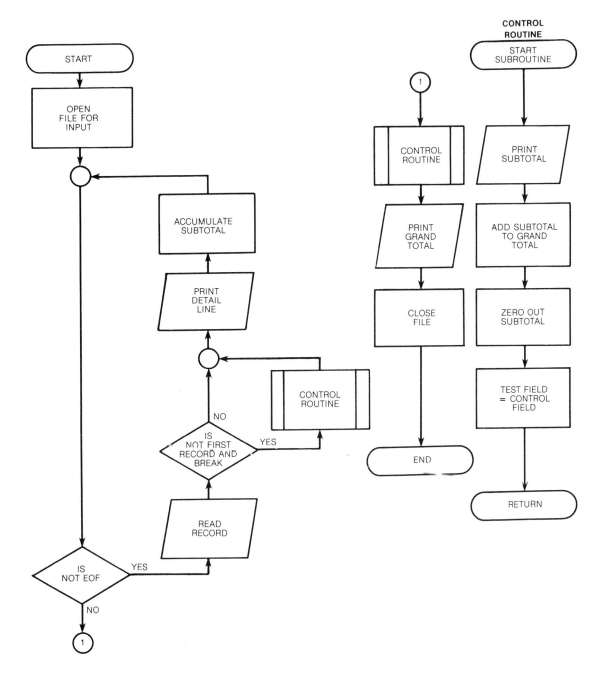

FIGURE 9-3
Flowchart of control break program.

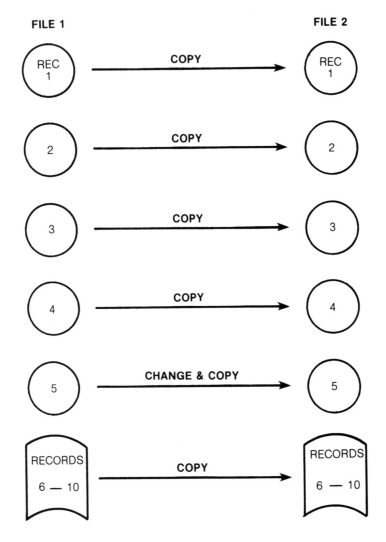

FIGURE 11-1
Sequential update.

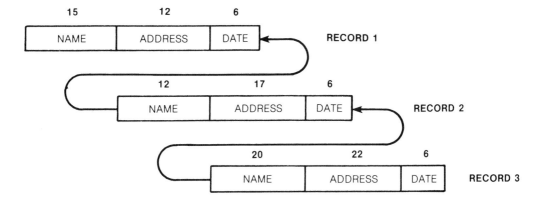

FIGURE 11-2
Example of sequential file storage.

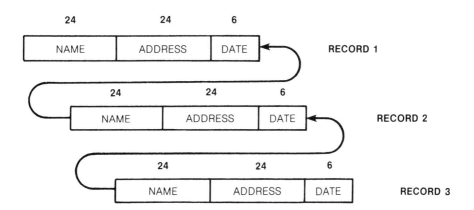

FIGURE 11-3
Example of random file storage.

From Coburn, *Microcomputer BASIC: Structures, Concepts, and Techniques,*
copyright © 1986 by Delmar Publishers Inc.

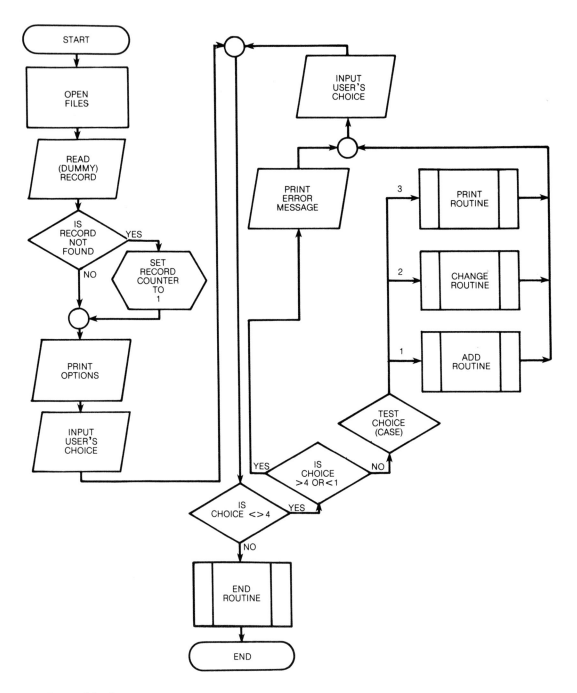

FIGURE 11-6
Flowchart of initial module.

From Coburn, *Microcomputer BASIC: Structures, Concepts, and Techniques,*
copyright © 1986 by Delmar Publishers Inc.

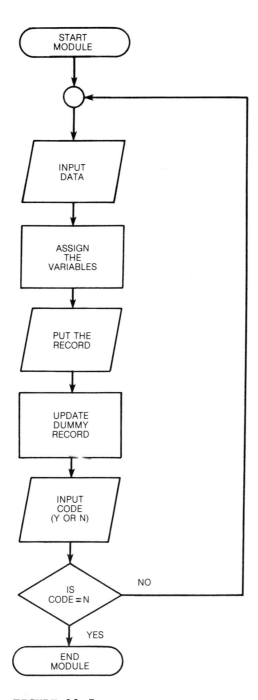

FIGURE 11-7
Flowchart of addition module.

From Coburn, *Microcomputer BASIC: Structures, Concepts, and Techniques,*
copyright © 1986 by Delmar Publishers Inc.

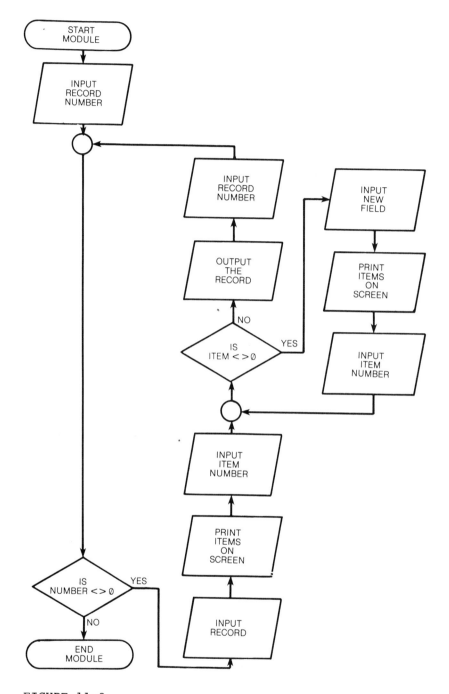

FIGURE 11-8
Flowchart of change module.

From Coburn, *Microcomputer BASIC: Structures, Concepts, and Techniques,*
copyright © 1986 by Delmar Publishers Inc.

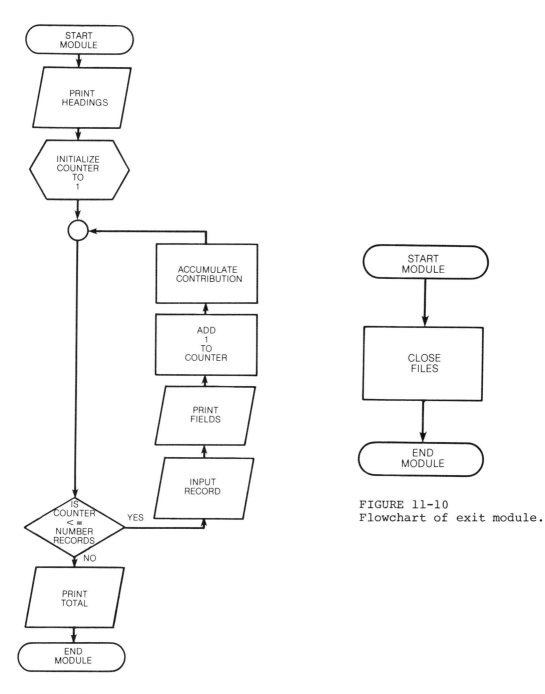

FIGURE 11-9
Flowchart of print module.

FIGURE 11-10
Flowchart of exit module.

From Coburn, *Microcomputer BASIC: Structures, Concepts, and Techniques*,
copyright © 1986 by Delmar Publishers Inc.

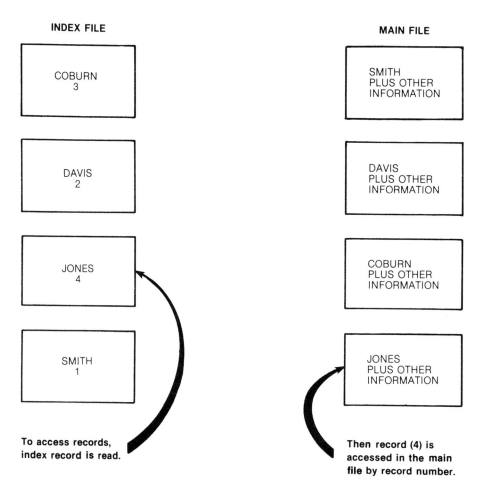

INDEX FILE

COBURN
3

DAVIS
2

JONES
4

SMITH
1

To access records,
index record is read.

MAIN FILE

SMITH
PLUS OTHER
INFORMATION

DAVIS
PLUS OTHER
INFORMATION

COBURN
PLUS OTHER
INFORMATION

JONES
PLUS OTHER
INFORMATION

Then record (4) is
accessed in the main
file by record number.

FIGURE 12-1
Illustration of index file processing.

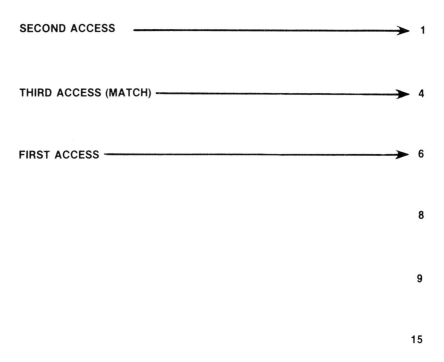

SECOND ACCESS ————————————————→ 1

THIRD ACCESS (MATCH) ——————————————→ 4

FIRST ACCESS ——————————————————→ 6

8

9

15

FIGURE 12-2
Illustration of binary search.

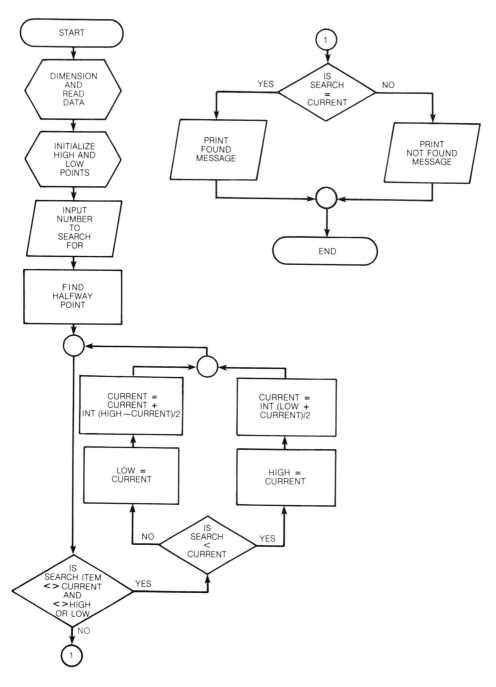

FIGURE 12-5
Flowchart of binary search.

From Coburn, *Microcomputer BASIC: Structures, Concepts, and Techniques,*
copyright © 1986 by Delmar Publishers Inc.

ORIGINAL LIST

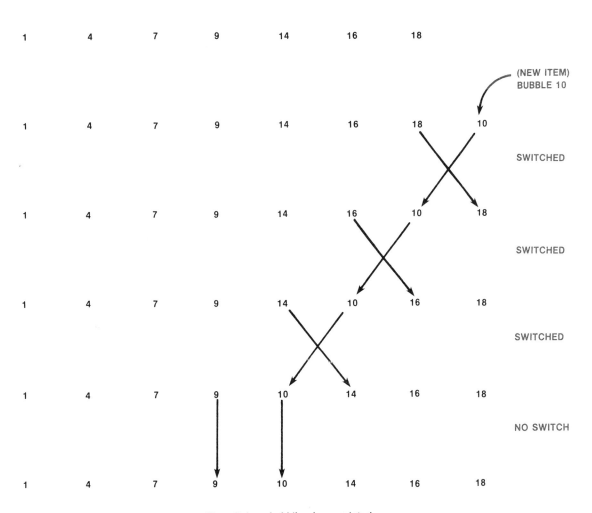

No switch so bubbling is completed.

FIGURE 12-6
Bubble technique illustration.

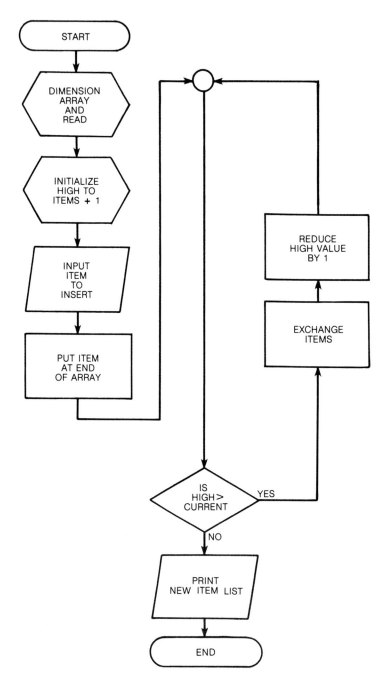

FIGURE 12-7
Flowchart of bubble insert.

From Coburn, *Microcomputer BASIC: Structures, Concepts, and Techniques,*
copyright © 1986 by Delmar Publishers Inc.

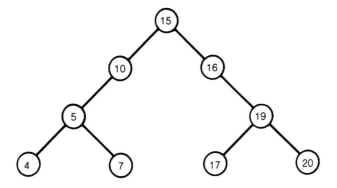

```
FIGURE 13-8
Final version of tree.
```

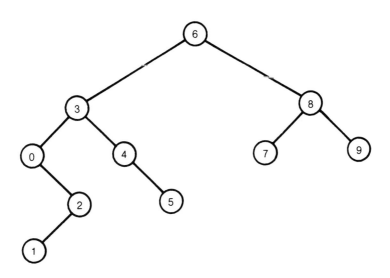

```
FIGURE 13-9
Second tree structure example.
```

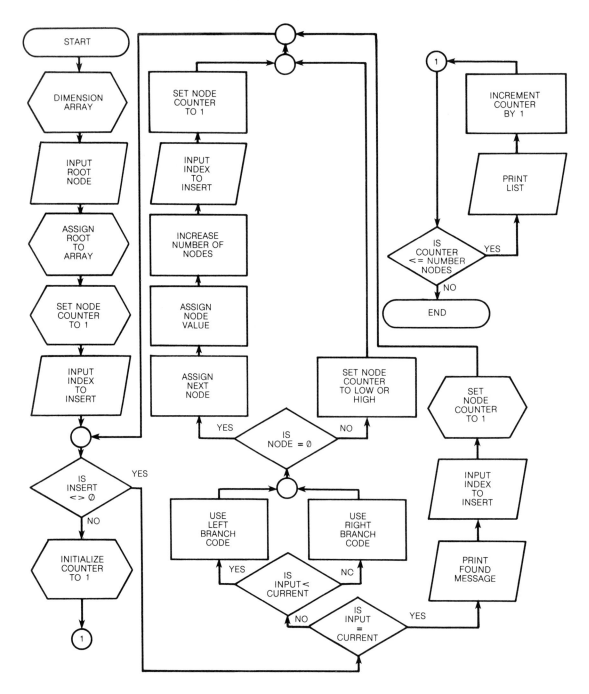

FIGURE 13-10
Flowchart of tree program.

From Coburn, *Microcomputer BASIC: Structures, Concepts, and Techniques,*
copyright © 1986 by Delmar Publishers Inc.

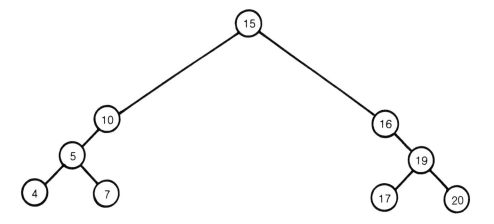

INITIAL STRUCTURE

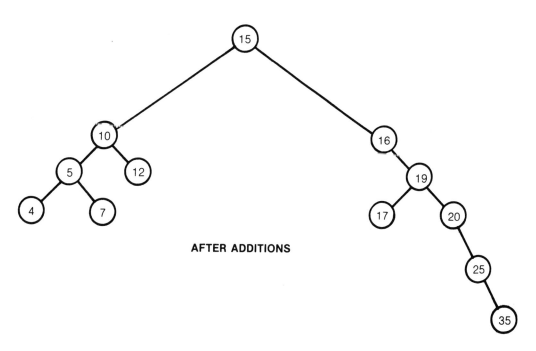

AFTER ADDITIONS

FIGURE 13-11
Tree before and after additions.

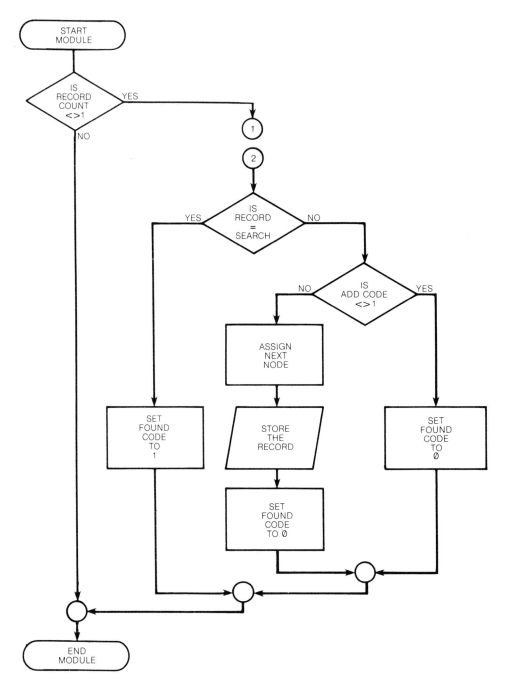

FIGURE 13-12
Flowchart of tree search module.

From Coburn, *Microcomputer BASIC: Structures, Concepts, and Techniques,*
copyright © 1986 by Delmar Publishers Inc.

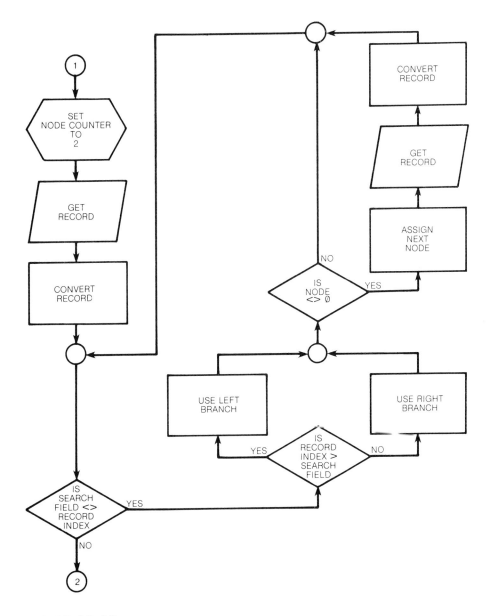

FIGURE 13-12
Continued.

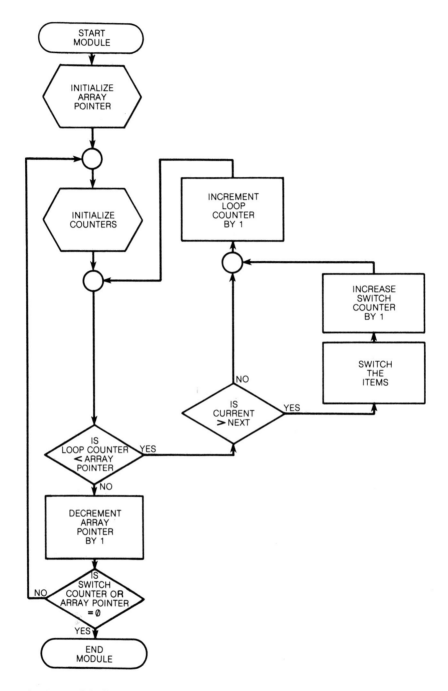

FIGURE 14-2
Flowchart of bubble sort module.

From Coburn, *Microcomputer BASIC: Structures, Concepts, and Techniques*,
copyright © 1986 by Delmar Publishers Inc.

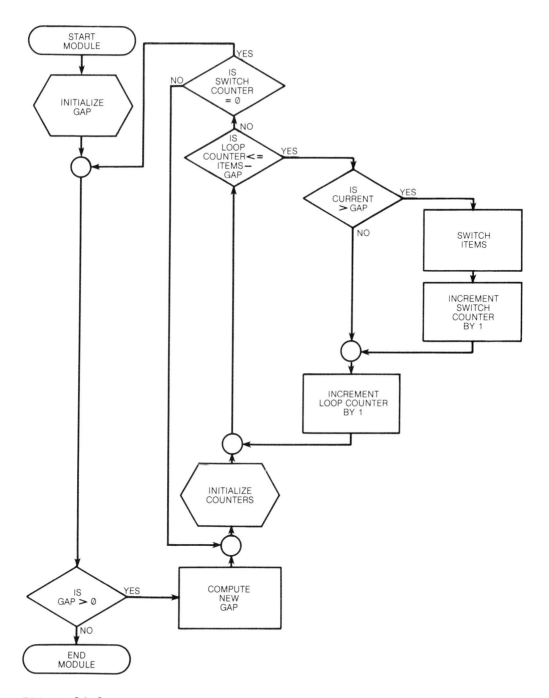

FIGURE 14-3
Flowchart of Shell sort module.

From Coburn, *Microcomputer BASIC: Structures, Concepts, and Techniques,*
copyright © 1986 by Delmar Publishers Inc.

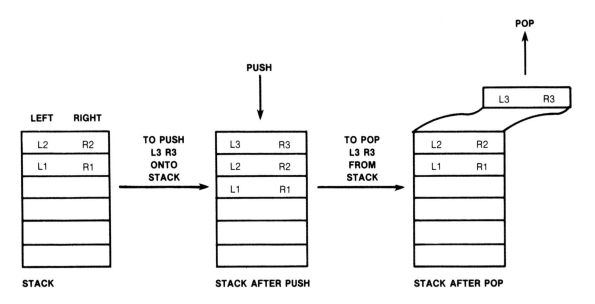

FIGURE 14-4
Pushing and popping a stack.

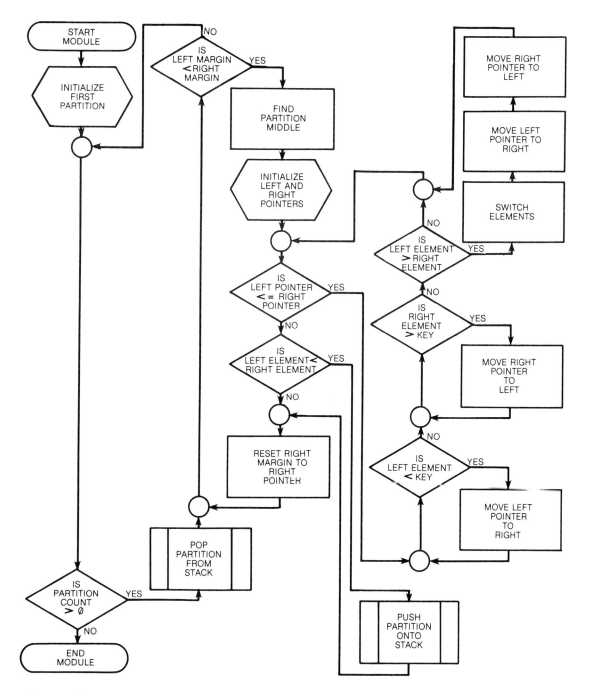

FIGURE 14-5
Flowchart of quicksort module.

From Coburn, *Microcomputer BASIC: Structures, Concepts, and Techniques,*
copyright © 1986 by Delmar Publishers Inc.

```
                    ┌─────────────────────────────────────────────────────┐
                    │                                                       │
                    │                    PARTITION                          │
                    │                                                       │
                    └─────────────────────────────────────────────────────┘


                          LEFT MARGIN           RIGHT MARGIN


                             A(1,1)                A(1,2)

          STACK
                             A(2,1)                A(2,2)


                             A(3,1)                A(3,2)


                             A(4,1)                A(4,2)
```

FIGURE 14-6
Using the array stack.

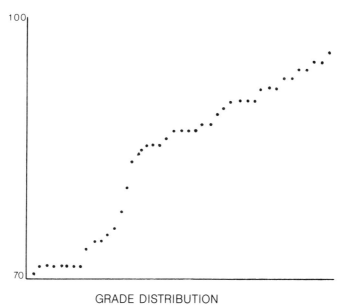

GRADE DISTRIBUTION

FIGURE 15-3
Radio Shack low resolution grade distribution.

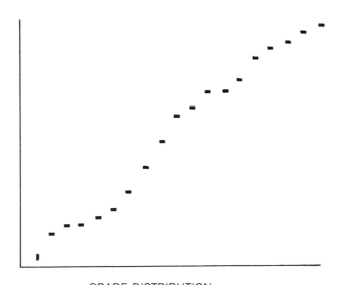

GRADE DISTRIBUTION

FIGURE 15-4
Apple low resolution grade distribution.

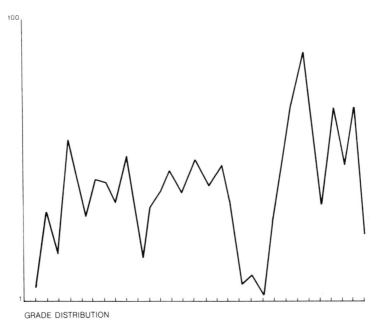

GRADE DISTRIBUTION

FIGURE 15-7
IBM high resolution graphics display.

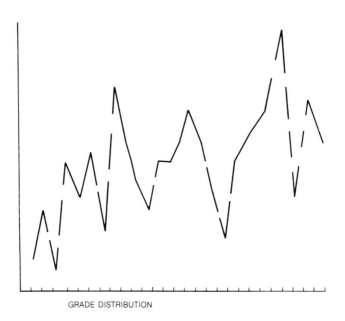

GRADE DISTRIBUTION

FIGURE 15-8
Apple high resolution graphics display.

From Coburn, *Microcomputer BASIC: Structures, Concepts, and Techniques,*
copyright © 1986 by Delmar Publishers Inc.